Mascu

YBRIDI~ ~~~3 8TT
2) ~

ME JANE

Masculinity, Movies and Women

edited by
Pat Kirkham and Janet Thumim

LAWRENCE & WISHART
LONDON

Lawrence & Wishart Limited
144a Old South Lambeth Road
London SW8 1XX

First published 1995
Collection © Lawrence & Wishart, 1995
Each article © the author(s), 1995

ISBN 0 85315 802 9

Cover designed by
Jan Brown Designs, London
Photoset in North Wales by
Derek Doyle & Associates, Mold, Clwyd
Printed and bound in Great Britain by
Redwood Books, Trowbridge, Wiltshire

Contents

Contents

For all our friends, especially
Wor Bill, Roy next door, Laraine, Piet and Jim,
and
Heather, Gin, Diana, Liz and Wendy

Acknowledgements

This book has had a long gestation: when we first planned an anthology of essays on masculinity, at the BFI Summer School bar in 1989, we envisaged both male and female contributors. As the project developed, however, it seemed to us that a focus on the gender of the writer – the reader of the films discussed – would be of interest and might be enabled by two volumes: hence *You Tarzan*, from the men and *Me Jane*, from the women. The absorbing differences in emphases between these two collections are discussed in our introductory essay, here we simply wish to acknowledge that this volume represents the completion of a project begun with *You Tarzan* and to thank, once again, the contributors to that volume many of whose insights have provided starting points for the essays in *Me Jane*

It has been a great pleasure to work with the fifteen contributors to this volume, many of them old friends who have long shared the engagement with practical feminism that provided the impetus for both volumes. All of the essays here have been the subject of lengthy editorial collaboration as, together, we attempted to articulate some of the tricky questions arising from sustained attention to popular cultural propositions about gender identity. We hope that out contributors will be as pleased as we are with the result, and thank them all for their efforts and their patience.

We are sorry that there are so few illustrations in this book. Apart from the perennial difficulties in obtaining permissions from most film copyright holders (except at impossibly large sums), we also had a conflict of interest between the length of the volume and the inclusion of pictures. We hope that readers will avail themselves of the many collections of film stills and add their own images to the book.

Finally, we should like to thank the staff at Lawrence & Wishart, in particular our editor, Ruth Borthwick, whose cheerful support and unfailing patience have helped to minimise the stress involved in what has sometimes felt like an unwieldy task and, even more important, to maximise the fun. Thanks, Ruth.

Pat Kirkham and Janet Thumim
April 1995

Me Jane

Pat Kirkham and Janet Thumim

'I don't know whether to look at him or read him ...' Lieutenant Elgart ... in *Cape Fear*, (Martin Scorsese, US, 1991)

Even before the completion of *You Tarzan: Masculinity, Movies and Men* (the anthology of essays written by men on masculinity and the cinema which we edited and Lawrence & Wishart published in 1993), we had invited a number of women to contribute to what would, in effect, be a companion volume. The last thirty years has brought new consciousness and explorations of what it was and is to be a woman – collectively and individually, politically and personally – and we invited those who were not already doing so to extend their feminist analyses to explorations of masculinity. We were as delighted at the enthusiasm of the response as we were at the range and quality of the essays themselves. We make no claims to this volume being representative of feminist film studies, but feel confident that what follows constitutes some of the most interesting writing currently by women on masculinity and cinema. Some essays are speculative and exploratory, some present detailed empirical research, discrete case studies or more well trodden theoretical paths: we hope that they will all spark new interests and insights. We offer them in the spirit of collaborative feminist scholarship, testing theory against the findings of empirical research and personal responses. In the films which our contributors have chosen to discuss masculinity is marked, time and again, as delicate, fragile, provisional; it is under threat, in danger of collapse; it is an impossible ideal – most of all it seems to be an impediment to the desirable human experience of pleasure-in-being. These signs of the masculine in the films are recognised by women viewers who are subject to patriarchal masculinity in their own feminine formation but *not* subject to it in the sense that masculinity itself is never a requirement, cannot be a goal, for us. Our brief suggested that the issue of *women's* viewing, studying and responding to cinematic representations of masculinity might be one of several points of entry into the topic. Hence the sustained probings of fictional masculinities – particularly their heterosexual constructions – and the reference to confirmations of the fictional in the real social order known through our own experience.

Christine Gledhill's *Women Reading Men* draws on her extensive knowledge of film and of melodrama in order to explore what is at stake in women's cinematic pleasures and fascinations with regard to masculinity. We are grateful for her ways of dealing with what can sometimes seem to be almost unanswerable questions. She writes 'while the pleasure of recognition depends on a certain "strangeness", for women consuming mainstream popular culture dominated by stories of male characters and actions recognition is often doubly "strange" because of the gender exclusions which debar us from large areas of social and political life'. In a slightly different vein Rikki Morgan suggests that a sub-textual proposition in Almodovar's *Tie Me Up! Tie Me Down!* (Spain, 1990) is that 'men are as oppressed and victimised as women by the straitjacket of patriarchy'. Kathleen Rowe, writing about post-classical romantic comedy, notes the increasing use of melodrama to tell of male suffering. Is this focus on melodrama simply a consequence of many of our contributors having chosen this familiar genre, canonically identified with the 'woman's film', to gain access to the 'problematic' of masculinity? Although it could be argued that the whole of fictional cinema, broadly, conforms to the codes of melodrama, it is nevertheless of interest to consider which genres *are* represented in this volume. There is certainly a difference between this volume and *You Tarzan* in which, as Gledhill observes, the films discussed 'offer a markedly different fictional space in which the hero can wrestle with society's demands'.

In *You Tarzan* discussion frequently focused on action and spectacular display of the male body, and the epic, war, horror and science fiction genres were each the subject of at least one essay; in *Me Jane* the recurring genres are thrillers, westerns and melodramas. Only one essay touches on the war film and there is no discussion of science fiction, the epic, nor – perhaps more surprisingly – the musical.

In the interests of our conception of *You Tarzan* and *Me Jane* as 'companion' volumes, we have used similar terminology though the emphases are different. Thus here we have *The Internal World*, the domain of the psychic construction of identity; *The External World* in which representations of masculinity in its public, social dimensions are played out; *The Body, Action and Inaction* and finally a discussion of *The Politics of Gender* which, in a volume of women's responses to filmic constructions of masculinity, seemed to us to require particular attention.

THE INTERNAL WORLD

Various terms recur in most of the essays which relate to 'the psychic' which we have designated *The Internal World.* The terms cluster round three sites: F/father, fragility, anxiety. The question of the F/father seems to produce a recognition or acknowledgement of fragility and vulnerability, which generates anxiety for the masculine protagonist, if not also for the male spectator. Although such terms – the 'F/father', 'fragility', 'anxiety' – are certainly acknowledged by the male contributors to *You Tarzan* it is striking how much more detailed attention, probing and speculation they have generated among the female contributors to *Me Jane.* Is it, perhaps, that female spectators, in investigating the spectacle of the cinematic construction of masculinity, are more readily prepared to examine elements of that construction which pose, in themselves, no threat to the (always already) disempowered female subject? We women know (because we have no penis) that we can never accede to the Phallus. Any social power we may wield must be differently accounted for. But to the male this is perhaps less clear since for men the conceptual separation between the Phallus and the penis is less obvious – at any rate in the psychic mechanisms informing their lived experience.

A problem faced by male subjects, it would seem, is the confusion experienced between concepts of the Father (patriarch, possessor of the Phallus, authority in the symbolic order) and the father (their father, their accession to the status of father, the Oedipal scenario experienced by the individual subject). Being a man implies acceding to (symbolic) patriarchal power but, precisely because this is a symbolic structure, it cannot take account of the contingencies of actual experience which may appear to deny this possibility. Thus masculinity is experienced as containing its own lacks, impossibilities – for the discrete individual. But the male spectator only *knows* this for himself – others, for all he knows, may be experiencing a less problematic transition to, or exercise of, power. The recognition of fragility, of vulnerability, generates an inescapable anxiety and also a fear of others in whom such fragility may not be present. Just as various 'phallic' fetishes, monuments, and structures both threaten and reassure the male subject, so also various wounds, scars, and disabilities signify vulnerability and the threat of its ultimate consequence, castration (the conclusive loss of both the penis and the possibility of the Phallus) – the fascination with the recent Bobbit trial had less to do with what he did to her than what she did to him. To paraphrase Bette Davis in *All About Eve* (Mankiewicz, US, 1950) 'Without that, you're not a man'.

This is a qualitatively different anxiety from that lived by female subjects. For the latter it is autonomy and the possible consequent access to power which would threaten their socially validated femininity: for male subjects, in contrast, it is precisely their socially validated potential for power which threatens them since for the individual subject such power seems, on the evidence of the films discussed here, always to be a provisional, temporary state. For male subjects their very masculinity may be an impediment to their experience of pleasure-in-being. Does this account for the melancholy, the sense of loss, of lack, of *dis*satisfaction noted in so many of these essays as a central component of screen masculinity? It is precisely this (disallowed) aspect of masculinity which has proved so compelling to our female reader/contributors. In a sense we might propose that the whole institution of cinema is in itself a dangerous enterprise for the masculine subject because, in constructing convincing and meaning*ful* representations of masculinity in its fictional characters, it focuses attention on the social construction of masculinity, on its trajectory from the promising to the tragic – from the quiescent to the statuesque to the depleted.

Susannah Radstone outlines Freud's propositions about the consequences, for public and psychic formations of masculinity, of the gap perceived between the patriarchal Father and the primal father – in an account of the relation of difference to be understood between phallic authority and ancestral origins. The anxiety generated by this relation can be accounted for by the recognition that, though the symbolic may propose an hegemonic ordering of reality, it can never account for experience of the real. Like other contributors she cites her 'fascination' with a star, Pacino in her case, as the starting point for her essay, his evident 'failings' in *Sea of Love* (Becker, US, 1989) producing 'a fascination that is undoubtedly tied to both triumph and mourning'. But 'triumph' and 'mourning' are terms which can describe delight in achievement, distress at failure, delight perhaps in the accession to phallic power implicit in the erect penis and distress at its waning. The language used to describe this physical trajectory is, to borrow a term from her essay, 'permeable' with the language of the Oedipal scenario in its significance for both sons and daughters; she concludes, 'Pacino rises from the flames, promising, perhaps, that fathers – and my father – will too'.

14

Though the problem of difference between the symbolic and the real may, arguably, be a fundamental, even structuring, constituent of the masculine, it is one which is particularly acute for young men, whose passage from childhood to maturity involves the terrible recognition that the Phallus may, after all, be inaccessible to them. Many of the male characters discussed in these essays are offered in this transitional stage, in relation to either their real or their symbolic 'fathers', hence the question of paternal models for adult masculinity is one which absorbs many of our contributors. In Janet Thumim's essay on *Unforgiven* (Eastwood, US, 1992) it is the Schofield Kid/Jaimz Woolvert's acceptance of his inadequacies, she suggests, which the narrative offers as a marker of his passage to maturity and with which the dominant narrative enigma is resolved. Coming to terms with adult masculinity requires acknowledgement of inadequacy; men must live with their 'teensy peckers', hence the film proposes the Kid's acceptance of his inadequacy as more satisfactory (because more realistic?) than Little Bill/Gene Hackman's inadequate (because fictional?) maturity.

The anxieties generated by recognition of the gulf between the symbolic and the real exercised many of our contributors, and the consequences of that recognition for an understanding of the individual's psychic makeup and of the collective structures ordering patriarchal society have led to some fascinating and productive insights into the conditions of that society. Gillian Swanson suggests these 'instabilities of the masculine' are figured visually in Burt Lancaster's persona and performances, drawing attention to what she describes as a 'dissolving corporeality' and referencing masculine anxieties about access to power and status in the social world – but with an implicit reference to the insubstantial and ephemeral nature of the penis. The delicate balance of the poignant and solid – 'the fragile opulence of Burt's body' – is understood in the typical angle of his massive neck which she pinpoints as the starting point for her 'attachment'. Something is promised, for her, in the solid poignancy of Burt Lancaster's performance of the Prince in *The Leopard* (Visconti, Italy, 1963), but it and he represent something fragile, something 'uncompleted in some way, unachieved'. The film's insistent discourse of Sicilian politics and history draws attention to what seems to be a perennial condition of anxiety in the masculine subject, to be accounted for, perhaps, in the impossibility for the male subject of reconciling his own being with the body politic of which he aspires to be a part. As Swanson suggests 'masculinity ... is unable to locate itself in a trajectory that escapes immobility; it is finally unable to assume a position'.

Similarly, Radstone's interest in Al Pacino is aroused by 'a certain fragility, a particular quality of fear, an edgy sense of collapse staved off' which she notes as a recurrent element of Pacino's persona. His portrayal of the limits of patriarchal masculinity explores the confusion over who possesses, and who lacks, the Phallus and, in Pacino/Frank's dealings with his partner and with his father in *Sea of Love*, offers the 'spectacle of patriarchal masculinity divesting itself of much of its sustaining apparatus ...', a common theme in the essays constituting this book. But this divestment is fraught with contradictions for the masculine subject because 'Frank/Pacino's plea for love ... seems to inch him (and us?) away from patriarchal masculinity's denials of emotional and corporeal lacks and inch him (and us?) towards an acknowledgement of masculinity's symbolic castration'. Morgan also notes the many destabilizing devices in *Tie Me Up! Tie Me Down!*, in particular the ambiguities surrounding 'saving' which, she suggests, 'serve as reminders of the fragility of the masculine ideal and its need for constant reassertion and reinforcement'. For our purposes what is so interesting is the recognition that masculine anxieties are not simply to be located in the awful spectacle of the castrated woman, but within the structures of masculinity itself. Both Frank/Pacino and the Prince/Lancaster experience their anxieties in relation to and as a consequence of their dealings with other masculine subjects and within the structures of patriarchal social order. Women rarely come in to this picture. Once masculine anxiety can no longer be displaced onto the female subject the prospect is indeed bleak, one might say tragic.

Writing about Jean Gabin's production of a paradigm for French masculinity, Ginette Vincendeau notes the 'generally doomed desire for rebellion and escape' of his early proletarian heroes, and suggests that their 'tragic destiny' was frequently motivated in the narrative by criminality. Does this suggest that the cinema's perennial fascination with masculine criminality could be explained as a means of allowing recognition of, or attention to, masculine anxiety and tragedy within the 'external' notion of a public law/transgression model while, at the same time, purveying an anxiety inhering far more deeply in the masculine psyche? It is also of interest to note, apropros Gabin, that his trajectory 'from rebellious proletarian to godfather/patriarch' offers precisely that which, according to the readings dominant among our female contributors, is actually denied to the masculine subject. Could this account for both his star and his paradigmatic status in French cinema? Vincendeau suggests that his success relates closely to certain social and political factors – both in French society and in the cinema industry – but perhaps there is more to it than that?

One source of male tragedy, then, is the inevitable trajectory of phallic power, another is its inaccessibility. As Thumim notes apropos Will/Clint Eastwood's recurrent struggle with his horse in *Unforgiven*, this inevitability is figured in the man of action's loss of prowess. And once *loss*, rather than prowess, is emphasised, we are returned to the terrifying instabilities of the masculine, to dissolving corporeality, to fallibility, vulnerability, and fragility and the masculine recognition that the Phallus is, in the end, forever out of reach; as Swanson so elegantly puts it 'the Prince/Lancaster can only become struck by an interminable grief for an elusive object'.

This fundamental anxiety appears in many guises – in the stoop of Lancaster's neck, the fearfulness of Pacino's edginess, in very the mise-en-scène within which fictional characters are offered. Sarah Street notes the claustrophobic settings in *Sunset Boulevard* (Wilder, US, 1950) in which William Holden/Joe Gillis is trapped, contained and restricted in various ways not only by events but also visually in the filmic articulations of camera and lighting. His anxieties are referenced in the narrative by his failing career and ambiguous relationship with Norma/Gloria Swanson, but the *visual* representations exceed these narrative requirements thus allowing a more dangerous recognition (for patriarchy) of the pitfalls of masculine subjectivity. Joe/Holden's position *as a man* is so compromised that it must be compensated by his voice-over which controls the narrative. Hence for male spectators, Street suggests, Holden's powerlessness within the diegesis is contained within an extra-diegetic position of supreme power. He holds power, finally, because *he* is telling the story.

Writing about more recent film, Rowe notes how *Pretty Woman* (Marshall, US, 1990) foists the evils of patriarchal masculinity and western capitalism onto its most odious characters, Edward/Richard Gere's father and his unregenerate lawyer. By this manoeuvre the representatives of phallic power (the father, the lawyer) are made responsible for the psychic damage to the central male character whom the film then recuperates by emphasising the distance between him and symbolic/phallic power. Thus both his weakness and fragility are valorised and, in such valorisation, compensated for in the text's preferred reading. The notion of compensation is, we think, a productive one in accounting for the social consequences of masculine psychic anxiety, and one to which Swanson, in her exploration of the psychic/political interfaces of patriarchy, devotes considerable space. In considering the consequences of masculine instabilities, she suggests that '*The Leopard* is a film which addresses the disparities in the way national alignments are individualised, the pragmatics of historical continuity and the vulnerability of political contracts to personal investments' and asks what it is about the sexual as a problem of masculinity which lends legibility to these terms. Here is a powerful argument for understanding the painful psychic recognition of the contingency of masculinity – its ephemerality – as the driving force behind more easily visible social structures commonly referred to as political and/or institutional. It bears out the truism of the women's movement that social structures in patriarchy are themselves an inscription of masculine power, masculine knowledge, and masculine understandings of being.

THE EXTERNAL WORLD

In films, power, patriarchy and privilege in the public world often stand for aspects of the inner, psychic world, but they also carry more direct meanings and reverberations. Power is central to the public, political sphere, to patriarchy and hence to any consideration of masculinity; indeed power and masculinity are virtually synonymous.

We noted in *You Tarzan* that it is not surprising that issues associated with power such as status, hierarchy, knowledge, skill, and success are used to inform our understanding of the operations of male empowerment and control, whether this be exercised over events, people or emotions. The question of worldly success and failure is central to both main characters in *Sunset Boulevard*, not just to Joe/Holden, who had a potentially glamorous career as a Hollywood scriptwriter. Street draws attention to the importance of his career failure, to his sense of inadequacy and to his fate as a kept man, the ultimate in male dependence. Even his surroundings are no longer those associated wih the public world of work: he becomes trapped in the domestic space of the faded female star. He has found a way to the 'good life' but it is marked as illegitimate because he has not earned it. By contrast, the worldly success of the Gabin characters, in the thrillers in which he starred in the 1950s, is something he has worked for but its criminality makes it illegitimate. But this is a man's man – not one kept by a woman – and he inhabits both domestic space and a range of public spaces from nightclubs and executive suites to the less plush but solid and 'male' courtrooms and police stations. The use of mise-en-scène as marker of bourgeois success moves into overdrive with *Pretty Woman*, arguably the most potent recent Hollywood rendition of the populist myth of the small (wo)man making it in free (white) America. The seduction of those markers, which include sumptuous clothes, superlative cars, decidedly up-market accommodation and gourmet food – to say nothing of lashings of dollar bills (Rowe comments that money is eroticised here more than 'true love') – is as powerful as the seductive Cinderella and Pygmalion narratives on which the worldly success and class transformation of the woman, Vivian/Julia Roberts, are based. There are objects of desire in abundance here for the female spectator, with clothes often out-doing Gere's particular brand of good looks. This is capitalism at its most worldly and at its most seductive; a cruel irony for those pulled into the narrative drive towards the 'happy ending' of riches and romance for both of them. But the routes to career and economic success are markedly different for the two main characters, the differences highlighting a central agenda for contemporary white male bourgeois masculinity. At first she is portrayed as not particularly successful at her job (prostitution) in financial terms; she is decidedly down at heel when by chance she meets Edward. It is only thereafter that she is shown to be professionally competent and receives what is for her good money (though, in fact, small pickings from his corporate profits) for a job well done. Her work, at one remove from the public world of its economic base, is constantly off-set against his. Like office cleaning, it is an integral part of business life but one which carries domestic and private references within the public sphere and is even more hidden away from the day-to-day activities of the public (male) world of business. By contrast, his enormous worldly success is seen to be the result of his talents and active endeavours, as opposed to being the lucky consequence of chance; hence the benevolent face of capitalism is fused with paternalistic lust and romantic love.

In cinematic representations career success is frequently imbricated with class and also with social mobility which are sometimes, though by no means always, closely associated. In *Pretty Woman* the proletarian woman 'moves up' out of her class through her charming personality, moral integrity, and prowess in bed. Her new class position, that of her husband-to-be, is not only sanctioned by the marriage but also sanitised by the associations of his job with 'good works', largely instigated through her influence. His job and class position are thereby legitimised for female entry into that class and for female approbation. The hero is dis/associated from the worst aspects of the 'old order' and capitalist greed, and their joint income is thereby made morally acceptable to Vivian/Roberts and to the female spectator alike.

Gabin's criminal heroes, on the other hand, gain the trappings of bourgeois life but are not successful at moving into respectable society because their business interests remain tainted with illegitimacy. These men play against a dirty system in dirty ways and inhabit the public world in a less than public way. Like the prostitute and the cleaner, they are tucked away from view; they too are ghettoised. They are often less an underclass than a parallel class; in the world of male power they do not occupy the same positions as their legitimate business and/or income equivalents. Represented as embodying the opposite of womanly attibutes, they are tough, ruthless, powerful and morally unscrupulous yet they too are kept at a distance from the respectable public world of work and, as such, some of their experiences are not dissimilar to those of many women.

Financial and career success are also crucial to the models of 'good' black masculinity offered by black director Oscar Micheaux in the 1930s and discussed here by Charlene Regester. But, again, legitimacy is all important, the 'easy' money of gambling and racketeering marking the moral decay of the black community in the USA. Micheaux's 'good guys' are respectable, they are attorneys, physicians, teachers, ministers, farmers/landlords and entrepreneurs using education and/or a will to succeed to reach for the America dream. 'Progressive' criticism acknowledges the 'positive' images of such black men but is less comfortable with Micheaux's call for blacks to emulate the white bourgeoisie. In a different article, and vis-à-vis transsexualism, Lola Young makes a point of some considerable bearing on this which significantly challenges the ways we think about 'moving up' the social order. She suggests that 'moving up' a hierarchy may be 'profoundly disruptive because it undermines the essentialist claims to exclusivity of the dominant, privileged group: the privilege based in the external signs of "race" or sex is demonstrated as being something which is appropriated rather than a natural and inevitable situation.

".Moving down" is not inherently more radical or subversive, as it may be read as a surrendering of power in order to abdicate responsibility.' Thus she offers a more open-ended response for viewers, women and men, in relation to ambitions, aspirations, worldly success and the assimilation of different cultural values, all of which have been and are difficult issues for radical politics.

In terms of social (and moral) status the Prince in *The Leopard* and the Earl in *Greystoke: The Legend of Tarzan, Lord of the Apes* (Hudson, UK, 1984), representing the 'old' order based on inheritance and innate breeding rather than merit, both outstrip the characters in those films that represent the 'new' order of capitalism and bourgeois politics, yet in *Pretty Woman*, the representative of 1990s corporate capitalism is presented as the ultimate ideal provider, companion and romantic lover. In general, however, our contributors have shown less concern with aristocrats or successful capitalists, big or small, than with more ordinary or flawed men. One of the ironies of *Unforgiven*, another tale of male work, is that the working gun-fighter, whose status came from his toughness and prowess, in the end gives it all up for, as the reference to the dry goods that he sells suggests, the emasculating occupation of shopkeeper. There is a hint of emasculation too, when the failed Hollywood scriptwriter in *Sunset Boulevard* turns gigolo. Vincendeau argues that so strong was the image of proletarian ordinariness that Gabin embodied in France in the 1930s that it continued to sustain him both as a proletarian hero and as a hero of the proletariat despite film parts, to say nothing of his own lifestyle, which worked against this image. The 'ordinariness' of the characters, and the way he played them, invites comparison with those Charles Farrell played out in 'naturalistic' styles in movies directed by Frank Borzage. Unlike Joe/Holden in *Sunset Boulevard* who cannot face returning to his home town in Ohio and leading an ordinary and uneventful life, Borzage revels in his heroes' ordinariness, as do Siletto (screenplay) and Reisz (director) in *Saturday Night and Sunday Morning* (UK, 1960). Seaton/Finney heralded the new proletarian hero and there is little of the old collective camaraderie of the male working-class world depicted in this bleak tale.

Besides men in entrenched or shifting class positions, cinema frequently deals with men in groups. Yet episodes of male bonding are not frequent in this volume, with the exception of two of Oliver Stone's war films discussed by Margaret O'Brien, and possibly, of the relationship between Jody/Forest Whitaker and Dil/Jaye Davidson in *The Crying Game* (Jordan,

UK, 1992). Yet filmic relations between (often small) groups of men frequently provide points of connection between the individual and the collective, the personal and the public. This interface, which allows exploration of broader public, political and social issues through the relatively safe means of individual voices and/or actions, is an established Hollywood device which draws on the rampant individualism of the American myth for much of its impact. Small groups of men in movies also provide examples of contrasting and/or conflicting masculinities, sometimes emphasising the pluralism of dominant masculinity/ies but, more often, privileging one particular type. *The Spider's Stratagem* (Bertolucci, Italy, 1970) plays around with this convention, using it to establish the superiority of the anti-fascist martyr over his comrades and contemporaries, only to have them and other voices from the past deconstruct the myth of his martyrdom, of his life as represented to the world after his death.

Swanson's study of Visconti's *The Leopard* (1963) and Lesley Caldwell's of Bertolucci's *The Spider's Stratagem* (1970), both explore masculinity via films concerned with nation/national identity and politics. Swanson develops a fascinating model of the relationship between the (collective) expressions of citizenship and masculinity which places the latter firmly in the public arena. Visconti's exploration of honourable politics and shifting authority is historically located in the move from the older order to the new – marked by the emergence of the nation state in the nineteenth century – but the agenda of conflict between principled positions and *real politik* clearly relates to contemporary concerns. Bertolucci goes back in time to a period still within living memory, to the fight against fascism, using a more fluid narrative structure to explore personal as well as national identity and to assert the links between past and present. A personal journey into memory of the past focuses on the friendship between a group of old men and the young male searcher after truth, linking the generations, the personal and the public, the past and the present. Caldwell's essay, like Bertolucci's film, finds the *process of becoming* more interesting than the *reality of being*. With reference to Gledhill's questions about how women access male cinematic concerns, this film seems to offer access via a rites of passage theme which emphasises the young man's exploration and construction of his own identity, while at the same time seeing that of his dead father *de*constructed.

THE BODY, ACTION, INACTION

Unlike in *You Tarzan*, there is relatively little focus here on the male body in action although O'Brien deals with Oliver Stone's 'Vietnam Trilogy', and Thumim with that deconstruction of the western, *Unforgiven*. In certain westerns and cop movies, the excessive violence of some male characters is critiqued so as to make more acceptable that meted out by the male lead. Vincendeau notes that this is the case in the thrillers in which Gabin starred from the 1950s but that, by contrast, in most of his 1930s films he was 'a victim ... paralysed, unable to move ...'. This, as Gledhill and others suggest, this might well have made him more accessible to the female imagination, particularly as he dreams of ways to escape despite the fact that his fantasies, like those of Seaton/Finney in *Saturday Night and Sunday Morning* (Reisz, UK, 1960), are doomed. Christine Geraghty's perceptive reading of Seaton/Finney in that film highlights the passivity of the beefy male so often taken as the epitome of 1960s tough British working-class machismo. *Me Jane* pays considerable attention to men's bodies – tall, small, strong, wounded, scarred, tattoed, naked, clothed, black, white, old, young – but, though many readings of those bodies (literal and metaphorical) are based on a great deal of looking, few focus on the direct display of the male body as spectacle. There is little here on the epic, on action, adventure or sports films, for example, which highlight the active male body and, it is argued, legitimise male as well as female gazing at men. Indeed sport, that major marker of masculinity, only really features in Pat Kirkham's discussion of Charles Farrell's star persona. Furthermore, in Griselda Pollock's discussions of Tarzan, there is next to no mention of Tarzan/Greystoke's body, which in both its adolescent and adult nakedness is not only spectacularised but differentiates the 'wild' and 'civilised' worlds.

The combination of good looks and being tall is repeatedly shown to have played an important part in representations of acceptable or preferred masculinities, black and white; the black heroes of Oscar Micheaux's 1930s films, for example, like the majority of male film stars then and since, were tall and good-looking. Height generally signals dominance and authority whilst attractiveness suggests the potential for counter attraction and, therefore, for romance or sex. Many of the essays feature stars who fit this bill, but equally fascinating are those studies of stars who do not quite measure up to these ideals.

Villains and other male characters of varying degrees of 'badness' can be small and/or ugly, heroes sometimes small – but they are rarely also unattractive and even more rarely ugly. In the case of the attractive Al Pacino, Radstone focuses on his smallness which had particular resonances for her. Pacino is one of those contemporary Hollywood stars rated, like De Niro, for his acting abilities as well as for his star qualities – although the latter, as Helen Stoddart points out, is not usually constructed as the object of romantic or sexual desire. Small men, and particularly small men not generally deemed to be heart-throb material, seem to need to prove themselves more as actors (or in certain movies as dancers or comedians) and by that very prowess assert their claim to masculinity. Strength as well as size is an important marker of masculinity. Three essays (on Farrell, Pacino and Lancaster) deal, in differing degrees of detail, with the tempering of strength: the softness and/or fragility of the male body being emphasised in order to suggest vulnerability. But not all male bodies are dealt with as totalities. The fragmentation and focus evident in the concerns with Burt Lancaster's neck, Albert Finney's beefy arms, and the expressive eyes of Gabin and Farrell, suggest an objectification of the male body – a practice too often assumed only to be employed for female protagonists. The physical body plays an important part in performance. The main modes of acting discussed in this anthology are either the melodramatic or various types of 'realism' – from 1920s Hollywood 'naturalism' and Gabin's famous minimalist performances to Lancaster's general hesitancy and De Niro's and Pacino's better known adherence to 'Method' modes of expression.

The voice occupies a curious position between the physical body of the actor and the ear of the film viewer (the very word 'viewer' privileging the visual over the spoken in film culture). We consider that its highly affective but disembodied and shifting nature makes it a fascinating topic of study (we were delighted at Gill Branston's choice of subject matter), but that those qualities possibly also explain the current lack of attention to it within film studies. Branston notes, for example, the impossibility of offering a 'sound-bite' as 'illustration' – perhaps we may look forward to this in newly emerging publishing forms such as CD-ROM. Critical attention is more frequently given to the voice-over which fits more easily into narrative traditions (see the essays by Street and Rowe) and is more generally dealt with in terms of narrative context rather than of the *quality* of sound. Voice, together with acting and body language, overall attractiveness and body form, play important parts in the 'to-be-looked-at-ness' of men. The 'male gaze' directed at woman as object, which dominated so much feminist film history and criticism in the 1970s and 1980s, is explicitly critiqued in *Tie Me Up! Tie Me Down!* through Almodovar's use of the pornographic film within a film, and several essays acknowledge the importance of the active female gaze. Oscar Micheaux's 'challenge to dominant cinematic practice' allowed for the female erotic gaze, and Farrell, Gabin and Eastwood are all here claimed to be objectified by the woman who dares to look; indeed Gledhill argues that Eastwood positively courts the female gaze in *High Plains Drifter* (Eastwood, US, 1972) and *Pale Rider* (Eastwood, US, 1985). Gabin, whose enormous popularity was partly built on his attraction of the female protagonist's gaze as well as that of the female audience and fans was, Vincendeau informs us, extremely anxious that he should not look 'effeminate' – inadvertently, perhaps, touching on what are for heterosexual men vexed questions related to ambiguities and instabilities within the representations of the glamorised or sexually attractive male.

The inadequacy of masculinity traced through the body is here discussed largely in terms of ageing and of invalidity (Eastwood, Hackman, Pacino, Farrell). Many male stars are able to maintain their status and prowess despite their having aged whereas the greater disruption of maiming or wounding to 'perfect' masculinity emphasises the central importance to it of physical wholeness, prowess and perfection. The cop in *Sea of Love* who fears mortality and is restored to a chastened version of wholeness through acknowledging his need for another, through love, bears similarities to the Borzage heroes, discussed by Kirkham, who find transcendence in love. But they, like the blind Pacino in *Scent of a Woman* (Brest, US, 1992), are often maimed or wounded. The penetration of wounding and its consequent invalidity, Rozsika Parker argues, places the male in the position of the female and allows for female recognition, empathy and the acknowledgement of sexual attraction. At the same time Borzage usually places considerable emphasis on competence and prowess, before and after the wounding, sometimes both, and also on a physical as well as an emotional transcendence of injuries or infirmities. The physical and psychological wounding of the male marks him as vulnerable, in the manner of the wounded Christ – an ultimate symbol of male vulnerability. To quote from our essay *You Tarzan* 'The crucified body is contradictory and perverse. In this image are united passivity and control, humiliation and nobility, eroticism and religious transcendence. "The epic hero ... demonstrates his control over his body through his ability to give it up". This is indeed a perverse ideal. The opposing agendas of duty and emotion, law and love, death and desire are united in sacrifice: this is the crucifixion, offered as the ultimate act of self control, thereby transcending control and producing the ideal'. However, it should be remembered that references to and/or representations of wounded men also evoke pre-Christian heroes, as Helen Stoddart notes in her discussion of wounded and scarred heroes from classical male mythological narratives – including those of Adonis and Odysseus, to say nothing of Oedipus. The names of those heroes call on their scars, rather than on the manner of their wounding. Like Christ's stigmata, the scars are the visible signs of their suffering.

Competence and prowess are important markers not just of masculinity in general but of the capable provider and ideal partner in particular. Prowess is such a significant marker that it does not always matter how it is manifested. On seeing a photograph of Frank Farmer/Kevin Costner in American football kit in *The Bodyguard* (Jackson, US, 1992), for instance, Rachel Marron/Whitney Houston asks 'Were you tough?' to which he replies 'No. I was fast'. What matters is that he was good at it.

Of all occupations, that of bodyguard most directly involves the spectacle of the body, usually male, as a physical protector and, because physical protection readily stands in for other forms of material and emotional protection, it is a powerful symbol when associated with gender relations. How many (female) desires for security are met by the fantasies associated with a lover who will protect you from all harm (and be good in bed too) which is what Costner appears to offer in *The Bodyguard*? Significantly, in *In the Line of Fire* (Petersen, US, 1993) Eastwood plays a bodyguard who attracts the attentions of Lily Raines/Rene Russo, in a text that in many ways parallels the ageing cowboy of *Unforgiven*. Much of the Eastwood 'presence' and stature are retained (and evoked) even though, or perhaps because, he is clearly ageing. Like the Costner character, the Eastwood bodyguard is a perfectionist driven to do his job as well as possible. The Eastwood prowess precedes him – in his star persona as well as through the narrative. He only has to appear on the screen in the 1990s for viewers to know that here is a man who can look after himself – and, by implication, can look after women too.

Somewhat more attention is paid to the clothing of male bodies in this volume than in *You Tarzan* but, like acting, body language and mise-en-scène, dress/costume deserves more attention in film studies. Clothes can serve to beautify and sexualise the male body and, as Young shows, can map out the body as 'feminine' to such a degree that its sex becomes ambiguous, if not completely misidentified. Not removable like clothes, although equally culturally contingent, skin colour and tone can not only sexualise but also stigmatise or validate. Regester cites the ironic example of black director Oscar Micheaux casting as male leads those very black men with light skin, straight hair and 'European' features who were rejected by Hollywood *because* they could be mistaken for white. Her essay also comments on the powerful sexual charge attributed to black masculinity which is coded within white culture as dangerous and threatening. Referring to the work of Richard Dyer and bell hooks, she makes points which connect with Gledhill's explorations of women reading men, noting not only the immense sexuality of Paul Robeson on screen but also Oscar Micheaux's acknowledgement of the desires of female spectators, by making black actors into desirable figures and incorporating the direct female gaze.

Black sexuality clearly plays a significant part in *The Crying Game*, but is the emphasis on 'deviant' or 'excessive' sexuality of a black male just another more sophisticated twist to the old tale – one which takes into account the fashionable 'gender bending' of the 1990s? Young argues that, despite all the pre-release hullabaloo about the sexual 'secret', in this film by a white male film-maker it is *race* rather than sexuality that is problematic, even though this is neither foregrounded nor problematised in the way that sexuality is. She writes about the 'racialisation of sexual transgression', of the fusing of the masculine and the feminine in a 'homo/transsexual black man masquerading as a woman: three kinds of Otherness captured in one'. The phenomenon of 'passing', whether as one sex rather than another or as belonging to one 'race' or culture rather than another, relates closely to the *construction* of identity as well as to masquerade. Interestingly, Swanson's observations on passing relate to a white (homosexual) character. She notes the lasting impression on many men of one particular scene in *Lawrence of Arabia* (Lean, UK, 1962) at the time of its release. That scene involved Peter O'Toole at the moment of his most emphatic assertion of the possibilities of identification with an 'other' culture as he changes his British military uniform for a billowing white Arab garment, giggling delightedly at the wonder of corporeal disguise and exotic self-fashioning. Lawrence/O'Toole's 'passing' is between cultures; from the ordinary, known, and domestic to the foreign which, Swanson argues, is part of the historical constitution of masculine subjectivity and definition. Drawing on Kristeva, she shows the centrality of the concept of the wanderer, the searcher ever open to new experiences, both to the opposition implicit in the idea of the foreign and to the construction of masculinity. Much as she argues, correctly, that we need to analyse the masculine in terms other than those which reference the feminine, however, one of the many reasons why the scene referred to is so resonant for western viewers is that it encourages participation in that liberating moment. And the moment is liberating partly because of the freedom the body, particularly the legs, is afforded by the garments. For the western male viewer it offers particular pleasures of being within a certain type of long, loose and flowing dress known mainly to women in his society; to a degree it offers a 'female' experience to the male just as it offers the foreign 'other' experience to the white person.

THE POLITICS OF GENDER

A dominant concern among the contributors to *Me Jane* is with the moral conflict which ensues once gendered values are 'lent' or 'borrowed' to inform filmic construction of social conflicts – not only the conflicts of gender but also those of race, class, age and citizenship. In a sense here is the female reader's perception of the psychic construction of masculinity writ large – written on the scale of the social itself. The complex imbrication of the symbolic and the real, so characteristic of popular cinema and central to active spectatorial production and re-production of patriarchal ideology, allows the interplay and exchange of gender specific values between fictional characters. But it also allows, through the gendering of the social, the spillage of such values onto the settings, locations, the very mises-en-scène to which characters are inextricably tied. Within the film image, after all, the character and her/his location have potentially equal status, and therefore signifying power. Gledhill is substantially concerned with the question of the production of ideology in the course of female readings which involve the processes of recognition and fantasy, and she introduces an important qualification in her observation that 'from D.W. Griffith onward, masculinity and femininity, rather than lending gender values to social conflicts may themselves be in moral conflict'. Whereas this 'lending' of values was assumed, fairly unproblematically, amongst contributors to *You Tarzan*, it is the consequent moral conflict which has exercised contributors to *Me Jane*. Emphasising the ideological work performed through popular cinema, she suggests that 'we need to focus on the film precisely as an elaboration of what the culture puts into conflict': clearly one of the important issues here is the negotiation of gender definitions – the specificities of culturally constructed gender – which is precisely the aspect of reading the masculine dominating the essays in this volume.

Gledhill's essay offers useful and sometimes provocative insights into these processes, exemplified by fragments of her own textual readings. That her insights *are* productive ones is borne out by their resonances in other essays, particularly those referencing social and/or historically specific events. Regester's discussion of Micheaux's representations of black masculinity, for example, shows how black men, both filmically *and* socially, were 'relegated to the realm of the feminine', citing, amongst other examples, the case of the prize fighter Jack Johnson who, following his 1910 defeat of the white fighter James Jeffries, was denied access to a major public sphere. No movie images of him were to be publicly screened; his victory had to be compensated by his relegation to the devalued, because not-public, and therefore *private* realm, an equivalent to the realm of the feminine. The binary oppositions of public/masculine, private/ feminine, signs of the gendered representation of the social, inform several essays. Young, for example, teasing out the complex web of exclusions which, she argues, constitutes *The Crying Game*, notes apropos the film's representation of the British/Irish conflict that 'the political is adeptly reconstituted as the non-threatening personal'. Put another way, her insight shows how the (feminised) private is used, by being made the site of displacement for a dangerous public transgression rendered harmless when it becomes private/personal, and therefore 'only' a *feminine*, transgression which cannot threaten the State – or the status quo. The public – political – transgression is made safe by being feminised, and feminised by being personalised. We would say 'privatised' but in 1990s Britain this term has lost its usefulness. Young elaborates on the complexities of this lending and borrowing of values characteristic of hegemonic claims, suggesting that 'ideologies of racial and cultural inferiority and superiority inform social and gender hierarchies' and pointing out the dangers, to the dominant group, in the willingness of any of their number to 'move down' in the hierarchy (which is what Dil/Jaye Davidson has done, in the terms of gender politics, by living as a woman, though, as we see, he is unequivocally a man) because such a move threatens the values informing the hierarchy itself. Thus the instabilities of the masculine, noted by Morgan, Swanson, Radstone and others, become instabilities of the social in so far as this is understood in gendered terms. The key proposition here is that the public sphere is identified with the masculine and the private, by opposition, with the feminine. Thus to distinguish between characters on the basis of their access to the public, is also to evaluate the characters' relation (to each other, to us, of their diegetic circumstances) in gendered terms.

This point is developed further in Branston's essay on the voice where she draws attention to Leary/Malkovitch's 'final shout of betrayal' in the last scene of *In The Line of Fire*, noting the fusion of the feminine with the masculine implicit in the broadcasting of the telephone conversation, when public and private modes of receiving sound are fused. The gendering of spaces through sound is thus confused, producing the implication that gender definitions are themselves fluid. By this clever means the opposition between the two men, Leary/ Malkovitch and Horrigan/Eastwood is itself produced as gendered, coded as the feminised versus the securely masculine, a coding which the narrative displaces onto the safer terrain of law versus lawlessness. One of the recurring pleasures of Branston's essay concerns, precisely, the additional insights into the gendering of the social which is allowed through attention to sound and particularly to the modulations of the voice. Leary/Malkovitch is feminised not only through the 'privacy' of his speech but also through his trangressive mimicry – his voice is fluid, unreliable because it is disguised – which recalls the duplicitousness of the self-productive device of female masquerade.

The 'feminine' device of masquerade has its counterpart, these essays would seem to suggest, in a masculine strategy noted in certain films which acknowledge the flaws in patriarchal masculinity and draw particular attention, as we have seen, to the suffering and anxiety induced in male subjects by their recognition of the impossibility of acceding to the Phallus. But in some films this acknowledgement of the dis-abling flaws in the patriarchal ideal is accompanied, or succeeded, by a claim that such flaws may be compensated by recourse to 'feminine' attributes. We are invited to understand that the tough or cynical exterior masks – it is *only* a mask – vulnerability which lies beneath/within. Maintaining the exterior is acknowledged to require constant effort, thus masculinity is not 'given', not effortless. It is susceptible to wounding, piercing, scarring, which will reveal it to be that which it is not: soft, fragile, provisional even. Gledhill notes, apropos Deckard/Harrison Ford in *Bladerunner*, that he is 'a man wounded by patriarchy but redeemable through his capacity to identify with the female character. For the female viewer such a figure may offer the gratifying spectacle of masculinity crossing the gender divide, revealing a vulnerability beneath a tough exterior'. It is a strategy, however, of which we should perhaps be wary, since the masculine crossing of the gender divide is an adventure largely conducted in the interests of the male subject. In the case of Deckard this may allow female sympathy or even identification with his dilemma, as well as pleasure at his transformation, but many other redemptions of masculinity are unequivocally at the expense of the female subject, as in the case of Joe/William Holden in *Sunset Boulevard* who, in his controlling voice-over, constructs Norma/Gloria Swanson as a 'monstrum' in order to compensate for his own humiliation.

Another, possibly more difficult, instance of the fusion of masculine and feminine attributes for the male subject relates to youth and the passage to adult masculinity. The male youth can be considered as feminised because he is not yet fully mature and he presents an ambivalent figure, a figure which invites the dangerous contradiction for masculinity implicit in the homo-erotic spectacle. This contradiction is similar to that noted by both Kirkham and Vincendeau, and to some extent also by Morgan, in their discussions of 'maternal', nurturing male characters whose 'femininity' must always, it seems, be compensated in the narrative. The dangers, for male subjects, of positioning the male in the inferior place(s) of the feminine subject are accompanied, for the female spectator, by an understandable fascination with the revelation that certain activities produce a disempowerment which is the consequence of positioning and circumstances rather than of sex.

The related questions of compensation and transgression appear, on the evidence of this volume, to be central to popular cinema's contribution to hegemonic struggle over gender. We might even argue that transgression is in itself 'feminine' since to transgress patriarchal law – social, moral, ethical, political – is to put oneself outside it, and outside the symbolic boundaries of the masculine is, precisely, the realm of the feminine. Young notes that, in cross-dressing, 'both transvestites and transsexuals contest the fixity of sex ascription' that is to say they refuse the symbolic borders of the masculine by disrupting sartorial boundaries which both enable and police public (therefore dominant, patriarchal) definitions of the masculine. For the male spectator this spectacle in itself can be a liberating pleasure, as some of our contributors to *You Tarzan* observed and as referenced in this volume by Lawrence/O'Toole, dancing delightedly in his Arab robes in the exotic desert landscape. Here surely is recognition of a welcome subversion of masculine fixity, a step across the borders into the limitless and therefore uncontrollable feminine, a form of adventuring.

But female spectators should also note that in this transgressive abandonment there is also an appropriation which leaves little place for the female subject. As colonial history shows, adventuring has very different consequences for the adventurers than for those amongst whom the 'adventure' is conducted. In an interesting acknowledgement of this limitation, for the female reader, of pleasure in the spectacle of transgressive masculinity, Gledhill suggests that it might be precisely the opposite of transgression which fascinates female viewers. She cites the 'unassimilability, separateness and invincibility of the Eastwood persona' which offers 'the pleasure of ego definition and boundedness which both separates the self from others and their needs and at the same time make(s) it possible to act on them'. Rather than the predatory forays into the realm of the feminine which seem so typical of filmic representation of masculine anxieties, identity formation and conflicts, Eastwood's persona offers a reliable *fixity* which recognises women as separate and other. This *recognition*, she proposes, is likely to be pleasurable to the female spectator since in so many fictions we (women) are present only as a marker to the symbolic realm of the masculine. This is particulary clear in *The Spider's Stratagem* of which Caldwell notes that there are, apart from the dead father's mistress, Draifa, no female characters yet the 'place of the woman is as central in the son's journey, and in the film's structure, as it is central to accession to the symbolic realm'. However, we should note that a woman's place is not at all the same thing as a woman, and Draifa herself is like a summary of woman's place on the borders of the masculine symbolic since she is 'ambiguous, ageless, sexualised'.

The notorious difficulties in theorising female spectatorial activity are a direct consequence of patriarchal investment in eliding the difference between the signifier – Woman – and the signified – the boundaries of the masculine – which narratives often work to produce (albeit erroneously) as equivalent to actual women. But though direct misogyny surfaces in narratives relatively rarely (see Gledhill) from the female spectator's point of view the usurpal of the signifier Woman is in itself a misogynist move because of its simultaneous appropriation and denial of female experience. Looked at like this we might conclude that a universal theme of popular cinema is, precisely, a misogynist denial of the feminine. Vincendeau notes that Gabin's 'pairings with women his own age tended to produce extremely misogynist narratives' in which 'mature women appear in humiliating or monstrous positions: bitter, dull "kill-joys", pointedly childless or else horrifying as mothers. Conversely, "feminine" values of tenderness, nurturing and vulnerability, are ascribed to Gabin'.

The valorisation of 'feminine' qualities in the romantic hero, noted in many of these essays can conceal a paternalist (patriarchal) misogyny operating through the mechanism of appropriation. Appropriating 'the other' implies a denial of the other's subjecthood. Further, since the romantic hero is often opposed, in narratives, to the patriarchal misogynist (a move explicitly described in Rowe's discussion of *Pretty Woman*) the concealment is doubly effective. Patriarchal misdemeanours (hatred of women) are acknowledged, and the correction (valorisation of the feminine) is claimed in the figure of the romantic hero. But he is still a man – hence woman is still denied as the proper site of the feminine which is thus maintained as guarantor of boundaries in the masculine symbolic economy. Morgan's insight concerning misogyny and romance – that 'the ideological foundations of these superficially antithetical notions share common assumptions about gender roles' – is germane here. The romantic hero's appropriation of the feminine can disguise the misogynist denial of woman's autonomous right to her own experience. In a development of this idea Rowe suggests 'another, darker scenario that recasts the story of struggle for women's rights into a melodrama of male victims and female villains – a direct reversal of the classic structure of melodrama outlined in Gledhill's essay and, therefore, an example of what Gledhill calls 'an active sense of culture as constant negotiation, process, fantasising, work'. If Susan Faludi's *Backlash* (1991) is to be believed, this strategy has contributed to the successful patriarchal recuperation of the women's movement during the 1980s. Vincendeau's discussion of Gabin and what she terms 'paradigmatic French masculinity' notes the longevity of such recuperative moves. In the earlier populist dramas Gabin 'invaded traditionally feminine spaces such as kitchens, dining rooms or children's bedrooms, and appropriated them' and throughout his long screen career he assimilated feminine characteristics to his own figure, denying, in the process, female autonomy. Even if the women suffer (as they often did) it is Gabin's own 'feminine' suffering which is the focus of audience attention. His 'victimisation of the heroine is adduced to *his* tragedy' and Gabin's star persona serves to mask his oppression of female characters. That this is a device familiar in French culture is illustrated in Depardieu's more recent and, it seems, equally successful adoption of Gabin's strategy. It may be one 'way in which patriarchal [French] culture has been able to reconcile the valorisation of femininity-as-difference with male hegemony' but as a strategy it is by no means restricted to French culture.

Transgressive adventuring and appropriation lead to the paradoxical but nevertheless widely noted filmic proposition – almost a trope of patriarchal cinema, we might suggest – that the perfect woman is a man. This is noted not only apropros Gabin and Depardieu, but also of Charles Farrell in the Borzage films discussed in Kirkham's essay, of the 'post-classical' romantic comedies which are the subject of Rowe's exploration and in Young's discussion of *The Crying Game*. Considering precursors of the gender tourism of the latter film Young notes, apropros *Some Like it Hot*, that 'the joke is on the old man, who in the quest for the perfect female partner, falls for a man in drag'. We should like to add that the competition for the affections of the rich old man in this film was none other than Marilyn Monroe herself, at that time widely acclaimed as patriarchy's ideal woman. In the more recent film Dil/Jaye Davidson is, in the terms of this ideal, a 'better' woman than the film's only 'real' female protagonist Jude/Miranda Richardson whose 'shrill characterisation as the ideologically dogmatic gangster's moll, wielding a retributive gun, stands in stark contrast to Dil, the soft-voiced transvestite version of femininity'. Moreover Jude uses her gun with a callousness and confidence which is at odds with patriarchy's preferred feminine mode in a way that her use of her sexuality to ensnare Jody/Forest Whitaker is not. By contrast, when Dil uses the gun to shoot Jude he/she is so distraught that Fergus/Stephen Rea protects him/her by assuming both guilt and punishment. The question which arises, and which Gledhill articulates, is 'what women in their millions are doing in the cinema where most of our time is spent in watching images of men rather than of women'. In one sense this volume is an attempt to answer that question, and there is a further clue, again from Gledhill's bravely speculative essay which unpacks the operations of melodrama – arguably a kind of meta-genre accounting for many of the characteristics of mainstream popular cinema. She writes 'recognition and naming are central to melodrama's epistemology': here, perhaps, is a key to the appeal of an often misogynist cinema for its female audiences, so often denied recognition in the patriarchal economy of the image and its referents. In the visual and aural 'recognition and naming' which constitutes popular cinema, female spectators can participate, in the course of producing understanding from image and referents, in the patriarchal economy of the image. In acknowledgement of this possibility Gledhill proposes a distinction between readings which 'deconstruct in a demand that [it] be accountable to analytic paradigms of the social formation or patriarchal psyche' and readings which 'work with the aesthetic dynamic and pleasure offered by the work'. She distinguishes therefore, and invites us to do so, between readings and analytical work which conform to the conventional requirements of patriarchy and its academy (including the academy's acknowledgement and subsequent appropriation of feminist scholarship) and readings and analytical work which privilege women's experience through explorations of and propositions about the meanings and pleasures available to female readers of popular (patriarchal) fictions.

... Viewer, I Listened to Him ... Voices, Masculinity, *In the Line of Fire*

Gill Branston

'One goes to see Clint to check out the current construction of masculinity in American culture.' Amy Taubin[1]

'You're the most attractive man I ever laid ears on.' *Sleepless in Seattle*

Taubin's comment seems at first glance to put an odd emphasis on a *Silence of the Lambs*-like political thriller with a 63 year old star, whose image was honed in westerns some twenty to thirty years ago. In the summer of its release in 1993 it was other films such as Stallone's *Cliffhanger*[2] and Schwarzenegger's *Last Action Hero*[3] which seemed to address the kinds of torso politics more widely associated with the construction of masculinity in the 1980s and 1990s. And cautiously aware of gender politics though the romantic relationship with Lily Raines/Rene Russo is, it seemed to me that the engagement with current masculinities did not find a focus in heterosexual relations, though the film did make me wonder about masculinity and the male voice. In this article I would like to outline ways of thinking about voices in cinema in their perceived relation to the body, and the relationship of voice to gender as it is structured vocally in cinematic and other institutions. I will then focus on the male voices in *In the Line of Fire*.[4]

BODILY VOICES

As Jane Gaines has pointed out, although voices are as imprinted with identity as faces, 'Sound imagery ... remains largely

37

"unapprehended", in contrast to the visual imagery on which consumer culture has banked so much, and to which we therefore attend with such expertise.'[5]

Recent work has done much to correct this imbalance, though even Altman's collection has only a little material on the construction of masculinity through voices in cinema.[6]

Turning first, albeit briefly, to psychoanalytic theories of pleasure of the kind dominant within Film Studies, we find arguments that the earliest pleasures associated with listening draw on heavily gendered sources of desire, bound up with the body. Mary Ann Doane has argued that:

> 'memories of the first experience of the voice, of the hallucinatory satisfaction it offered, circumscribe the pleasure of hearing and ground its relation to the fantasmatic body ... The first differences are traced along the axis of sound: the voice of the mother, the voice of the father ... The mother's soothing voice, in a particular cultural context, is the major component of the 'sonorous envelope' which surrounds the child and is the first model of auditory pleasure.'[7]

Kaja Silverman suggests, along similar psychoanalytic lines, that in 'classic cinema' the female voice is held to the interior of the diegesis (as women are held to interiority in other spheres) while the male subject has more access to exteriority, including the authoritative, *because disembodied*, voice-over.[8] Other accounts, however, have played the body-authority connection rather differently. For example in Barthes' beautiful essay (on the singing rather than speaking voice) *The Grain of the Voice*, authenticity, the authoring body, and masculinity get articulated as a particular kind of evidence:

> something which is directly the cantor's body brought to your ears in one and the same movement from deep down in the cavities, the membranes, the cartilages, and from deep down in the Slavonic language ... The 'grain' is the body in the voice ...[9]

It matters greatly of course that it is not the (hysterical?) female body but rather the power-full male body which is the source of this pleasurable, even erotic 'evidence', but Barthes makes an important point about the relationship between a body and the sound it produces.

For cinema, the voice in both sexes seems to be more naturalised than, say, the face which is more readily seen as coded, as 'made-up', but in both there are of course systematic codes at work, often inherited from theatrical melodrama, and often in relationship with assumptions about appropriate male and female voices in the rest of our social lives. The 'evidentiality' of masculinity is often signified by a deep voice, and this in itself supports and recreates cultural over-emphases on real biological differences between men and women. As Graddol and Swann suggest, vocal gender images directly affect the lives of those (often women) whose voices are perceived to lack authority.[10] Women speaking in public will often call upon their bodies (especially hands) to support what they have to say. And similarly the waving, gesticulating hands of the 'Latin', male or female, is often a source of comic disturbance, at least in much non-Latin cinema, as the speaker is suggested to be somewhat outside the realm of the authoritative, controlled norm. Likewise women are sometimes perceived to have 'over-excited' voices in meetings etc., (perhaps because they expect at any moment to be interrupted or otherwise silenced and therefore have to rush to make their points?) Such sets of association led Margaret Thatcher to undertake a programme of voice training when the broadcasting of Prime Minister's Question Time had her characterised as 'shrill' and therefore lacking in authority. She achieved, through the training, a reduction in pitch of 46 Hz, almost half the average difference in pitch between male and female voices.[11]

This area shades over interestingly into theatrical and cinematic codings. The place where evil hung out in nineteenth century theatrical melodrama was in a villain who was conventionally male, swarthy, wore a cape and had a deep voice. Inheriting such sedimented histories, Robert Mitchum's voice, for example, is a key part of his star image, drawing as it does on those melodramatic codes for villainy. Played for certain women stars, though, the deep voice works differently: the very young Lauren Bacall was trained by Howard Hawks to deepen her voice with a punishing series of exercises so that she came to embody that particular male fantasy which combines young woman's body and experienced/older woman's deeper voice. Does Tom Hanks' deepish voice in *Sleepless In Seattle* (Nora Ephron, US, 1993) in combination with his boyish star image help make possible a 1990s updating of the woman's film, with its dream of the new romantic and therefore, to an extent feminised man, in a film with a very traditional, even ultra-family centred agenda? Does this securing of the masculinity of such a New Man via a deep voice depend too on the 'little girl' 'bubbly' voice, performance, costuming and star image of co-star Meg Ryan? Two of the recent 'nervous romances' cited by Neale star Melanie Griffiths, complete with 'little girl' light, high, lispy voice, a kind of vocal equivalent of batting eyelashes.[12] (After all, key parts of the dumb blonde stereotype have usually been vocal as well as visual.) Perhaps this works in such generic contexts (and even in *Something Wild*) to undermine Griffiths' powerful sexuality, or at least, to secure it, for the male, in childlike dependency and lack of power?

Behind the more obvious codings of deep/high, loud/soft, precise/lispy or halting there lie other cultural inflections. As Barthes indicates, the voice is also geographically and culturally formed: the 'Slavonic language' of his essay on the voice is formed from a region, with a particular climate, geography, altitudes and relationship to the lungs, and to the vocal chords, which could be said to be pre-discursive though inhabited and perceived culturally. In other words, a land, a terrain, a culture and its various struggles, and stereotypes, have shaped the language, so that when a speaking voice is at stake, in a language, a vocabulary *we* inhabit, the histories of class, gender and region seem much clearer, and, of course, combine together, articulate, differently.

Friends and students discussing male stars' voices in cinema, for example, have expressed their enjoyment of Scottish accents, and suggested that the star image of Sean Connery is crucially nuanced by such an accent. Would the same response be true for non-English or even non-British viewers? Moreover there seem to exist contradictory connotations of Scottishness in the male voice, broadly: Edinburgh as precision, clipped control, austerity, and Glasgow as 'macho hard drinking'. How do these get perceived, further stereotyped, misrecognised, and then how do they relate to, say, the screen presence of Connery and to broader discourses around Scottishness? Could we perform a commutation test, and imagine him with a Texan or a French accent, and if so, how different would the visual image then become? Or take the cultivated Welsh male voice. Geoffrey MacNab quotes an expert on the subject on its 'inherited quality derived from the mines: 'Generations of coal workers have lived in cramped, acrid environments … The consequence … is that they breathe very deeply and use dilated nostrils and a stretched and open air passage.'[13] There is clearly some truth in this as part of an account of the physical inheritance of some South Wales voices, and consequently certain notions of masculinity at work in certain star images. But as MacNab asks, how then to account for Ivor Novello, or Ray Milland, or Donald Houston, presumably both in terms of their less stereotypically 'Welsh' vocal resonances, and, where these resonances exist, how they combine with very different, even absent connotations of Welshness in the whole image? How does 'educatedness' (defined usually in very English, even Oxbridge terms) combine with such assumed evidence of industrial work in the most famous 'Welsh' star voices? And how do these particular voices articulate with the rest of the bodily star images of those icons of cinematic Welshness – Burton, Baker and, in a different way, Hopkins?

GENDERING MOVING VOICES

Most of those who have written on the voice suggest how difficult it is to separate out any one strand of signification for exploration. Script, recording technology, the inextricable elements of ambience and often music included in the recorded voice all easily get caught up in memory and discussion of voices. Even basic primers for theatrical voice production list a bewilderingly long set of components for analysis, from timbre, pitch, intonation, volume through to varieties of accent. Full accounts of gendered sound in cinema would further need to take note of histories such as those of the voice training manuals for actors which early silent cinema inherited from the theatre, the assumptions of sound technicians, script writers, and directors as to 'appropriate' voices for men and women in particular roles and genres, as well as what might be called, particularly in relation to contemporary cinema, a spectacularisation at the level of the aural as well as of the visual.

Recent work suggests that nineteenth century sound technology already gendered voices, especially in relation to class and ethnicity.[14] (White) male voices were important enough to preserve by phonographs, to dictate, while female voices were groomed to serve and soothe, on the telephone, and in other service jobs. (By the same token, of course, 'non-soothing' voices were perhaps thereby more easily stereotyped as less 'feminine').

Lina Lamont/Jean Hagen's voice is deployed in one of the classic accounts of the innovation of sound in Hollywood, *Singin' in the Rain* (Stanley Donen, US, 1952), as signifier of all that is to be rendered outside the feminine norm: 'harsh', 'over-loud', with a Bronx accent clearly signified as vulgar and lower class. It's one of the frustrations of writing about such sound effects that I cannot even offer a freeze-frame equivalent to consider. And one of the ironies that Jean Hagen, acting the part of Lina Lamont, dubbed the singing voice of the Debbie Reynolds' character, Cathy Seldin. As Peter Wollen writes: 'It seems that, after all, the ear is more easily ensnared than the eye.'[15] Interestingly, Lina's inability to benefit from studio elocution lessons is paired in a gendered relation to Don and Cosmo's glorious triumph over the normalising solidities of class, cultural and linguistic status in the *Moses Supposes* number, which crescendoes with a ridiculing of a card illustrating 'The vowel sound "a" ' – exactly what Lina has been unable to pronounce in the scene preceding the number, which is dissolved into its opening.[16]

Alan Williams suggests that the explanation for the decline in certain silent male stars' careers at the coming of sound because their voices were 'unsuitable' evaporates when one listens to the actual voices of John Gilbert and others.[17] He goes on:

> the 'bad voices' of the most notorious Hollywood stars were probably in part a product of their association with melodramatic *sensibilité*.
>
> It was, most notably, certain of the men who suffered, those whose acting was most expressive, whose screen personas were somehow feminised … It is, for example, around the time of the transition to sound that male characters begin to cry far less frequently – and that crying begins to signify, not admirable sensitivity, but hysteria and sexual ambiguity.[18]

It's tempting to suggest that 'camp' male voices, of the kind which Malkovitch's occasionally approaches in *In the Line of Fire* (I am thinking of Kenneth Williams, Harvey Feinstein, Julian Clary) are signified not necessarily by a higher pitch, but by a greater mobility than the 'masculine', by a vocal apostrophising and innuendoising of certain words and phrases, by a refusal to claim authority, and by a moving in and out of that camp mode. The bearers of those voices are also designated as being full of a feminine garrulousness – often talking about such 'feminine' matters as shopping, fashion, style and other 'trivia'. Interestingly the 'ole timer' in westerns likewise has his now supposedly deficient masculinity signalled partly by garrulousness. Having referenced 'ole timers' and westerns, I will now consider *In the Line of Fire* and how 'ole timer' Eastwood is vocally constructed to avoid such deficit.

IN THE LINE OF FIRE

The relationship between the characters played by Clint Eastwood and John Malkovitch is at the heart of this film. It is mostly conducted over the phone, though also through Horrigan/Eastwood's intuitive sense of when Leary/Malkovitch is present, which, together with the telephone torture, the killing of the bank clerk and her friend, and elements of the mise-en-scène, moves the film in the direction of the horror genre. Within this horrifying relationship, Leary/Malkovitch occupies a position partly coded as feminine, a codification partly achieved through the voice (as well as via audience recollections of *Play Misty For Me*, Eastwood's 1971 thriller which centred round a late night radio DJ being harassed over the phone by a woman). Malkovitch's voice, with far greater range and mobility than Eastwood's is almost flirtatious, a feature also constructed by the script ('I was worried about you ... We have so much in common ...'). His postmodern shape-shifts, even blending into computer generated effects, and untrustworthy bodily surface are orchestrated with a voice which veers unnervingly from a volatile phrasing, pacing and pitch, almost camp in its deconstruction of the authoritative male monotone, through to a blank intonation for some of his more Nietschzean speeches. The blankness perhaps epitomises the ultimate 'hard man', the robot, and articulates with Leary's association with high technology, while the arguably camp vocal flexibility emerges from a stonily impassive face. Yet his voice, insofar as it is 'bodied' and never internalised, will still 'give him away', even as his brilliant shape-shifting accelerates. As he shouts of betrayal during his final telephone message, Horrigan comments questioningly on the final lack of control in it – perhaps a clinching of its 'femaleness'?

Leary speaks the private, whether knowledge of the secret-yet-public work of government agents like Leary and Horrigan, or of the details of Horrigan's private life, and yet he pushes Horrigan into public exposure in the amphitheatre of phone calls 'broadcast' round the workplace, as if to emphasise the fusion of the 'feminine' and the 'masculine', the public and the private which he embodies so troublingly. He saves Horrigan's life in a *Bladerunner*-like melodramatic sequence, on top of the city, during which he climactically takes Horrigan's gun into his mouth. His fury in his final scene seems bound up with Horrigan's betrayal of their relationship by appearing to speak to him while actually directing Agent Raines over the concealed microphone.

The gendering of the relationship also operates through Eastwood's voice which, in timbre, pitch and accent recalls, at times more vividly than his appearance, his roles in that key genre of masculinity and Americanness, the western. It is also a voice which has delivered some of the most celebrated and brutal lines in that other key masculine genre, the urban detective thriller. (Such lines, of course, being 'portable' for their audiences, can be used easily as signs, as conversational mementoes or triggers for the whole structure of feeling of such films: 'Go ahead – make my day.')

His voice, together with John Wayne's, perhaps best epitomises what Jane Tompkins[19] suggests may be one of the most potent pleasures of the western, namely its offer, to both men and women, of what she calls seriousness, of being in boundary situations. She suggests that men in westerns often look like the hard landscape – and, I'd suggest, have voices which are also constructed and/or come to sound like it: hard, parched and strained. Eastwood's voice updates Wayne's as iconically 'western'; sharing a parched quality, it is slightly softer and has less volume; it lacks the ease with which Wayne's voice could modulate into a shouted order to other men. The drawl is there, but less pronounced than Wayne's, which embodied physical ease in situations of extreme danger or testing, as well as contempt for both the proper, 'cultivated' speech which the realm of the western's female ('schoolmarm') would inculcate, and also for the clipped precision of a class-differentiated male voice.[20] It seems that the same kinds of changes as Martin Pumphrey has suggested occur at the level of dress and style may also be constructed vocally as the western takes on new modes of masculinity in the 1980s and 1990s.[21] The question here is whether or not Eastwood's voice has changed in those years, or whether the lack of change is what gives it impact when carried into movies which do different ideological work around masculinity.

In such play between 'newness' and all too familiar 'old style' masculinities, perhaps the voices of male stars, especially those out of the western, in their perceived status as evidence of the body, and given the lack of detailed discussion of voices, and how they might have changed, seem to add to the stability of their star images. The body/voice/interiority connection suggested by Doane and others can be read as in place here: when Horrigan/Eastwood, showing off his Old Man rather than New Man uncertainty, bets to himself whether or not Lily/Russo will 'give me that snooty look', the lines are delivered as external rather than internal speech. Even while an updated coding of heterosexual relations, or a necessary admission of some of the vulnerabilities of older age is attempted, such an externalised voice seems to root the star's power and status in older but still potent genres.

I suggested earlier that the garrulousness of the 'ole timer' in westerns may be coded as part of his move out of the realm of the masculine. No such fate has befallen Eastwood as old 'un. His star image has inherited and intensified the 'strong silence' of the western's heroes. This generic and highly masculinised silence is on the one hand very different to, say, the denial of language in slurred, incoherent male speech or to those silences so objected to in the early reception of male 'Method' actors. And, of course, it is very different to the strength of the silences wielded by female characters such as Ada in *The Piano*[22] or the three women heroes of *A Question of Silence*.[23]

Horrigan/Eastwood's detective partner in this film, Al D'Andrea, (whose lightly coded Latin ethnicity may intensify the following points) is rendered terrifyingly and humiliatingly speechless (not the same as silent, for these purposes) in the opening scenes, and meets his death by a shot through the mouth from Mitch Leary/John Malkovitch, having earlier wept on screen for the strains, the 'demons' with which he and his family, unlike strong and silent Horrigan/Eastwood, cannot in the end cope. Though it was announced by some critics that Eastwood weeps in the film, in fact he allows the vocal to give out nothing so close to the body, the pre-verbal: only the slightly quivering mouth signifies the trauma which Leary/Malkovitch verbalises for him and at him.

One fascinating possibility for further research might be the construction, within cinematic and other voices, of a distance from or closeness to vocal but non-verbal releases of the body such as laughter, and what they are perceived to reveal of character. Does a particular voice seem to be often close to or far away from a chuckle, a sneer, a full or a thin laugh? It's startling, for instance, to think just how rarely, if ever, Eastwood laughs in his films, and how laughter tends to function in the western more generally. The aggressive and bonding laughter in *The Wild Bunch*[24] for example, (rather like a mass spitting in public) is as expressive of a kind of masculine territorialising power as the laughter of the women in *A Question of Silence* or *9 to 5*,[25] is evocative of a release of shared, enforcedly silent observation of the absurdities of that power.

Eastwood's voice and speech maintains the restricted range of a western hero, deeply distrusting vocal mobility, 'fancy words' and the exposure of such intimate, fluid conversation as can embrace comfortable silences. Horrigan/Eastwood describes himself, as one might have described much of Eastwood's western persona, as 'a borderline burnout with questionable social skills'. Westerns often seem to prefer such strong silences or, at most, verbal and vocal restraint in combination with a choral masculinity of either characters or soundtrack. Rosolato (cited in Doane *op.cit.*), is suggestive in this context, arguing that vocal harmonies (like the choral singing so often found in westerns) can be seen as embodying 'the entire dramatisation of separated bodies and their reunion'.[26]

But *In the Line of Fire* is a thriller, not a western. The male voice in thrillers has often had at least the kind of mobility which allows a deadpan wit to be delivered, and it will often work in a brilliant, equal play with the deadly wit of the femme fatale. Here, though, the underdevelopment of the female lead is as much present in the marginalising of the vocal-verbal evidence of her professional effectiveness (for example via the mobile phone in the crucial final scenes) as it is in her role in publicity shots and the narrative generally, or her inability to give the intimidating glare which Horrigan/Eastwood sketches as part of his equipment in the piano scene. 'Stick to the sunglasses' he advises (perhaps also referring humorously to his own earlier role as Dirty Harry). The line comes at the end of a scene simultaneously drawing on the trope 'Piano Playing by Tough Male as Evidence of Sensitivity Underneath' and seeking to evoke, while failing to develop, the Bacall-Bogart echoes from *To Have and Have Not*[27] as well as some from *Casablanca*.[28] There, the black singer, famously, has to verbalise in song what Bogart's strong silence will not allow to pass his lips.

But the film's central relationship, that between Eastwood and Malkovitch, is reminiscent of *The Silence of the Lambs*[29] whose motto 'Hurt. Agony. Pain. Love It.' might equally apply to Eastwood as Horrigan, or rather, might illuminate the Horrigan role as being similar to that played by Jodie Foster in *Silence*. The Eastwood persona (and actual body) here is markedly aged and vulnerable, and filmed as beng physically dazed, even silenced by the public-political sphere of US election politics of the 1990s. There seems to be a close relationship here, as in some of his earlier roles, between the pleasures of action and those of suffering. In this it resembles those recent horror films discussed by Clover who suggests their pleasures include identification with the 'feminine' or passive terrorised position for audiences of both sexes. Intriguing in such a context is Clover's quotation from Dika's political allegorical reading of the Final Girl in contemporary horror movies, (of which Jodie Foster is one): 'She is a symbol for an enfeebled United States, but one that, when roused, is still strong.'[30] I need hardly labour points of similarity to Horrigan/Eastwood, throwing off at one and the same time in the film's climax his cough, his doubts about his ability to stand in the line of fire, and his doppelganger closeness to the sexually ambiguous Leary/Malkovitch, who voices those pertinent (if fairly unspecified) objections to US Secret Service operations of the last thirty years in a film fairly bristling with US flags and erect Washington monuments.

But if the vulnerability, the ageing has to be admitted, if only to be overcome at climax, that vulnerability is only allowed to go so far, and again it is interesting that the voice is part of the image that is to be controlled and patrolled. Eastwood's voice, which fans often cite as special, pleasurable, is never given telephonic distortion in the movie. In fact the only time he changes it is in the long 'a' he gives to 'dance' when asking Lily 'Would you care to dance?' and that is half mocking, and perhaps an echo of how a cowboy might approach a schoolmarm, (even if she weren't coiffed to resemble Jackie Kennedy, in this Kennedyian revivalist context). Would it perhaps be too major a transgression for a male star, especially one associated with the western, to mimic convincingly a very different voice or to be able to take on a 'false' let alone a feminine voice convincingly? For Malkovitch and Eastwood to be thrillingly matched, Malkovitch, however feminised has to have comparable status. (To pursue the *Silence of the Lambs* comparison for a moment, he has to be *both* Buffalo Bill and Hannibal Lecter.) He never has to disguise his fluid but deep voice, and it is he rather than Eastwood whom we wait to see at the beginning of the film, in the manner usually reserved for The Star.

Does the persistence over a range of films of a particular voice in a star (particularly a male star) work to signify a bodily continuity which is able to anchor the overall image, however nuanced or self-reflexive, in a perceived bodily truth and authority? It certainly seems a key part of the horror of the two Terminators that their voices are as mobile as the Terminator's body in the second film.[31] (Indeed, one of the most striking special effects in both *Terminator* (James Cameron, US, 1984 and 1991) films involve the cyborgs impersonating women – in fact, mothers – first vocally, then visually.)

Eastwood's voice, if it is read as 'evidence', emerges from, and is consonant with, a filmic body carefully constructed as one of 'male youthful maturity'. Despite the film's heart attack joke, such sequences as those used in publicity of Eastwood jogging beside the Presidential limo construct him as impressively fit. But that joke, as well as the vocal signifier of his cough, along with a couple of positively boyish smiles, allows gestures on the part of Raines/Russo which are part professional, part maternal concern for this 63 year old man. At the end of the film we are left to imagine Clint as retired house husband, in a reversal of the status quo at its start. The characteristically husky, slightly straining voice, like a bass under pressure, here seems to function, in conjunction with the visibility of his ageing, as sign of authenticity, as well as of 'masculinity under strain' which Amy Taubin suggests is signified so effectively by the rigidity of his upright body.[32] It seems that for Clint, as for many other male stars, the unexplored vocal image allows complex work to be achieved in the securing of the whole, ageing star image for masculinity at a time when both might be assumed to be under some pressure.

Thanks to Janet and Pat for their helpful and encouraging editing, and to Christine Gledhill, Val Hill and Andy Medhurst for being so worth listening to on this and most other matters.

NOTES

1 Amy Taubin, 'An Upright Man', in *Sight and Sound*, September 1993.

2 Renny Martin, US, 1993.

3 John McTiernan, US, 1993.

4 Wolfgang Petersen, US, 1993.

5 J. Gaines, *Contested Culture: The Voice, the Image and the Law*, BFI, London, 1992, p126.

6 Rick Altman (ed), *Sound Theory, Sound Practice* Routledge, London, 1992.

7 M.A. Doane, 'The Voice in the Cinema: The Articulation of Body and Space' in *Yale French Studies* no 60, 1980.

8 K. Silverman, *The Acoustic Mirror: The Female Voice in Psychoanalysis and Cinema*, Indiana University Press, Bloomington, 1988.

9 R. Barthes, 'The Grain of the Voice' in *A Barthes Reader*, S. Sontag (ed), Cape, London, 1983.

10 D. Graddol and J. Swann in *Gender Voices*, Basil Blackwell, Oxford, 1989.

11 *Ibid.*, p38.

12 S. Neale, 'The Big Romance or Something Wild?' in *Screen* 33, 3 1992.

13 G. Macnab, 'Valley Boys' in *Sight and Sound*, March 1994.

14 A. Lawrence, *Echo and Narcissus: Women's Voices in Classical Hollywood Cinema*, University of California Press, Ca. 1992.

15 Peter Wollen, *Singin' In The Rain*, BFI Film Clasics, London, 1992.

16 Such normalising processes, or 'technological advances' may also be argued to have formed part of the marginalising of women's talk.

Women's voices talking together in the often supportive, relational, exploratory way which feminist sociolinguisticians have suggested may be a cross-class factor, often get characterised in cinema as babble, cackle, gossip, and garrulousness. An example from a woman's film would be the scene in *Mildred Pierce* (1945) where Mildred first goes to Ida's cafe to look for work. Various auditory (and narrative) manoeuvres construct the waitresses as gabbling, squabbling and generally existing outside the realm of the narratively authoritative norm, that centred, clearly audible, cinematically class differentiated conversation between the vamp-voiced Mildred/Crawford and the bantering Ida/Arden.

The most extreme construction of 'unacceptability' in this area of the film works via ethnicity, in Butterfly McQueen's role as Mildred's maid, against whose 'inadequacies' Mildred's pretensions are perhaps most keenly judged.

17 Alan Williams, 'Historical and Theoretical Issues in the Coming of Recorded Sound to the Cinema' in R. Altman, *op.cit.*, pp134–135.

18 However, even in sensitive heroes a respectable/acceptable depth of tone was necessary and in the case of Charles Farrell, a leading man of the late silent and early Hollywood sound cinema, discussed elsewhere in this volume by Pat Kirkham, he had voice lessons to reduce his high-pitched voice and Cape Cod 'twang'.

19 J. Tompkins, *West of Everything: The Inner Life of Westerns*, Oxford, University Press, 1992.

20 Wayne later objected to reports that he did not speak correctly. 'Have you noticed me dropping any "g" at the end of words, like "gonna"? ... Writers do that to me sometimes. It's belittling, a cheapening thing....'. Quoted in D. Lepper, *John Wayne, Star Dossier 2*, BFI Education, 1987.

21 M. Pumphrey, 'Why Do Cowboys Wear Hats in the Bath?' in *Critical Quarterly*, Vol. 31, No. 3.

22 Jane Campion, Australia, 1993.

23 Marleen Gorris, Netherlands, 1982.

24 Sam Peckinpah, US, 1969.

25 Colin Higgins, US, 1980.

26 Doane, *op.cit.*, p45.

27 Howard Hawks, US, 1945.

28 Michael Curtiz, US, 1942.

29 Jonathan Demme, US, 1990.

30 C. Clover, *Men, Women and Chainsaws: Gender in the Modern Horror Film*, BFI, 1992, p63.

31 Other examples of the problems of vocal mimicry for male characters might include Dustin Hoffman's voice-shifting in *Tootsie* (Sydney Pollack, US, 1982), though the character is constructed as having enormous problems of sexual control with such a successful impersonation, and the role is partly set up as tribute to Hoffman's own virtuosity. The character played by Robin Williams in *Mrs Doubtfire* (Chris Columbus, US, 1993) is constructed slightly differently, with much more emphasis on family values. Williams' previous success with *Aladdin* (John Musker and Ron Clements, US, 1992), seems to partly motivate the opening scene but also interesting is the way as godlike, disembodied vocal dubber (vis-à-vis the cartoon characters) he spontaneously corrects the unhealthy smoker in the cartoon, a capacity for ideological correction which the whole film seems eager to give to Williams as 'Father Knows Best Even in Drag'. Women playing men, on the other hand, (*Orlando*, (Sally Potter, UK, 1992) being only the most recent example) hardly need to change their voices, or at least, the area seems to be not an issue, surely because so much less authority has been invested in the woman's voice?

32 A. Taubin, *op.cit.*

Relations Between Men: Bernardo Bertolucci's *The Spider's Stratagem*

Lesley Caldwell

A distinguishing mark of the European cinema has often been the association of the film-making process with personal identity and with the imaging of a national culture. In Bertolucci's *La Strategia del Ragno* (Italy, 1970), hereafter *The Spider's Stratagem*, an investigation of personal and national identity is linked to the historical moment of the late 1960s. The film's themes, and the mise-en scène through which they are explored, announce the significance of the past. The present politico-social moment becomes one framework for an exploration of postwar Italy and for the preoccupations of the film-maker, a director known for his continuing concern with identity, masculinity and paternity. This film, while presenting itself as an intensely personal evocation, offers a sustained commentary of the impact of the one upon the other.

The representations of masculinity made available, testify to the personal concerns and beliefs of Bertolucci, at the same time as offering a more general set of reflections, incorporating a national/regional emphasis. For each perspective being and becoming a man is signalled as central. This is especially the case if certain forms of masculinity are understood as linked to the production of a social self whose validity and appropriateness are seen as forming part of a general cultural ethos. In this film a familiarity with particular forms of knowledge, in the shape of the discourses of art, literature and history, provides one such parameter. *The Spider's Stratagem* assumes, and could be said to depend upon, intellectual and cultural expertise as one way through which being a particular kind of man can be understood and developed. This is common to certain class locations and

51

expectations but, arguably, there is also a cultural specificity in its close associations with a particular Italian political tradition. Through Bertolucci's focus on the father and on forms of masculinity organised around the fantasy of paternity, this tradition is subjected to an examination which has implications for the ways social and political change might be envisaged.

In *The Spider's Stratagem*, the son of a local anti-fascist hero killed in 1936 is summoned to his father's hometown by his father's mistress. There he encounters his father as the hero of collective anti-fascist memory, and begins the search to resolve the mystery of his death. He discovers that his father betrayed his political comrades and then staged his own death. The film's enigmas extend well beyond the solution of who was responsible for the killing of his father, and the film is very much an internal search where fatherhood is the organising fantasy. It is one associated with heroism, with betrayal, with pretence, with spectacle, with myth, with friendship, and with longing. Ultimately it is associated with repetition and disappointment. In the space constructed by the son's return to the father's town, Bertolucci uses themes central to Italian culture to reflect upon the Italy of past and present. The family and its place, the relations between fathers and sons, and the power of the *idea* of the father are all explored. The film offers a sustained meditation on the implications of this *idea* both for forms of friendship between men and for political forms in general. In its emphasis on the link between politics as an encounter with the self and ideas of the self as bound to local, regional and national memories, it highlights one peculiarly Italian preoccupation. Its interrogation of staging, performance and theatricality also gives a national dimension to the issue of politically effective forms. Together they illuminate how the interlocking identities of Italian male and political actor are constructed and woven together as a set of propositions about masculinity for contemporary Italian men.

Apart from Draifa/Alida Valli, the father's lover, who occupies a primary place, in that she initiates the son's return and encourages, seduces, and enmeshes him, there are no other women characters, no other women at all, except in the staging of the climax. Yet the place of the woman is as central in the son's journey, and in the film's structure, as it is central to accession to the symbolic realm. The relation between Draifa and the son is a central dynamic of the film. As a signifier of the other levels at which the film operates it may be seen as an external visualisation of the primacy assigned to the mother in the researches conducted by the child in his/her encounter with the realities that first shape external and internal worlds.

With the exception of Draifa – ambiguous, ageless, sexualised – this is a drama played out between men, the real male characters in the film's present, their earlier selves, and the two Athos Magnanis, father and son, who, played by the same actor, Giulio Brogi, emphasise the sense of confusion between the generations and between past and present which is one of the film's consistent preoccupations.

The organising narrative is centred around the adult son and his discovery of his father and himself. This is both offset, and contributed to, by the focus on the landscape and on the town, for the concern with the town and the landscape offers one version of the history of a generation. This wider history diminishes the impact of the dreadful aspects of the father's story, while implicating the recognition of self in the discovery of place. The film is structured around the links between a moment of the Italian past, Fascism, a particular locality, and the determining push of psychical reality. Told in a mixture of flashback, memories and associations, unfolded through a narrative and a camera style that run together past and present, what is thought and what is said, what did happen and what may have happened, the son's story emerges on a number of levels as the encounter with the father, and with himself.

Many of the ideas about masculinity are developed through the friendship between the father and his three friends: Gaibazzi, the salami-maker, Rasori, a primary school teacher, and Costa, who runs a cinema. The friends, clearly characters of interest in their own right, may also be regarded as representing aspects of the son's unconscious mental structures. In addition to the characters of the diegesis and their relationships with the actual father, they, like Draifa, may be seen as representations of the dynamics between an internalised father and a variety of subject positions through which the son's own reactions come to be identified. Taken as existing in both registers, they offer two different ways of apprehending the son's dilemmas and realisations. This is one way the film's structure may be said to parallel the dream and the process of dreaming, a parallel which, it has been argued, is appropriate to all of Bertolucci's corpus.[1] Dreams provide the clearest access to the sheer randomness of the unconscious and the different logic of primary process thinking it employs. By deploying some of its features, *The Spider's Stratagem* makes central the child's initial questions about the relations between the sexes and gives some sense of the quality of the knowledge then gained. Recognition of sexual difference and the consequent loss of infantile omnipotence attendant upon its realisation are both implied by the film's structure.

The investigation is organised around a relationship with a woman, and with a town, its history, and its environs, through a past identified and elaborated through male friendship. The affectionate associations conveyed by the geographical location, the warmth and humanity of the characters, the setting with its evocation of the sheer heat of summer, are all captured by the meandering camera and the carefully constructed light effects. In the spaces established within the frame, the timelessness of the unconscious is made available and pondered without haste.

In a sense the son is the only man in the film who is neither too old nor too young, the only real adult; but his adult existence, the reality of being a man among men and women, is postponed in favour of the ongoing, internal search for the past. In the film's present, the father is partly an absence, existing as he does, partially and selectively, through the reminiscences of those still living. His friends' memories are suffused with affection and with their explicit recognition of his difference, but the encounters between the film's male characters are never really those of equals. For the three friends and the father, being a man among men is primarily presented as a matter of the group and its leader, and this dynamic is present, for the most part, in its positive dimensions. While Bertolucci's later films are often bleak in their portrayal of the fate of men, and the fear and futility sometimes associated with contemporary masculinity, the darkness and the pessimism of *Last Tango in Paris* (France/Italy/US, 1972) or of *1900* (Italy/France/W.Germany, 1976) do not feature here.

Soon after the beginning of the film the son, Athos, is having a drink in the bar of the piazza. He asks his fellow drinkers if there are any young people in the town. In the immensely good-humoured scene which follows, two old men approach him.

> First old man: How old do you think I am?
> Athos: About seventy.
> Old man: Seventy-five and my girlfriend's pregnant!
> Second old man: I'll buy a drink for anyone who can piss further than me.

The group of old men break into a revolutionary chorus. Athos laughs and laughs, slightly hysterically. We, the audience, laugh too. From the old men and their adolescent boasts to, significantly, the adolescent boy who smokes Athos' cigarettes and recites Pascoli but cannot tell the sex of his rabbit, to Draifa's helper – a girl whom Athos mistakes for a boy – the characters, and the town itself, inhabit a space where the realities of age, sexual difference and time can be, and are, ignored. Denial, incomprehension, confusion, the negation of sexual and generational realities, are encountered and juxtaposed unproblematically. It is this which replicates not only the landscape of the dream, but a more general visual rendering of the timelessness Freud ascribes to the unconscious, and the childhood researches stored there.

One understanding of an analysis, significant for the film, is the reinscription and negotiation in the present of the child's initiation into the world of difference and of origins. Through this perspective, the relations between the sexes and their inescapable links with generational difference are linked to the son's researches in the film. The cinematic pleasures the film makes so readily and prolifically available, however, relegate to the margin the anxiety normally attendant upon that first negotiation – subsequently endlessly repeated – of what it means to be a *boy*, not a girl; a *man*, not a woman. The film's exploration is mostly light-hearted and good humoured, the filmic process paralleling Draifa's stratagems with the son as it enmeshes the viewer in its sheer luxuriance and pleasure.

Although *The Spider's Stratagem* presents unaccounted for, potentially threatening and mystifying events – the son is locked in a stable, woken by a fist in the face and an ominous inscription on his door, attacked by the fascist Beccaccia's men – these moments do not carry major disturbance. Again, such a failure to register as overly troubling or ominous is more comprehensible if, rather than events requiring explanations in themselves, all these moments are regarded as secondary elaborations of the fundamental psychological and cultural enigmas which the Freudian project describes as universal.

The first memory/flashback is an illustration by Draifa (who was not present) to a question of the son's, 'What was my father like?' The four friends walk along at dawn; the father crows and the cockerels, deceived, begin to crow in their turn, anticipating the day's beginning. The father has succeeded in misleading nature! On this occasion, as on almost all the others where they appear together, the behaviour of Gaibazzi, Rasori and Costa, is playful, boisterous, rumbustious and adolescent. The father appears as a friend among friends but also exceptional, one of them, but also singled out as different, both by the camera and by what is said and done within the shot. The friends are revealed, and reveal themselves, as captivated followers. Their admiring descriptions reverberate with the pleasure and the nostalgia of fond memories, and the mise-en-scène implicates the viewer in the indulgence. In all that these old friends recount of him, and in the ways the camera reveals that recounting, reconstructing the mood and the settings of the past, the father's exceptional status, his absolute difference, is insisted upon: an idealised father, the father as hero.

As the narration of the events proceeds, the father, this figure of fascination who activates both desire and love, is successively reduced and exposed. At first he appears as the repository for their (and our) fantasy of an idealised masculinity, a universally positive vision of charm, courage and power, further embellished by its condensation of the maternal associations of love, protection and wisdom. But the delusion and the anger of the friends' memories insinuates itself until their implications can no longer be evaded by the son. His first response is to attempt to erase his own and his father's birthdates from the tombstone. He then seeks, in a variety of ways, to delay what has to be known: 'Your father said it wasn't the truth that mattered, what was important was its consequences', says Gaibazzi. Athos runs away. He rejects Draifa's attempts to ensconce him in her house, to have him literally replace his father. He seeks to leave town.

At the station, he is drawn back by the opening bars of *Rigoletto* and, the film has already indicated, its identification with the moment of knowledge. The discovery of the truth of his father's death carries with it the resonance of other discoveries, the acquisition of other moments of knowledge in the acceptance of what it means to be a boy and become a man. Even as Athos approaches the theatre, he delays, he wavers, he turns back, he speaks with the old women sitting on the dray, who have been brought in for the performance. Cinematically, Bertolucci enlarges these extra significations by having him enter the opera house for the performance of this painful opera of fathers and daughters at the moment in Act Two where Gilda is singing, 'Tell me, your poor daughter. Such mystery as surrounds me/is oppressing. I'd like to know something of my family.' But the son's knowledge of *his* family is gained, not through *Rigoletto*, but through the confirmation whose delayed discovery is announced in the off-stage performance between him and his father's friends.

In his first meeting with Draifa the son is sceptical about her summons but, having decided to pursue his origins and the mystery of his father's death, Athos meets up with each of the friends in turn. Among the first words of Gaibazzi, the salami-maker, are, 'Hey, don't you know me any more?' It is the same confusion between past and present which underpins the film. In one of the most warmly affectionate of sequences (so successful that Bertolucci restages a version of it in *La Luna* (Italy, 1979)), Gaibazzi takes Athos first to investigate his salamis and then, like the other two immediately after, off to eat. His words are full of warmth and humanity as they resonate first with his pleasure in his work, then with the dynamics of the relationship of the friends with the father.

> We were anti-fascists, possibly we didn't even know what it meant; we didn't have a programme, couldn't have had, given the three of us, none of us very bright ... What was our anti-fascism based on? We fancied conspiracies, like the Ernani, like Sam and Tom in *Un Ballo in Maschera*. We thought of ourselves like that, but we understood nothing. Your father, no ... he was very different, he knew ... when we listened to him talk, it was fascinating; so refined, cultured, educated, so full of knowledge, so full of facts: intelligent. It was him who paid, not us. They knew we counted for nothing ... He was always with us. We, well, we were three idiots really ... you'll see the other two ... but we were the only ones to try and understand this extraordinary man.

The second friend he encounters, Rasori, is more childlike, more impressed. His words and his tone are accompanied by a shaking of the head, a still-present amazement: 'your father ... *your* father' shaking his head, 'an ex-tra-or-din-ary per-so-nal-ity! And his death. It was on a par with his life, an *exceptional* death, an *exceptional* life.'

In *Group Psychology and the Analysis of The Ego* (1921), Freud argues that two complementary dynamics govern group behaviour, the relation between each member and the leader, and the relations of the group members among themselves. He ascribes the power of the leader to a love where, through a kind of seduction, each member gives over his freedom. Each puts the leader in the place of that with which he identifies, his paternal ego-ideal.[2] Abandoning what one would like to be to the same other then permits a relation of fraternity, equality and symmetry among the members who had given over their freedom to the same figure. This second dynamic is fuelled by the fantasy illusion that he loves them all equally. The breaking of this libidinal tie induces panic in the members and dissolution follows. Freud's insistence that the basis of the group is love describes the relationships that this film portrays and reveals. It identifies one understanding of how the loved and longed-for father, rather than the feared and terrifying father, forms the fantasy basis of this film. This may possibly be regarded as proposing one dominant form around which Italian political culture of both left and right can be represented. 'It is easy to show that the ego-ideal answers to everything that is expected of the higher nature of man. As substitute for a longing for the father, it contains the germ from which all religions have evolved.'[3] Were this to have a specifically Italian dimension its rationale might tentatively be sought in the links between the pre-eminent place ascribed to the mother and the force of Catholicism. Draifa invites the friends to dinner with the father's enemy, the fascist landowner Beccaccia, now ancient himself. The son, lit in blue, is asleep in the foreground, the group at dinner behind him, staged like the visual rendering of a dream. In the banter of the three friends, there is now additional intent underlining their references to the past. The change in tone and the bitterness of the knowledge of betrayal is movingly signalled by Renato's painful aria, 'Ero tu' from Act Three of *Un Ballo in Maschera*, and, a few minutes later, the Miserere from *Il Trovatore*. The operatic references draw upon Verdi in such a way that a taken-for-granted place is assigned to the music, but even without that operatic knowledge, the music here carries another level of dread and premonition.

With these three as protagonists, these three boisterous, naive, well-intentioned locals, the aspiration to conspiracy and assassination is indeed laughable. When, in an earlier scene, Costa expostulates that the last thing their god-forsaken town needs is a visit from the Duce, Rasori says pompously, 'You don't understand anything! It's the fascists from Cremona who have arranged this. You just don't understand the dialectic of things!' And after Athos has announced that they must kill the Duce, Costa, with deadly seriousness, says, 'So long as we don't get caught. We're more useful alive than dead.' Their proposals are laughable, full of boys' adventure yarn bravado. Equally, however, in these fantasies of drama, of life as drama, is contained an examination of the place of theatricality in Italian life which the film pursues throughout. If life is staged spectacle, politically effective choices may also be dramatically staged ones. On yet another occasion it is again Costa who, as they sit in the darkness of the conspirators' meeting place, its own meagre dimensions stage-lit, says, 'Oh the stage, the theatre! So beautiful, in the dark, mmm, we'll go and shoot him there. We'll get parts.'

An impossible plot by impossible conspirators, who, while never in any doubt of their difference, know themselves. In that knowledge they make available to the son, and to the spectator, an overlap between discomforting political and personal issues.

Despite the boasts of the old men and the son's researches, the only figure who mobilises desire in the film is the mythic anti-fascist hero, yet he is the one who has disappointed and betrayed. The son, once apprised of his father's betrayal, participates in the deception so that the status of the father is publicly preserved. Just as the film's investigation of the power of myth, and of the place of theatricality and spectacle in Italian life, appears to expose one set of awkward political issues while effectively sidestepping another, it also remains equivocal in ascribing a judgement to the son's actions. The value of the father's death and his acute political pragmatism may be also vindicated by the continuing power of his hero's death as a local symbol, not only of anti-fascism but of ongoing political struggle. This, however, is both ethically and politically problematic. After all, what is the contemporary weight to be ascribed to the myth of a hero in a town lost to the modern world and inhabited by the old? *The Spider's Stratagem* suggests that neither men's motives nor the contemporary implications of the anti-fascist inheritance are ever straightforward.

The film is dominated by the unreliability of memory and by the recovery of memories of a father who proves inadequate to the weight he carries for others. Athos, confronted with the solution to his father's death in the box at the opera house, says, 'It all seems a sham.' What remains to him is a father who is a false hero, a sham, as is the early, pre-conflictual fantasised father that fuels the film's concerns. While Kristeva locates motherhood as an adult fantasy of a lost continent, a fantasy that derives from a primary narcissism, this film's mobilising fantasy is the search for a paternal figure of similar dimensions.[4] About this, in both its personal overtones and its relation to political myth, to male heroism and to national identity, the film remains openly equivocal.

These issues provide a starting point for the son's immersion in his own story. There the generational dynamic is presented as unclear and uncertain, but engagement with it appears as the only route, either forward or backward, in the acquisition of an adult male identity. This is personal, rather than political or social.

In their different ways of confronting themselves and what it means to be a man, the son and the three friends pursue, but also evade, the elusive figure of the father. The film is its own commentary upon this, for it is here that one focus for the discussion of masculinity arises. The process of becoming a man, rather than the reality of being one, is a key association for the son in his ongoing encounter with the father. The history of the father's betrayal, with its calculation, with its hollow but effective gesturing, does reveal the reality of a real man, and his choices among men. This is a choice for a kind of masculinity associated with heroism and fame, but the film remains equivocal about this too. This equivocation depends upon a mise-en-scène where an excess of visual and other cinematic pleasures is so insistently highlighted that political issues are subordinated to the creative choices of the director, to the apparently personal one of the character of the son.

In the trust and desire placed in the father by his three friends, and in the son's investigation of the reality of his apparently unknown paternity, paternity is presented in two different but similar psychic configurations. Disappointment and delusion is common to both. The friends insist upon this as what the son must discover and come to know if he is to be a man himself. They feed and reminisce and tell and share, their position as guides through the maze of past and present also identified around these qualities with their feminine associations. Friendship between men, shared memories, organised by love and a kind of family around the pleasures of food, the opera, politics and a sense of location, these are the bases for an immensely warm investigation of some of the issues that were central for the late 1960s generation of Italians.

In contradistinction to the benevolence of the bonds between men, Draifa's ultimately self-directed stratagems resonate with other, more sinister implications. Unlike the old women who recount the predictions before Athos enters the opera house, Draifa's place, regardless of her age, is a sexualised one. Despite the colour and the light, the engulfing maternal imago from which the child turns to the father as escape from its all-inclusiveness is present in her overgrown villa, in her motivations and actions, in her location as the centre of the web of narratives, in the pan that announces this threat. Bertolucci's later film, *La Luna* (Italy, 1979), ostensibly his filmic encounter with the mother, also presents the urgent need of the father as the condition of escape from the mother whose desires threaten and enfold. Both desire of and need for the father and the threat of psychological chaos without his presence are pursued there through the mother-son relationship and its mirroring onstage in the operatic segments which occupy a substantial part of the film. In different ways both these films, made nearly ten years apart, highlight adolescence, or the adolescent within the man, as a significant moment in the acquisition of a male self. They emphasise its necessary renegotiation of the earlier Oedipal moment through the living out of the interiority of personal, psychological issues, in a context of specific socio-cultural expectations. Through this emphasis both films acknowledge and also question the taken-for-granted status of the Italian family, and the earlier one in turn uses this to probe Italy's heroic anti-fascist past.

The form of *The Spider's Stratagem* and its spatial and geographical articulation so closely bind this acknowledging and questioning with psychical reality that all the themes of the film – fathers, betrayal, the weight of the past, the relations between men, the mystery of woman, the difference between the sexes and the generations – serve as so many instances of an exploration whose personal basis within the diegesis speaks uncertainty and innocence. The film itself, with its cinematic strengths and its cultural expertise, speaks mastery and knowledge. This contradiction exemplifies one dilemma for men in their espousal of the alternatives offered by contemporary understandings of masculinity. Through its juxtapositions of past and present, personal and social, knowledge and uncertainty, *The Spider's Stratagem* offers an open examination of the issues at stake.

NOTES

1 T. Jefferson, Kline, *Bertolucci's Dream Loom*, University of Massachusetts Press, Cambridge, Massachusetts, 1987.
2 S. Freud, (1921) *Group Psychology and the Analysis of the Ego*, Standard Edition, Volume XVIII, pp67-143.
3 S. Freud, (1923) *The Ego and the Id*, Standard Edition, Volume XIX, p12-66.
4 J. Kristeva, *Tales of Love*, Columbia University Press, New York, 1987.

Albert Finney: a Working-Class Hero

Christine Geraghty

In an article on *Victim* (Basil Dearden, GB, 1961) in 1984, Andy Medhurst in a characteristically trenchant aside refers to the discourse of 'spectating-as-rapture' which collapses 'the viewing experience into a single blissful surrender to some nebulous *jouissance*'. He comments, a touch ruefully perhaps, that in *Saturday Night and Sunday Morning* (Karel Reisz, GB, 1960) 'this surrender assumes the concrete form of swooning into the beefy arms of Albert Finney – a pleasant prospect, undeniably, but hardly a cogent argument against ... criticism of the film's sexual politics.'[1]

This essay seeks to address two questions in relation to the hero of *Saturday Night and Sunday Morning*. Firstly, I want to examine, without surrendering too much, what 'swooning into the beefy arms of Albert Finney' might mean by looking at the ways in which the star/hero of this realist film is presented to the audience. Secondly, I want to comment on the handling of the social and sexual determinants on the hero in a narrative which ends with Finney established as a star and Arthur Seaton, the character whom he plays, settling for compromise.

The editors of *You Tarzan* commented in their introduction to that volume that masculinity in the films under discussion seemed to be signalled at 'certain recurrent sites' which they identified as 'the body, action, the external world and the internal world.'[2] I intend to use this schema as the basis of my discussion and show how the figure of Finney/Seaton, a composite created out of the star persona and the fictional character, is mapped across these sites. *Saturday Night and Sunday Morning* was one of the films from the British 'new wave' of the 1960s which changed the concept of what was desirable or indeed acceptable in a film hero. In the Finney/Seaton composite there is, on the one hand, Albert Finney, the pin-up whose face graced thousands of bedrooms alongside the pop stars and footballers of the period[3]. On the other hand, there is Arthur Seaton, a fictional character taken from a realist novel, part of a 'new wave' washing across British culture. It is this amalgam of star and character which is the object of this study. The points at which the two work together and those at which they are in conflict provide an indication of the tensions around masculinity which were being expressed through a new type of British hero in the 1960s.

THE BODY

The most striking aspect of the use of the hero's body in *Saturday Night and Sunday Morning* is how little of it is on display and yet how much his physical presence controls the film. In the main, the focus is on Finney's face which at key points literally dominates the screen. It is the face which is offered to the audience for pleasurable contemplation of its star qualities and it is the face which we have to learn to read in our attempt to understand Arthur Seaton.

The film focuses on Finney right from the start, even before the credits appear. Using a camera position which is returned to throughout the film, the first shots show Finney/Seaton at the workbench, framed slightly from below so that his shoulders, upper arms and face impose themselves on the screen. There is little facial movement as Seaton, through an internal monologue, comments disparagingly on his workmates and asserts his aggressively individualist philosophy for getting by. In these opening moments, a star is being constructed through a clearly marked visual presentation and a character is being created to whom the presentation of self is of vital importance. It takes some time for this self-consciously impassive demeanour to break. A key scene in this connection is the first pub scene where Seaton is involved in a 'boozing match', a competition over the number of pints that can be drunk. Finney's face is stern and challenging as he taunts the other drinker. Sweat gleams on his face with the effort of control and when he does move, to get another pint, he holds his body stiffly. He registers no flicker of remorse at the upset he causes by spilling beer over the other customers. Even in victory, his face remains hard and impassive, demonstrating a masculine capacity for control in contrast to his girlfriend Brenda who breaks into laughter. In the final shots of the scene, Finney's rigid face and shoulders are framed from below as he stands at the top of the stairs. Only after he falls does the audience (but no other character) get a private glimpse of his face relaxing, the boyish smile finally flickering as he registers his collapse.

The dominance of Finney's presence is established in other ways in the opening scenes. His face and body are contrasted with those of other men as a way of showing off his aggressive handsomeness. During the credits in the factory, Arthur comments on the older men – 'They got ground down before the war and never got over it' – while the camera emphasises the shrunken bodies of the older men, picking up three of them in line, wearing overalls, flat cap, spectacles. Back home, Finney/Seaton's vitality as he prepares for an evening out is contrasted with his father's worn demeanour as he sips his tea in front of the television, the camera framing his slumped shoulders. In the pub, during the drinking competition, Finney's aggressive features are contrasted with the more conventionally handsome features of the pop-singer, whose more animated expressions as he courts his audience seem to appeal for approval in a way which Finney/Seaton would disdain. A further comparison, in these opening scenes, occurs again in the pub, the following morning, when Seaton meets his cousin Bert and the head and shoulders of the two men are framed in one slightly low-angle shot. The contrast is striking. Bert is at the edge of the frame, his head coming up to Arthur's shoulder, his face in profile as he looks at Seaton. Finney's head is central, with its American-style quiff of hair, and he looks directly out of the frame so that his face can be clearly seen. Here is the character actor set against the star and there is no question as to who comes out on top.

The early scenes, in addition, offer the audience the sight of Finney's body. After his fall at the pub, Seaton arrives at the house of his girlfriend Brenda who is married to one of his workmates. Finney's body is close to the camera while Brenda moves about in background tidying up. As he embraces her, he turns his back on the camera and the conventionally realist sleeveless vest he is wearing gives a view of his 'beefy' arms and shoulders. This teasing of the audience is resolved in the subsequent bedroom scene when Finney is vestless and we finally see the front of his upper body before Brenda places her head on his chest.

These glimpses of his body establish Finney's credentials as a pin-up but as the narrative takes a grip and the story moves away from the pleasures of Brenda's bed, Finney's body is less obviously on display. Much later in the film, for example, after Seaton has been beaten up because of his affair with Brenda, another bedroom scene starts with Arthur in bed, recovering from the attack. Initially, he is alone and has his pyjamas on, the jacket open to give sight of his chest but hiding his shoulders and arms. His move from a prone position to sit at the side of the bed restricts further the audience's view of his body. He stands up and looks at himself in the mirror but his body is still largely hidden and our attention is drawn to his face by his angry eyes and, in contrast, by the tender way in which he touches his face to feel for damage. When his new girlfriend, Doreen, arrives to visit he is back in bed, the eiderdown well up. He teases her a little. For once now, the camera frames him slightly from above, his face fresh and clean, his white teeth glinting in a smile, both hands joined as if in prayer and tucked under the pillow. It is from this childlike position that he proposes to Doreen – 'I'll buy you a ring next week if you're good'. His body is hidden, the chest and upper arms which have so strongly signified masculinity are tucked away and Doreen's move down to kiss him is obliterated by a cut. It is as if the audience, like Doreen, is being teased again as Finney's body is removed from display. This association of desexualisation with the domestication of Seaton's character at this point is typical of the realist narratives of the new wave in which marriage undermines and drains off sexual energy; in *Saturday Night and Sunday Morning*, however, as we shall see, the constrictions of the narrative on the character cannot entirely subdue the audience's engagement with and contemplation of Finney as a star whose image has so clearly been constructed around sexual presence.

ACTION

Kirkham and Thumim suggest that action is an important way of demonstrating masculinity as an expressive and dynamic force. 'Chivalrous deeds, sports, combats and violence'[4] offer the opportunity to demonstrate the male body in movement and to develop stories about training, rites of passage and violent action. Action thus allows the male hero to demonstrate his masculinity in his own space.

The films discussed in the *You Tarzan* anthology, however, tend to be genre films often operating at quite high levels of fantasy. Male epics, sports films, war films and science fiction are all genres which, however differently constituted, offer a markedly fictional space in which the hero can wrestle with society's demands. In *Saturday Night and Sunday Morning* we have a rather different situation. The film was made in a British realist tradition which tended to emphasise the hero's typicality rather than his exceptional qualities; its resolution, however, is that of a romance narrative in which Seaton eventually settles down with Doreen. Both elements seem to operate against making the demonstration of masculinity through action a possibility for Finney/Seaton.

In the realist tradition, *Saturday Night and Sunday Morning* offers a portrait of a young man in a specific social context. Its claim to significance rested on the accuracy of its representation of working-class life (the factory setting, the emphasis on popular forms of entertainment such as fishing and the pub) and its ability to delineate a range of differences between characters in the same class. Seaton's masculinity is rooted in rebellion but his actions take place within the confines of this realist mode. He goes fishing but in this film fishing offers more opportunity for conversation than action. He speaks defiantly to men such as Jack, Brenda's husband, whom he despises, but in the end Jack's actions are more effective. Even the moments of violence in the film are heavily undercut by their context and undermine the heroic claims of the character. When Seaton seizes a gun it is to shoot air pellets at a woman – his neighbour, old Ma Bull – to repay her for her nosiness and it is his father who defends him when she comes seeking reprisals. The one fight sequence takes place when Jack, Brenda's husband, gets his army friends to beat Arthur up after an accidental meeting with Brenda at the fairground. It is filmed in long shot, in semi-darkness, so there is no opportunity for masculine display and Seaton is heavily beaten, sagging between the squaddies as they use him as a punchbag.

If there is little opportunity for exuberant action in the film's emphasis on social observation, Seaton is also surprisingly passive in his relations with the two key women, Brenda, his lover when the film starts, and Doreen, his fiancée by its end. In Brenda's story, after the initial lovemaking at her house, Finney/Seaton is shown in a slightly comical way, scuttling out of the door as Brenda's husband arrives back unexpectedly early. As the narrative develops around Brenda's accidental pregnancy, Seaton is seen to become more and more helpless. He is excluded by Aunt Ada from her attempt to terminate the pregnancy and in the end Brenda rejects his money and muttered offers of help with a painfully accurate 'Nothing much you can do.'

Similarly, the story of Seaton's relationship with Doreen shows the hero in an equally passive mode. Although it is Seaton who begins their first conversation in the pub, Doreen is adept at handling his mocking banter. She sets out the terms of their courtship and she seeks him out twice when the relationship is in jeopardy, once after her mother's display of hostility towards him and again after the fight at the fair. Sexually, Doreen also takes the initiative; when Arthur visits her home, she suggests that they act out his departure for the benefit of her mother upstairs and she shows no coyness in her sexual response.[5] Her behaviour can be framed, as we shall see, in a discourse of female dominance but its effect is to show Seaton as acted on rather than taking action. It maybe that this passivity is important for Finney as a star in establishing the sense that he is on display for the audience's contemplation but it does not establish him as a dominant figure in terms of narrative action.

THE EXTERNAL WORLD

In laying out the sites across which masculinity is structured, Kirkham and Thumim place emphasis on the external world as an arena in which masculinity is associated with issues such as 'status, hierarchy, knowledge, skill, language and success.'[6] This concern with the public world is reinforced in *Saturday Night and Sunday Morning* by a realist emphasis on the external details of a particular culture. The film goes to considerable lengths to map out the world which Seaton inhabits. It shows him at work, in the pub, out fishing with his mate, dancing with Doreen in the back room. It shows the boredom of Sunday afternoons – tea with the family, walks in the park – and the high spot of the fair with its bright lights and hidden dark corners. In addition, as John Hill has shown, the film seeks to represent a working-class community at the point of change. It lays out the boundaries of old communities, the aspirations of those who have moved to the suburbs and the tensions between generations. It attempts then to present an external world, marked out by class, 'at a time when the traditional working class is perceived as being in decline, supplanted by a modern working class whose identity is most tellingly revealed in consumption rather than production.'[7]

The hero of *Saturday Night and Sunday Morning* is clearly presented as being central to this world; he is indeed the object of its concern, someone whose power is feared because he appears to threaten change. He has more money than the older workers; he challenges the traditional values of sharing and attacks the community for being petty minded and interfering. 'I've got some fight in me,' he tells Bert and he castigates his parents for being 'dead from the neck up.' In fact as the film progresses, it becomes clear that all Seaton has is words; he has no power. Though he earns his money he cannot use it except to buy beer. He teases and abuses women but in the moment of crisis over Brenda's pregnancy all he can do is turn to one of the matriarchy, his Aunt Ada, for help. He asserts his rights as an individual but makes no attempt to combine with or to lead others. Just as Seaton is blocked off from action so also is he blocked off from access to power in the external world.

It is possible to read Seaton's defiant rejection of older traditions as part of the film's concerns about the consumerist culture of the 1950s, the fear that the spending power of young people would weaken their links with family and community.[8] But we can also see here a gap which increasingly opens up between Finney/Seaton's words and gestures; his inability to act effectively can be understood as a sign of loss of masculinity. One example of this is the episode in which a man breaks a shop window and is held by the women of the community who call the police. Seaton argues that it is unjust and urges the man to run. But he is unsuccessful and the man fails to escape. Seaton is reduced to bitter invective against Ma Bull 'She's a bitch and a whore' he cries to Bert. This violence of language recurs through the film – 'They can get stuffed', 'Bastard', 'It's a bloody lie'. This aggressive dialogue allows Finney/Seaton to dominate the soundtrack just as his face dominates the image but it nevertheless becomes increasingly clear that he is powerless to dominate his world.

THE INTERNAL WORLD

All this may suggest that *Saturday Night and Sunday Morning* centres on a crisis of confidence for Seaton over what kind of future he is to have, what kind of man he is to become, 'the absorbing question of male anxiety' which runs through many of the films discussed in *You Tarzan*.[9] This is indeed set up in the film through the commentary of other characters who are continually predicting that Seaton will 'learn one day'. But these are external comments and the film gives us surprisingly little information about what is going on in Seaton's head.

The structure of the film appears to offer access to the central character. It starts with a voice over which immediately outlines for the audience Seaton's philosophy of life and his views on the 'poor beggars' who have failed to live by it. The voice-over reoccurs at various points, most significantly when Arthur is lying in bed, recovering from the beating. But it becomes clear that what we are being offered is not access to inner feelings but the same bombastic overdriven rhetoric of his external speech – 'I'm me and nobody else. Whatever anybody says that I am that's what I'm not.' The voice-over does not help the audience to understand Seaton's actions. Why, for instance, does he propose to Doreen? Is it because she 'looks nice' (if we pick up on the 'never bite unless the bait's good' fishing reference in an earlier conversation with Bert about marriage)? Is it because he finally agrees with Bert that 'everyone's got to get married some time' and society gives him no choice? Or is it because Doreen (and her mother) have trapped him as a reading which stressed the film's misogyny would tend to suggest?[10] Seaton's inner world remains closed to us, the apparent openness of the voice-over device is deceptive. The audience is left to study Finney's impassive face, to try to make sense of the character's behaviour by reading the changes in expression, the look in the eyes, the smile, the scowl.

CONCLUSION

Studying the star/character of Finney/Seaton across the categories of the body, action, the external world and the internal world helps to pinpoint some of the contradictions at work in the film. Here we have a star whose physical presence dominates the screen, whom the camera looks up to and whose impassive face is presented for our study; we have a character who aggressively asserts his claim to be above and outside the working class community in which he lives. At the same time, this star/character is placed in a double romance narrative (the first with Brenda ending with the abortion, the second with Doreen leading to the engagement) in which his physical actions are circumscribed and he can neither influence nor control the external world. By the end of the film, he is joining the 'poor beggars' he so despises and facing the prospect of starting married life in the unwelcoming home of his mother-in-law.

This compromise, particularly around sexuality, is typical of British new wave films of the period and can be read as a social problem being brought to the audience's attention by a realist film. In terms of class, Seaton is presented as a young man, coming to terms with the collapse of a culture based on the traditions of his working-class community and asserting his individualist philosophy in an attempt to fill the gap. In terms of gender, John Hill points out that the films of the British new wave centre on 'female inadequacy', on the 'problem of securing an adequate "female counterpart" for the angry hero with the result that their endings (abandon) male heroes to isolation or (impose) upon them "solutions" which primarily consist of compromises.'[11] While this aptly describes the way in which the sexual and erotic appeal of the working-class hero is undermined, I would like to suggest that as far as *Saturday Night and Sunday Morning* is concerned, the concepts of class and gender at play here need also to be read in terms of the film's visual presentation of the hero and the narrative organisation in which he is caught in order to shed light on the impasse reached at the end of the film.

The masculinity embodied in Finney/Seaton is experienced outside the narrative action and is based on what we see and hear. The image and soundtrack are dominated by Finney. His physical presence provides an object for erotic contemplation while the interior monologue grounds our looking, not in the revelation of his inner world but rather in the verbal display of an aggressive personality. The audience's pleasure is caught up with the presentation of Finney's face and body, characteristically held in the upward gaze of the camera, and with the defiant, uncompromising stance of Seaton as a character. The character's passivity, his inability to act effectively, are not an issue in this pinup mode of looking but problems do arise when this figure is caught, as in *Saturday Night and Sunday Morning*, within two narrative modes, both based on change and compromise. In the realist narrative typical of films like *Room at the Top* and *A Kind of Loving*, the young working-class man either moves out of his class or accepts that he has no way out. In both cases, the hero has to change and develop some kind of ability to judge his own position in the external world. In the romance narrative on the other hand, the hero has to come to terms with the internal world and recognise the emotions and feelings which the heroine wishes to share with him.[12] In this narrative, the hero also changes and acknowledges that change in his expression of love for the heroine. But neither of these endings would be satisfying in *Saturday Night and Sunday Morning* because the changes they imply would undermine the status of the Finney/Seaton figure as the pin-up, the defiant hero; resolution, based on change, is thus necessary for the narrative but blocked by the need to maintain the hero's static masculinity.

John Hill, quoting Ken Worpole, suggests that the weakness of the working-class heroes of the new wave is 'avoidance of engaging with the reality of personal and sexual relationships'.[13] I would suggest that the weakness of *Saturday Night and Sunday Morning*, and perhaps of British new wave cinema generally, is the avoidance of a working-class male figure who can combine visual power and narrative effectiveness. The hero is trapped not by the woman but by the trammels of a narrative which, using realism as its alibi but class fear as its rationale, denies the audience the full measure of a working-class hero. The integration of masculinity in body and action, a common fantasy in American cinema, is thwarted in *Saturday Night and Sunday Morning* because images of sexual power are cut across by a narrative of class position. The end of the film tries to find a way out of the dilemma by refusing to acknowledge it. The narrative drives to an ending in which Seaton is tamed by the uselessness of his rebellion and the practical skills of Doreen in settling him down. The image and soundtrack, however, still insist that Finney/Seaton has remained the same. As he talks to Doreen about their new home, Seaton throws a stone. 'It won't be the last thing I'll throw,' he tells Doreen, reiterating his refusal to change, while the camera for the last time captures Finney's head and shoulders, shot from below and dominating the screen. The final line of dialogue wraps up the narrative 'Come on, duck, let's go down.' Arthur Seaton, the character, takes his girl down the hill, but Albert Finney, the star, stays up there throwing his stones.

NOTES

1 Andy Medhurst, '*Victim*: Text as Context', *Screen*, Vol. 25, Nos. 4/5, 1984, p24.
2 Pat Kirkham and Janet Thumim, *You Tarzan: Masculinity Movies and Men*, Lawrence & Wishart, London, 1993, p11.
3 In a later film, *Charlie Bubbles* (Finney, GB, 1968), his link with other pinups was more explicitly made when Finney as the eponymous hero, Charlie Bubbles, goes to watch George Best playing for Manchester United.
4 Kirkham and Thumim, *op.cit.*, p15.
5 I would disagree with John Hill's reading of Doreen as fearful in *Sex Class and Realism British Cinema 1956-63*, BFI, London, 1986, p160.
6 Kirkham and Thumim, *op.cit.*, p19.
7 Hill, *op.cit.*, p154.
8 *Ibid*.
9 Kirkham and Thumim, *op.cit.*, p22.
10 Hill, *op.cit.*, p162.

11 *Ibid.*, p162.
12 See Alison Light ' "Returning to Manderley" – Romance Fiction, Female Sexuality and Class' in *Feminist Review*, Volume 16, Summer 1984, and Janice Radway, *Reading the Romance*, University of North Carolina Press, Chapel Hill, 1984, for influential accounts of the romance narrative.
13 Hill, *op.cit.*, p163.

Women Reading Men

Christine Gledhill

The central concern of this essay is the possible meanings of images of men for women. My goal is neither a catalogue of masculinist stereotypes nor a celebration of favourite moments with male images, although I touch on both since I am seeking a way of thinking about popular culture that will acknowledge its pleasures and meanings without losing a critical edge. In this respect the invitation to contribute to *Me Jane* offers a welcome opportunity to bring together a series of scattered thoughts which have cropped up over years of engagement with feminist film theory and latterly, melodrama. My essay falls into two halves: first, a series of theoretical/methodological questions and propositions and second a series of 'moments' from popular Hollywood films through which I attempt to construct a framework for analysis.

READING NOT JUST LOOKING

By signalling reading rather than looking I do not want to deny the centrality of looking to the production of meaning and pleasure in the cinema. However, the term has become identified with the cine-psychoanalytic construction of main-stream narrative as a series of looks which, organised around woman as object of an active male gaze, masculinise the spectator. Although this approach offers a compelling explanation of the objectification of 'woman' in the cinema, it has had notorious difficulties in theorising the female spectator in the text or dealing with historically constituted female audiences. Given the preponderance of male characters in film fictions, except for those few special and marginalised genres made with women in mind, an emphasis on the masculinisation of the look raises for me the question of what women in their millions are doing in the cinema, where most of our time is spent watching images of men rather than of women.

More recently a growing body of work seeks to deconstruct dominant images of masculinity as contradictory products of patriarchy – notable among these, this volume's predecessor, *You Tarzan*. But judging from the paucity of writing on the meaning of images of men for women, even by ethnographic researchers, it would seem that this has been a difficult question to pose. However, its neglect not only risks overidentification of women as victims of patriarchy, but refuses recognition of women as makers of meaning out of male images. I think a major problem blocking such exploration has been the equation of the 'look' with sexual power to the neglect of other constructive principles such as character and plot which extend beyond visual materialisation, taking life in the viewer's imagination and turning looking into reading and fantasising. As Ian Green argues, 'character' is a key mechanism in our experience of film fiction, drawing together social stereotyping, fictional production and the viewer's own experiences and fantasies.[1] Secondly, while feminist theory has produced highly sophisticated analyses of 'woman-as-image' constructed by and for male fantasy, it has often seemed to me that the hero of film analysis who controls the unfolding of narrative and image, replicates rather too neatly the social male whose power is theorised outside the cinema. Men in movies somehow remain men. If, however, 'woman' is image – a fantasy – is this not true of 'man' too? The failure to put this question arises, I think, from the assumption that the 'fantasy' of a popular work belongs to the dominant and therefore patriarchal imagination. Thus the hero in dominating the narrative reflects the dominance of the social male, the fantasy producer. For example my analysis of *Klute* (Alan Pakula, US, 1971), focused on the narrative power of the noir detective hero over Jane Fonda's would-be liberated prostitute, Bree Daniels,[2] to the neglect of the intractible presence of Fonda herself, whose star image exceeds the film and as I found later held an important, if contradictory, place in the perception of many female viewers.[3] Could it be that the male figure performs an equally contradictory function for female audiences?

MELODRAMA

Working on melodrama intensified these issues for me. When writing about *Coma* (Michael Crichton, US, 1977), for example, I became aware of a critical contradiction: as a feminist I wanted to contest the film's patriarchal recuperation of women's liberation.[4] As a student and avid consumer of melodrama, I was fascinated by the staging and working through of conflicts between the melodramatic moral and gendered personifications of villain and heroine. Two critical comments on nineteenth-century melodrama exercised me in particular: first, Peter

Brooks' claim that 'virtue is nearly always inevitably represented by a young heroine'[5] and secondly Thomas Elsaesser's comments on melodrama's 'metaphysical interpretation of class conflict as sexual exploitation and rape'.[6] As statements about representation, both are clearly – and perhaps rightly – unattuned to feminist sensibilities. Peter Brooks' formulation, in particular, appears to block an immediate move into ideological critique through his more pressing concern with melodrama as a symbolising and aesthetic dynamic. But what these statements do imply is the *dual* function of the human body in popular fictions. On the one hand the human figure commands recognition by its reference to social, cultural and psychic attributes – gender, age, class, ethnicity, sexual orientation, and so on – on the other hand the human body functions metaphorically, symbolically, mythically. Moreover, this is as true for male as for female bodies. Opposed to Brooks' heroine as virtue stands villainy, which is 'a swarthy cape-enveloped man with a deep voice'.[7]

Approaching Hollywood from the perspective of nineteenth-century melodrama suggests a tension between representation and aesthetic function, when socially defined bodies perform symbolic enactments. The triangular conflict between villain, heroine and hero which structures not only many nineteenth-century melodramas but is restaged throughout Hollywood's history, from *Way Down East* (D.W. Griffith, US, 1920) to *Coma* or *Jagged Edge* (Richard Marquand, US, 1985) enacts an aesthetic, emotional and moral dynamic to which gender is central. The concept of representation has in my view proved inadequate to the task of opening up the work of this dynamic for its audiences because it precipitately refers the work and its reception to a reality constituted and theoretically known outside the work – for example, the unequal relations of patriarchal society as understood by historical materialism, feminism or psychoanalysis. Attention to the aesthetic requirements of melodrama, however, suggests a gap between imaginative and representational functions, which should delay the immediate translation of the one in terms of the other. It is necessary then to consider the provenance of fantasy and aesthetic structures in order to bring ideological analysis closer to the actual pleasures of audiences.

REFERENCING, SYMBOLISING, FANTASISING

Recent work on fantasy, drawing on Freud, refuses the

common sense opposition of the real world and fantasy defined as simple make-believe. Rather it argues that fantasy has to be understood as a process through which public and private, social and psychic, the real and the fantasised intersect and interact in a series of 'secondary elaborations' woven out of source material derived from material and psychical experience.[8] In a similar way, the melodramatic mode draws on issues, figures, events, objects from the social world and everyday experience and reworks them according to a different set of aesthetic, emotional and moral priorities.[9] However, despite highlighting some of the mechanisms of fantasy – displacement, condensation, the fluidity of subject positions – the concept of 'representation' and its over-riding concern with what is represented persists. The variety and intricacy of cinema's 'secondary elaborations' are regarded as indeed secondary, and translated back to their psychic substrate in the primal scene and Oedipal scenario.[10] Ideology is found in an originating source rather than in lived experience and the processes of fantasising.

However, what audiences encounter is precisely these elaborations in their endless variety. It is the work of elaboration itself that is my concern; what interests me are the meanings and emotional affects made possible by the dramatic conflicts, stereotypes and fantasies of film fiction. As an aesthetic of polar conflict, melodrama requires *dramatis personae* who embody starkly defined and opposed social and aesthetic values. The dramatic frisson of melodrama lies in the startling encounters, confrontations, reversals, *coups de théâtre*, blinding recognitions, which these emblematic figures enact. In this respect it could be argued that ideology, which codifies social and cultural values in concrete representations – stereotypes – serves the aesthetic dynamic of melodrama as much as melodrama produces ideology. For exmple, the popular appeal of *Dallas'* JR may lie less with his justification of American capitalism than the capacity of capitalist ideology to produce a dynamic villain whose acquisitive drive flouts the social proprieties of the business world and the bonds of the bourgeois family. Treating this dynamic as representation enables ideological analysis to identify stereotypes, myths and misrepresentations but leaves untouched the pleasure of popular texts. I want to argue that the aesthetic forms, emotional dynamics, and fantasied conjunctures of such fictions are meaningful *in their own right*, not simply as displacements for something else. If we want to know what mainstream cinemas make available to their audiences we need to focus on films precisely as elaborations of, negotiations between, discourses put into conflict by the culture or the unconscious. What I am interested in, therefore, is what experiences are offered and what is being said in the '*as if*' scenarios of fantasy and the particular figures, images, situations and actions they use. These questions need to focus on the aesthetic and affective work such figures can be made to perform.

CRITICAL READINGS AND THE 'DUAL TEXT'

How can one think of the sensationalising and personalising dynamic of popular culture in relation to a critique of gender relations? Looking at popular films within the framework of melodrama reveals a contest between politics and the mythic functions of representational art which steals, as it were, the bodies of historically and socially constituted figures for the symbolising functions of fantasy. When oppressed groups claim their image back in the name of social change, not only has social representation to change, but popular fictions which seek to retain audience recognition are forced to negotiate with newly emerging social identities while hanging on to the mythic functions performed by the image. Feminists, both black and white, confront this dilemma acutely in, for example, Spielberg's film of Alice Walker's black feminist novel, *The Color Purple* (US, 1985) in which Miss Celie's triumphant cry, 'I'm poor, black, I may even be ugly, but dear God I'm here, I'm here', remythifies a black feminist liberationary figure for public fantasy. There seems to me no way out of this mythologising process except through an active sense of culture as constant negotiation, process, fantasising, work.

Negotiation is a key concept in thinking about the dual activity of the text as referencing and symbolising.[11] What interests me in the notion of 'women reading men' are the processes of gender negotiation made possible in the fantasising activity represented by popular texts and their engagement by female audiences. I want to approach the male figure in films not simply as a source of ideological norms and stereotypes but to consider both what the culture has vested in masculinity as an element in collective fantasy and what functions such figures might perform in the economy of female fantasy. Only by forestalling an immediate reference to 'real' social relations, is it possible to ask what emotional or aesthetic effects the values embodied in male figures – ambition and aggression, for example – might play for female pleasure and fantasy.

However, before proceeding, I need to make three caveats in relation to my title, 'Women Reading Men'. First I do not propose 'women' as an essential category but I am assuming that given the historical and contemporary operation of gender difference, female audiences read and fantasise from different social, cultural and subjective positions to men. Second I use the term 'reading' as itself a 'secondary elaboration' of a diffuse and multiple experience which includes looking, emotional and visceral response, fantasising, as well as reflection and reminiscence. In this sense 'reading' is not synonomous with response but is the product of mental reflection. If readings are determined by the social and subjective formation of the reader, then the readings themselves tell us less about the text, than what for a particular group of readers the text makes possible. This introduces my final point, which is the status of my readings in an exercise which lacks the scale and funding necessary for the ethnographic research such a project clearly warrants. What is the status of the readings made by one white, middle-class, professional woman? First textual and ethnographic research do not necessarily exclude each other. Ethnographic work can change the questions we ask of a text; for example the question this piece explores has been made possible by the ethnographic investigation of Janice Radway and others into female readerships and the romantic hero.[12] Second, textual analysis is not simply a rarified, academic activity, but participates in the cultural production, negotiation and circulation of meanings. We 'read' texts and stake so much energy in debating images and meanings, because meanings matter, and although as professional 'readers' we may work in a privileged and relatively individual way, nevertheless we look for and put into public circulation meanings important to a particular cultural and social context. Critical work is thus part of a social debate and inevitably, in its turn, contributes to the questions asked by ethnographic researchers. The modest ambition of this piece is to put the question of 'women reading men' on the agenda, using my own responses as a starting point.

I begin this process in the exploratory spirit advocated by Pat Kirkham and Janet Thumim in their introductory essays in this and its companion volume, *You Tarzan*. As is implied in my broadening of the term, 'reading', I do not approach the film 'text' as a purely formal construct, but as the space of engagement between film and viewer which includes a range of personal and cultural processes. I want now to propose a framework through which to examine these different processes by distinguishing between four levels of text-viewer engagement and exemplifying their work through particular filmic moments. These levels, of course, co-exist and intersect, but for the purpose of analysis I want to deal with them separately. These levels are: 1) Recognition, 2) Symbolic Figuration, 3) Ideological Negotiation and 4) Fantasy.

REFERENCE AND RECOGNITION

Although I am primarily interested in the aesthetic and symbolic work of a text, the force and relevance of this work is grounded in reference to the social world and appeal to audience recognition. All recognition is based on a mixture of familiarity and difference in what is essentially a process of re-*cognition*: we need to see the familiar differently in order to see it at all. For women, excluded from so many areas of male dominated social life, the play of familiarity and renewed recognition has a double force. My first film example is just such an exclusionary moment: the scene in *The Deer Hunter* (Michael Cimino, US, 1978) of the three heros – Mike (Robert De Niro), Nick (Christopher Walken) and Stephen (Chuck Aspegren) – 'drinking and joshing' in their comrade's bar prior to Stephen's wedding and their departure for Vietnam the following morning.[13] But this is not just a moment of gendered exclusion, it is also a moment of privacy and intimacy for the men which celebrates two male rites of passage – stag night and initiation into war. For the female spectator, doubly excluded, such a scene invites curiosity. It offers women a 'fly-on-the-wall' spectatorial pleasure thereby enabling us, in Joseph Bristow's phrase, 'to occupy another's gender'.[14] It is perhaps an anxious anticipation of the presence of the female spectator which rebukes such eavesdropping in the heavily caricatured entry of Stephen's mother who comes to drag him off to prepare for the wedding to the mockery of the others.

So how is recognition invited here? What might women in particular recognise and what are the pleasures of such recognition? The element of difference which permits recognition is based on the familiar strategy of using supporting types played by character actors as a foil for the central protagonists, Mike, Stephen and Nick, who are realised through a mixture of star presence and the greater naturalism of 'Method' acting. The cultural codes of recognition at work in this scene – stag night, beer, the pool table, the juke box – are those which both permit and constrain male bonding and expressiveness. In the general rowdiness of the group as a whole – 'the drinking and joshing' – there is much that women might recognise with a heavy heart. But the search for recognition through the central players in their more nuanced performance of gesture, body movement, behavioural traits, 'grain of voice', turns of phrase, etc., both holds masculinity up to view while also aestheticising it. If the uninhibited expenditure of energy of the comrades, their self-assured command of space and the airwaves as of natural right, enacts an empowerment unfamiliar to many women, the privacy of this moment offers a relatively unthreatening access to masculinity. These exchanges between male figures who are ostensibly off duty and off guard produce moments of self exposure which hint at the hidden person beneath the armour of masculinity. Central to this scene is the androgynous performance of Christopher Walken as Nick who, singing his heart out and swinging his body and cue in time to the juke box, momentarily escapes the constricting male stereotypes of leader or led.

However, the same-sex bonding of men differs from the intimacy of women. Despite the expenditure of energy, the mise-en-scène serves to constrain. Stag night is used less to tell Stephen's heterosexual story than to set going undercurrents of unexpressed male desire between Mike and Nick who, in his exuberant rendition of 'I Can't Take My Eyes Off You', becomes a central focus of the camera's gaze. The sentiment of the song is held in tension with the choreography of body movements and edits in which looks between the two seem to be exchanged without eyelines exactly meeting. The paradoxical pleasure of these near exchanges for the female viewer may well be the expression of desire without objectification – desire between subjects. Whether this be so or not, the pleasure of recognition in this scene hinges on the gestures and codes which suggest a different form of gendered existence.

SYMBOLIC FIGURATION: MALE ARCHETYPES

Recognition in *The Deer Hunter* is premised on the claim to authenticity of method acting which, it has been argued, promises access to the personality as the primary post-Enlightenment source of meaning and value in the western world.[15] Masculinity is specifically personalised here. But as the self-conscious symbolism of the film makes abundantly clear, *The Deer Hunter* is not a naturalistic film. The behavioural detail which grounds *recognition* coalesces with stereotypes circulating in the culture to produce male images as narrative functions and symbolic figures – turning, for example, Mike into the Leader and Nick and Stephen into different versions of the Wounded Man (see below). The shift from authenticated character to archetype is presaged by the huge photographs of the boys hung aloft at the wedding feast and the unexplained, lugubrious entrance of the Green Beret (recalling Coleridge's Ancient Mariner) who has only two emblematic words to offer them – 'fuck it'. Whereas individualised characters who authenticate recognition, and stereotypes which offer short cuts to it, are rooted in particular historical and cultural conditions, the archetype exceeds its socially specific sources, emerging as a distillation of stereotypical features and evolving through an accretion of uses across decades, forms and national cultures. In this sense the archetype is not so much universal and eternal as trans-individual, trans-historical, and trans-cultural: a figure whose reappearance can be used to chart relations between past and present, and between different cultures.[16] Through the orchestration of the narrative and the ritualistic enactments of the plot, Steve, Nick and Mike cease to function as characters who require reading in terms of psychological motivation or stereotypical representation. The narrative forces these figures into positions of symbolic magnitude, over which the shadow of previous archetypes hover – most notably John Wayne, as the All American Hero and symbol of Invincible Masculinity – but which, in the 1970s, these protagonists of Vietnam can scarcely fill. Nevertheless, the film strives to find in them the symbolising functions that will sustain by highlighting the culture's loss of the dramatic emotional and moral economy for such a scenario. It is at this level that we can begin to speculate on the myths that masculinity sustains and on the pleasures and meanings such mythic uses of male images make available to female readers.

Like female images, male figures can be classified according to a range of types – Romantic Hero, New Man, Older Man, Villain, Crusading Hero, Wolf, Wounded Man, and so on, which may be treated as patriarchal stereotypes. But analysis of this sort often discounts the aesthetic and symbolic work the cultural type can perform in popular art. For example, a distinction between these figures, which is important for feminist analysis and may be lost in their reading simply as stereotypes, is the different relations they permit with the heroine. Whereas the Romantic Hero is constructed in relationship to the heroine, the Crusading Hero's power is premised on his invulnerability to women while the Wounded Man may or may not accommodate the opposite sex.

The Romantic Hero has received most attention from feminist critics as part of the re-evaluation of women's cultural forms where, as one of those male figures constructed with the female audience in mind, he is most frequently found. For female audiences, it is argued, the imaginative value of such figures is that they recognise or will come to recognise the heroine's true worth, often despite herself.[17] In this respect they offer the fantasy of similarity or rapprochment between the sexes. At one extreme, the Romantic Hero promises to become the Soul-Mate who recognises from the outset the worth of the heroine, because he is in many ways like her – he is feminised. A variant of the Soul-Mate is the Maternal Man or New Man, whose role may be to recognise and confirm a worth in the heroine she does not recognise herself.

In many ways these feminised figures are more legible by feminist analysis because they are already organised for female reading. More challenging are those figures which embody a masculinist ethos, such as the Crusading Hero or the Villain, who because of their separateness from the heroine, dramatise the attractions and repulsions of masculinity more starkly for the female audience. In particular, they represent lessons in the forms and exercise of power – physical, material, psychic or moral, and often violent. The figure most closely associated with power is the villain, who demonstrates both its fascinations and dangers. If power defines masculinity, the ultimate measure of power, its place of deepest public recognition, has traditionally lain in the abjected female. Thus it is possible for feminism to invert Peter Brooks's melodramatic paradigm. If virtue is represented by a young woman and the villain is male, masculinity becomes villainy. We can see this developing in many of D.W. Griffith's films where the Heroine, sometimes supported by a Mother figure, sometimes by a male Soul-Mate, engages in a moral and sometimes physical battle with a Father conceived as Patriarchal Tyrant. The figure of Battling Burrows in *Broken Blossoms* (D.W. Griffith, US, 1919) makes the identification of masculinity and villainy explicit by challenging Victorian morality in its own terms and demanding that the male display a similar virtue to the female. In more recent times, in the medical thriller, *Coma*, Richard Widmark, who plays Dr George Harrison, Chief of Surgery, wields patriarchal ideology as an instrument of villainy against the heroine, Dr Susan Wheeler (Genevieve Bujold), who is close to uncovering his racket in body parts and whom he threatens as much by manipulating the sexism of his colleagues as by hiring a killer. In an interview with the junior doctor he manipulates the psychotherapeutic discourse of feeling as a means of making Susan break down as she remembers her dead friend, thereby forcing her back into an appropriate femininity and, he hopes, the containing arms of her lover on a diversionary weekend. After she has made her apologies and left, his silver-haired mask of benevolent paternalism is suddenly torn aside as he spits a misogynist aside to the audience: 'Women, Christ!' The perversely subversive power of this villain for the female audience lies in Widmark's enactment of an all-knowing, all-understanding paternalism which is both seductive and life-threatening.

CONTRADICTIONS AND NEGOTIATIONS

The redefinition of villainy as sexism in *Coma* exemplifies the way in which the stereotypes and archetypes of popular culture are not simple ideological products but counters put into contradiction and negotiation by the ideological work of producing popular representations. Nineteenth-century melodrama which offered a relatively secure equation between gendered bodies and moral values comes under pressure as women increasingly struggle with the burden of maintaining social virtue and at the same time fight for female emancipation. While the dramatic need for bodies to enact moral confrontation is as strong as ever, changing social relations disrupt the relation between gender and moral value, producing a series of dislocations, negotiations, reframings, involving Romantic Heros and Villains, New Men and Independent or Liberated Women. It is at this level that we can ask what is ideologically at stake in terms of the text's work. Certain male roles, for example, are clearly the product of such negotiations between changing gender roles in society and the symbolising work of gendered figures in popular fictions. D.W. Griffith uses Richard Barthelmass to personify Woman's Soul-Mate in both *Broken Blossoms* and *Way Down East* in an early twentieth-century construction of the New Man, whose function, it would seem, is to preserve the True Woman from the polar extremes of the New Woman and Victorian Patriarch.[18] The Older Man, performs a similar function, mediating between the needs of the unprotected, threatened, or would-be independent heroine and a destructive patriarchal world. Where male power represents a threat to the woman, a benevolent paternal representative is required to open up a space for the female protagonist.

Significantly, however, it is rarely the father himself who plays this role. The Older Man may appear in the role of doctor or priest, roles which permit relatively 'safe' interchanges between woman and man.[19] For example in *Now, Voyager* (Irving Rapper, US, 1942), Bette Davis as Charlotte Vale, like Olive Higgins Prouty, her creator, uses the space that Dr Jacquith (Claude Raines) can authorise away from her family to overcome a nervous breakdown.[20] Where heroines take a more active role in conventionally male genres such as the private eye thriller or police film, an elderly male side-kick may take on this mediating role. Through such figures who combine maternal with male power, the heroine may address patriarchy, get to 'talk with God', and even contest his power: for example, exchanges between Bette Davis and Claude Raines in *Now, Voyager*, between Susan Weinblatt (Melanie Mayron) and the Rabbi (Eli Wallach) in *Girlfriends* (Claudia Weill, US, 1977) and Teddy's (Glenn Close's) exchange with the older male sleuth, Sam (Robert Loggia), in *Jagged Edge*.

Figures such as the Older Man who function to mediate between patriarchal representation and the demands of women implicitly recognise the disjunction between 'woman' and women. This disjunction, now made vocal through campaigns by the women's movement and feminist analysis of sexism, has forced melodramatic confrontation onto new ground. As the ideology of separate spheres, which built gender so unproblematically into a polarised moral schema, is challenged by feminism, masculinity and femininity, rather than lending gender values to social conflicts may themselves be in moral conflict. Thus contestation in the social arena causes reverberations in the symbolic economy of popular fictions which affect male as well as female personae.

Clint Eastwood's films offer an interesting barometer of contemporary turmoil in gender representation. For example, if *The Deer Hunter* in the scene I have quoted above appears uncomfortable about the intrusion of the female look, *High Plains Drifter* (Clint Eastwood, US, 1972) and *Pale Rider* (Clint Eastwood, US, 1985) seem positively to court it. In both films, a slow ride into town – which intercuts different takes on the Eastwood figure with shots of townspeople reacting – is staged as a performance for a waiting, recognising, female look. In *High Plains Drifter* the woman recognises in Eastwood the return of a Marshall long ago beaten to death by the townsfolk. In *Pale Rider*, the female look, which is not located in town but in an outlying homestead, is integrated into Eastwood's approach by cross-cutting between separate locations, while recognition is suggested by the daughter's readings from *Revelations* and the mother's look to the window as if in anticipation of his arrival. The ramifications of these moments would reward detailed investigation, but given Eastwood's reputed rise to stardom through his appeal to young working-class men, this figuration of a female spectator in the text begs for feminist consideration. Indeed, Eastwood's films seem increasingly aware of the sexual politics they flout with their assertion of the all-sufficient male, and self-conscious sexism. For example, *Play Misty For Me* (Clint Eastwood, US, 1971) sets up a highly ambiguous play with feminism. Here Eastwood, playing the role of DJ, constructs himself as a male sex object who calls into play the desires of an obsessed female fan his character seeks to disown. As the Eastwood character lives out macho fantasies of alternately rape and sentimental paternalism, the orchestration of gender roles and looks suggest an uncomfortable awareness of the female gaze and conscious-ness, which plotting and mise-en-scène attempt in different films to bully, cajole, reason with and rationalise away but, by the same token, recognise. It is almost as if these films seek dialogue with the imputed female spectator, out there, watching, and with feminism.

READING AS FANTASY

Eastwood's films offer acute exemplification of the contra-dictions and negotiations entailed when male archetypes seek renewal in dramatic enactments that will command assent from audiences in a context of contested gender roles. How then do the elements of recognition, symbolic figuration and contradiction fielded by such films come together in the workings of female fantasy? What desires and fears do such figures cathect or enact? What do they tell us of the ties that bind us to atavistic social and psychic structures? How do they contribute to resistance and the imagining of something different? Sexual politics creates new drama among the archetypes. Both masculinist and romantic archetypes come under pressure, forming two major routes for female fantasy: one that turns on difference and distance, the other on similarity and rapprochement.

DIFFERENCE, SEPARATION, FIXITY

Clint Eastwood's films exemplify the former. Eastwood

represents an intensification of the Westerner as outsider, separated, and unassimilable. As the 'Man with No Name', he is produced in an imaginary space outside the social structures of patriarchal power which uses violence in support of greed, exploitation, and corruption. The Eastwood Westerner does not reform the codes of masculinity like the New Man, but abstracts masculine power as a purifying instrument in the service of an invincible authority. In the opening of *Pale Rider*, for example, he appears as a magical defender against male violence, a figure of imaginary empowerment for the dispossessed miners and waiting women alike, who exercises a purifying violence to withstand the horrors of corrupt masculinity.

Within the aesthetic and moral economy of the drama, the capacity of the Pale Rider to perform this function depends on his separateness. How might this function for female fantasy? It is suggested that a major pleasure for the male audience in the fetishised image of woman is her promise of a return to an original maternal plenitude and fusion. Arguably women have little need of fantasies of fusion – quite the reverse, for women as the caring gender are over-sensitised to the presence and needs of others. In this context, the unassimiability, separateness and invincibility of the Eastwood persona suggest the opposite might appeal to women in images of men. Rather than fusion, Eastwood offers the pleasure of ego definition and boundedness which both separates the self from others and their needs and at the same time make it possible to act on them.[21]

In this context it becomes possible to revisit Donald Sutherland's impassive detective, John Klute, who in a masculinist persona tinged with 'new mannishness' provides for Jane Fonda's drug and sex exhausted prostitute, Bree Daniels, thankfully silent ministrations. The fixity and decisiveness of his masculinity is counterposed both emotionally and aesthetically to the shifting social and sexual identities of the liberated woman, figured as at once prostitute, actress and liberated woman, providing security and comfort in the context of her confusion.

RAPPROCHEMENT: CROSSING THE GENDER DIVIDE

The contemporary polarisation of masculinity and femininity makes particularly alluring the figure of The Wounded Man, who may cross over the gender divide, playing to a fantasy of similarity and rapprochement. Rozsika Parker goes back to the nineteenth-century novel to explain the prevalence of the Wounded Man in women's writing and painting, suggesting that one attraction in this figure is its capacity to redress the power balance between the sexes – to force the male into the position of the woman.[22] In so doing the wounding of the man, whether physical or psychological, makes the male figure accessible to the female imagination.

The first encounter of Harrison Ford as Deckard with Rachel, the replicant, in *Bladerunner* (Ridley Scott, US, 1982) possibly offers the frisson of such rapprochement. Ford's character starts out as a futuristic version of the Chandleresque private eye – the Romantic Hero for men, now a postmodern technocrat when computer technology, tinged with gothicism, threatens to take over reproduction. Ford as Deckard, a one-time operative in this society as a hunter of renegade replicants, is a moral loner who, disillusioned with the system, has tried to drop out. Ford's world weariness and anxiety creates a chink in the armour of male competence, self-sufficiency and machismo. Rachel's sudden appearance exposes, in his hasty rejection of her help, the underlying vulnerability of the Marlowesque Private Eye. However, here it is in her very function as the symbol, 'Woman', that Rachel disturbs. She is doubly a construct: first as a replicant and secondly as the ultimate fetish with the high fur collar that surrounds her perfectly made up and soft focus face, with its large staring eyes and crimson lips. But just like the robot that wants to be human, the fetish gestures at the pathos of the 'real' woman it displaces. Rachel's pathos lies both in being a male construct and in the denial of motherhood – a denial enacted in Deckard's brutal exposure of her memories as mechanical implants. But the film's nostalgia loaded onto the photograph of a longed for natural mother unites male and female figures. Deckard's attempted retraction of his emotional brutalism indicates a rare moment of male recognition – almost an apology? – and as Rachel retreats from his apartment Deckard begins to shift from male to female Romantic Hero: a man wounded by patriarchy but redeemable through his capacity to identify with the female character. For the female viewer such a figure may offer the gratifying spectacle of masculinity crossing the gender divide, revealing a vulnerability beneath a tough exterior. Furthermore, the director's cut might suggest Deckard as Soul-Mate, with the implication that he, like Rachel, may be a replicant.

'OTHERING' MASCULINITY

The attempt by contemporary fictions to incorporate an active heroine or adjust patriarchal fantasies to notions of liberated womanhood, not only puts a strain on traditional gender types but raises interesting questions about 'otherness'. For if in melodrama the heroine represents the valorised virtues of a culture, the villain represents the return of a repressed 'other'. The aesthetic charge of melodrama is precisely the capacity of its polarised aesthetic to bring positive and negative others into play and confrontation. The development of the active 'liberated' heroine puts on the agenda the question of the male figure as female 'other', emerging into public discourse through the campaigns, rhetoric and mythmaking of the woman's movement. The separation, egoboundedness and silence of the hero may well signal positive qualities of the male 'other'. But the point at which separation signals disconnection, the 'other' becomes a threat. *Coma*'s commitment to the thriller over psychotherapy summons up such dangers in images of corrupt medical science and death which reveal not only the misogyny shrouded within paternalism but implicate the romantic hero too. Pursued into the hospital's anatomy lab, Dr Susan Wheeler may have to deal with a killer, but at least there is no mistaking who he is, and her intellect can function coolly to devise ingenious methods of escape. But as is made clear by the shock cut between the killer and her lover Mark (Michael Douglas) into whose arms she falls, it is the father figures and lovers who threaten to undermine her.

If Eastwood's persona seeks to purify masculinity, the Michael Douglas persona seems increasingly to open up a neurosis in the Romantic hero. *Basic Instinct* (Paul Verhoeven, US, 1992), like *Fatal Attraction* (Adrian Lyne, US, 1987), updates the femme fatale by arming her with an articulate claim to sexual activity and to pleasure on equal terms with men. The question for feminists is not whether such figures are fantasies – it is the premiss of this piece that they can be little else – but how we understand the male hero who engages in battle with this figure. What does each new activation of the femme fatale call into play in the male personification who opposes her? Like the Eastwood persona, Michael Douglas as Detective Moran is out of kilter with the structures of patriarchal power but, unlike Eastwood, he is also adrift on the sea of sexual identity. The femme fatal is 'coming for him', but declaring and demanding a recognition of similarity. Despite hints at an inner corruption, the good-looking arrogance of the Douglas persona in *Coma* is left intact by the film and he is given its last word – 'I know, Baby'. In *Basic Instinct*, however, this image is thrown into torsion, offering a spectacle of masculinity at war with itself; unable to read the female images his character is torn between, destined to make the wrong choice – she still has the ice-pick under the bed at the end.

FANTASY RESOLUTIONS: 'NO' TO THE ROMANTIC HERO

Finally, *Jagged Edge*, a film which relates both to *Coma* and to *Basic Instinct*, invites a return, given acknowledgement of the aesthetic and emotional dynamics of mainstream cinema's secondary elaborations, to the question of ideology. The film features Glenn Close as the reluctant attorney, Teddy, who seeks to redeem a past prosecution case (compromised through her submission to the false practices of District Attorney Krasny (Peter Coyote)) by defending the urbane Jack Forrester/Jeff Bridges on trial for the brutal murder of his rich wife. Like *Coma*, the film puts the would-be independent career woman in the role of virtue. But, whereas *Coma* leaves the audience in little doubt about Dr Wheeler's insight into the medical truth, in *Jagged Edge* Teddy can only access the truth – whether a husband murdered his wife – through a reading of the male. As in *Coma*, misogyny provides an array of *dramatis personae* and plot twists. Krasny, like Richard Widmark's Harrison, is early identified with patriarchal corruption, to contest whom Glenn Close's Teddy is drawn back into the lawcourt, although here she has the benevolent support of an Older Man, her erstwhile investigator, Sam. Also as in *Coma*, a link is made between Krasny's villain and the Romantic Hero, Jeff Bridges, but whereas this link is only implied in *Coma*, in the world of *Jagged Edge* the link is real and the heroine's desires impede her vision: both Krasny and Sam, villainous and benevolent patriarchs, are right as to the guilt of Jack Forrester, and the Romantic Hero turns out to be the worst villain of them all.

A literal reading might well take this as a slap in the face for the woman attorney, but this would be to ignore the emotional and aesthetic dynamics of melodrama. Glenn Close's embodiment of the heroine is surrounded by parasitic men, including not only Krasny and Forrester but also her guilt-inducing son and new mannish but separated husband. As a heroine of melodrama, her impaired vision is a product of the innocence necessary for ethical resistance to patriarchy. As a contestant in a gender struggle her myopia is a gesture of our desire for the Romantic Hero, quintessentially embodied in Jeff Bridges, so that although we must logically know he is the murderer we still hope to be mistaken. Thus, in her final confrontation with Jack Forrester, Teddy destroys not just the villain but the fantasy itself. Sam's presence in an ideologically driven reading may well seem to undercut her action, but, for the emotional and aesthetic dynamic of the melodrama, it is essential.[23] Sam acts as public witness to the heroine's recognition that Villain and Romantic Hero are one – recognition and naming being central to melodrama's epistemology. Without that witness, the fact of recognition would be meaningless, the destruction of the Romantic Hero an act of nihilism. But while Sam bears witness to the trauma undergone by the heroine, he, like Mark in *Coma*, is left outside the dramatic centre of confrontation and recognition. For a moment, as the realisation of Forrester's guilt and her own danger grips her, Glenn Close's Teddy rings for help. But during the call, the signs of panic dissipate as Glenn Close's features relax into an enigmatic, calm determination, and she declares to the now anxious Sam that she is fine.

Her final confrontation with Jeff Bridges destroys less a killer, than the grip on female fantasy of a male image. The mise-en-scène is diagrammatic in its construction of the moral conflict between constructions of masculinity and femininity. Glenn Close, showered, robed in white, is almost transfigured as she rests on the bed, awaiting the final moment, unafraid because morally secure. The calm she radiates is shattered by a shock cut echoed by crashing glass as the killer gains entry. His figure and face masked in black, his movements automated, he embodies a villainous masculinity. Teddy speaks of lost love, but shoots as the killer lunges for her. Sam arrives in time to perform the removal of the mask and bear witness to the final denouement as the face of Jeff Bridges is revealed, confirming what we knew but wanted to deny, the Romantic Hero as Villain. A shot-reverse shot exchanging looks between heroine and the dead but still appealing Romantic face of Jeff Bridges completes the articulation of the emotional and moral drama. Teddy acknowledges Sam's paternal recognition of her trauma – the nod and chuck under the chin – but walks past him and away from the camera, her exhaustion a sign of purgation. Like Mark in *Coma*, Sam services and makes patriarchal acknowledgement of a recognition produced out of the heroine's struggle with male archetypes.

CONCLUSION

I have arrived back at making ideological readings of these conflicts between male and female figures, but readings which attempt to work with the aesthetic dynamic and pleasures offered by a film, rather than demanding they be accountable to analytical paradigms of the social formation or the patriarchal psyche. I have used a model derived from the melodramatic aesthetic, because I think it enables us to understand the relation between ideology and popular culture as a mutual dynamic, rather than the series of ideological distortions suggested by a focus on representation. If representations are always constructions, they must also be ideological, so the naming of stereotypes as ideological misrepresentations is only a first step. Rather we need to think of stereotypes, images, representations and myths as the material of culture struggle. The confrontational structure of melodrama implies ethical struggle and a concept of justice, however limited – it always matters who wins. And the need to remain relevant, to retain sufficient credibility to ensure suspension of disbelief, to retain changing audiences, requires a constant readjustment both of stereotypes and images as well as concepts of justice. While ideological contests around legal and social definitions provide the means of renewing the dynamic of melodrama, the play of mis- and re-cognition at the heart of the melodramatic aesthetic enacts a struggle between the ideological positions implied in its *dramatis personae*, challenging the grip of gender, class or ethnic definitions. Patriarchy is not thereby routed – and may well be repositioned, reconfirmed in the fiction's ending. But if we take popular films as cultural products rather than as critics' texts, they represent a space of engagement in which audiences enter into a process of aesthetic contest, emotional struggle, and fantasy. From this perspective we would do well to pay attention to the recognitions and attractions held out to female audiences by male protagonists, the dynamics they sustain in relation to female protagonists, the possibilities of projection and introjection which they offer, and the evidence of ideological struggle which they provide.

NOTES

I would like to thank the many colleagues, friends and my two editors who read or listened patiently to various experimental presentations of this paper and offered useful resistance, constructive criticism and always encouraging support.

1 Ian Green, 'Malefunction', *Screen*, Vol. 25, Nos 4-5, July/October 1984.
2 Christine Gledhill, '*Klute* 1: A Contemporary Film Noir and Feminist Film Criticism' and '*Klute* 2: Feminism and *Klute*' in E. Ann Kaplan (ed.), *Women in Film Noir*, BFI, London, 1978.
3 Tessa Perkins, 'The "Politics" of Jane Fonda', in C. Gledhill (ed.), *Stardom: Industry of Desire*, Routledge, London, 1991.
4 Christine Gledhill, 'Pleasurable Negotiations' in D. Pribram (ed.), *Female Spectators*, Verso, London, 1988.
5 Peter Brooks, *The Melodramatic Imagination*, Yale University Press, New Haven, 1976, p32.
6 Thomas Elsaesser, 'Tales of Sound and Fury: Observations on the Family Melodrama' in C. Gledhill (ed.), *Home Is Where the Heart Is: Studies In Melodrama and the Woman's Film*, BFI, London, 1987, p46.
7 Brooks, *op.cit.*, p17.
8 See Elisabeth Cowie, 'Fantasia', *m/f*, No. 9, 1984; James Donald (ed.), *Fantasy and the Cinema*, BFI, London, 1989.
9 See Brooks, *op.cit.* and Elsaesser, *op.cit.*
10 For example Elisabeth Cowie's application of her highly illuminating account of the structuring processes of fantasy to *Now, Voyager* dismisses the film's diegetic fantasies as 'banal wishes' (p90) in order to disclose an underlying Oedipal trajectory which reveals the 'perversity' of Charlotte's desire to have a child without sex: 'When Charlotte foregoes the moon for the stars she fulfils every child's wish for the mother to forgo the father' (p93). To my mind it is the psychic substrate that is banal and the character's wish that is significant.
11 See Christine Gledhill, 'Pleasurable Negotiations', *op.cit.*, and Homi K. Bhabha, 'The Commitment to Theory', *New Formations*, No. 5, Summer 1988.
12 Janice Radway, *Reading the Romance*, University of North Carolina Press, Chapel Hill, 1984.
13 Rachel Kranz, '*Apocalypse Now* and *The Deer Hunter*: The Lies Aren't Over', *Jump Cut*, No. 23, October 1980.
14 Joseph Bristow, 'How Men Are: Speaking of Masculinity', *New Formations*, No. 6, Winter 1988.
15 See Brooks, *op.cit.*, p16, Richard Dyer, '*A Star is Born* and the Construction of Authenticity' in C. Gledhill (ed), *Stardom: Industry of Desire*, Routledge, London, 1991, pp132-5, and Christine Gledhill, 'Signs of Melodrama' in *Stardom*, pp217-9.
16 See, Laura Mulvey, 'Changes: Thoughts on Myth, Narrative and Historical Experience' in *Visual and Other Pleasures*, Macmillan, London, 1989.
17 Radway, *op.cit.*, p97 and Maria LaPlace, 'Producing and Consuming the Woman's Film: Discursive Struggle in *Now, Voyager*' in Gledhill *Home is Where the Heart Is*, *op. cit.*, pp159-161.

18 See Carol Christ, 'Victorian Masculinity and the Angel of the House' in M. Vicinus (ed.), *A Widening Sphere: Changing Roles of Victorian Women*, Methuen, London, 1980.

19 For a nineteenth-century example see the role of the doctor in mediating between the Countess and her authoritarian husband, the Minister of Police and in reuniting the separated sisters and Louise's mother in John Oxenford's adaptation of Adolphe D'Ennery and Eugene Cormons' melodrama, *The Two Orphans*, London, printed and performed by E. Rimmel, 1874.

20 Olive Higgins Prouty, *Pencil Shavings*, Riverside Press, Cambridge, Massachusetts, 1961.

21 Nancy Chodorow, 'Family Structure and the Feminine Personality' in M. Zimbalist Rosaldo and L. Lamphere (eds), *Woman, Culture and Society*, Stanford University Press, Stanford, California, 1974.

22 Rozsika Parker, 'Images of Men' in Sarah Kent and Jacqueline Morreau (eds), *Women's Images of Men*, Pandora, London, 1990.

23 See Brooks, *op.cit.*, pp31-4.

Loving Men: Frank Borzage, Charles Farrell and the Reconstruction of Masculinity in 1920s Hollywood Cinema

Pat Kirkham

'Everywhere ... in every town ... in every street we pass, unknowing, human souls made great by love and adversity'. *Street Angel*, Frank Borzage, US, 1927.

When I first saw the surviving silent films directed by Frank Borzage I was greatly struck by their representations of 'ordinary' men changed by love and adverse circumstances and I was particularly intrigued by those which coded men as maimed and/or maternal.[1] This article focuses on issues of masculinity raised in a group of films released between 1925 and 1929 when Borzage was one of the best known and best paid directors in Hollywood,[2] namely *Lazybones* (US, 1925), *Seventh Heaven* (US, 1927), *Street Angel* (US, 1927), *The River* (1929), *Lucky Star* (US, 1929). I was moved by the lyricism, expressivity and sensuality evident in them, particularly in the tender love scenes described by Jean Mitry as 'amongst the most beautiful ever filmed'.[3] I was also more than a little taken with the male lead in four of the five, Charles Farrell, a popular heart-throb who, at the height of his fame, commanded the then astronomical salary of $3,000 per week.[4] With Janet Gaynor he formed 'one of the most successful romantic couples in the history of cinema; adored by millions of fans'[5] and played an important part in

Borzage's success as a director of the melodrama of the 'ordinary' – of 'human souls made great by love and adversity'[6]. One glimpse of Farrell in torn vest and body covered in snow (Fig 1) was all it took to knock Marlon Brando from his number one position in those of my sexual fantasies devoted to men in T-shirts. To cut short a long story of erotic gazing, archival research, and cultural and textual analysis, I often realised that not only did Farrell's appearance and star persona remind me of my only and elder brother but so too did the film characters he played. This article therefore includes two parallel investigations – one 'academic', one much more subjective. I consider it important to investigate the ways in which personal histories affect responses to and readings of films and I offer my own responses and speculations thereon in the hope that they might add in some small way to our increasing understanding of how films affect us as individuals.[7]

Borzage's was a rags to riches story.[8] From a poor family of fourteen children, he worked in the mines of Utah before becoming an actor. In about 1913 he joined the New York Motion Picture Company, becoming one of the youngest leading men in the business, and by 1916 was established in Hollywood as both actor and director of westerns and

Fig 1 Charles Farrell as Allen John in *The River*, 1929.

melodramas. Like D. W. Griffith, William De Mille, Erich von Stroheim and others, however, he increasingly felt the need for cinema to shift from situations being the main or only determiners of character and wanted to exploit the special qualities of the medium in order to achieve more subtle characterisation and greater psychological realism. Borzage considered melodrama to be an important mode of cinematic address, arguing against its critics in much the same way that defenders of soap opera do today, that 'life is made up largely of melodrama ... yet when these true to life situations are transferred to the screen they are sometimes laughed down because they are 'melodrama'.[9] He saw nothing wrong with 'tugging at the heart strings'[10] in his dramas of ordinary people (just like the milkman or the neighbours, to cite his own examples [11]) and much of his success sprang from his powerful expression of the inner feelings and emotions of such people – men as well as women.

> It is my aim to develop characters on the screen that everyone in an audience will recognize. I want a man to say when he sees a character in one of my pictures, 'Well, that's awfully like Johnny Jones', or ... 'Gosh, I did the same thing myself, yesterday'. That is the kind of character that makes a hit on the screen. A character that everybody recognizes and loves,[12]

Borzage's leads – male and female – were distinctly proletarian and/or poor. At a time when the relatively young film industry had only just consolidated more middle class audiences by, amongst other things, turning to more 'refined' stories and characters, he argued for a shift to what one might characterise as a new type of proletarian cinema which portrayed the joys and sorrows in the daily lives of ordinary people. His particular ability was to present them in ways that emphasised the universality of their experiences, particularly those relating to romance, love and separation, thus making the material more palatable to the broad social mix that then constituted American cinema audiences, and particularly to the women. Although his characters were rooted in American populism, his sympathy with and admiration for poor people was conveyed within a framework which was far from radical in class or political terms. Hervé Dumont has recently emphasised the influence on Borzage's movie making not only of his religious beliefs but also his freemasonry;[13] suffice it to emphasise here that the films continually suggest that love, openness to emotions and the transcendence of adversity, rather than collective action or culture, is what ennobles and 'makes great' ordinary people.

Much of the impact of the films comes from the conjunction of melodrama and 'realism' – different and sometimes divergent cinematic modes which Borzage and Farrell each deftly negotiated. The central concerns of the 'realistic' characters, male and female, were personal ones; wider issues such as prostitution, poverty or the horrors of war mainly functioned as dramatic scenarios within which to explore personal anguish and resolutions. Feelings and values were exposed and dissected in the traditions of melodrama which dealt with broad sweeping issues such as good and evil. Yet wicked and predictable villains, the traditional motor of melodrama, are noticeably absent from Borzage's films in which a main site of moral contest was the very nature of masculinity itself. Farrell and other male leads were called upon to convey deep and tender feelings through characters devoid of cynicism. Borzage was nothing if not a positive thinker yet he represented shifts and changes not as the result of actions associated with over-determined 'macho' masculinities but, rather, through softer, more interiorised means. Love is what matters to the heroes of these films; the fully rounded man is one who can love. Love acts as a catalyst, enabling the characters to find the strength to deal with emotionally painful situations. They achieve greater realisations of self, others and 'true' values in life and it is this that transforms them into 'heroes'. Such portrayals were achieved through the unashamedly affective and narrative mode of melodrama and, crucially, also through acting styles that by contemporary standards were extremely modern in their 'naturalism'. This, the music, the lyrical and expressive cinematography, special effects, atmospheric set design and sensitive location shooting make the films beautifully poetic multi-layered experiences – ones wherein the feelings of a man in love with a woman (and vice versa) are given the attention such emotions deserve without seeming soppy or self indulgent.

Given Borzage's central concern with 'ordinary' people and 'natural' characters, it is not altogether surprising that he cast a relative unknown 'of a disarming, almost naive, candour, who won the part without even trying'[14] for the male lead in Seventh Heaven (which won Borzage the first ever Academy Award as best director). During my research I was continually struck by the similarities between Borzage and Farrell to whom he gave the much coveted part of Chico, the somewhat cocksure and cynical but caring and protective young man who finds it difficult to express love yet transcends being blinded in war by learning 'female' ways of being and subsuming himself in a selfless uncynical love. Besides both being tall, curly haired, athletic, handsome and deciding to be an actor at an early age, Borzage and Farrell appear to have been similar in character. Borzage, described in 1914 as 'a thoroughly whole-souled clean young chap',[15] must have been reminded of his younger self when meeting Farrell, 'one of the finest most likeable chaps', who was invariably described as pleasant and unspoiled.[16] Farrell radiated the 'naturalness' Borzage had brought to his own acting and seems to have epitomised the same essential good within ordinary men that he was so keen to portray as a director.

It is sometimes claimed that his height (6 feet 2 inches) was what won Farrell the role opposite Gaynor (5 feet) who looked even more fragile against Farrell's frame.[17] But Hollywood was full of tall actors and Borzage would never have cast for height alone. The part demanded sensitivity to the affective and dramatic elements of melodrama and an ability to convey both the 'masculine' and 'feminine' within men and within heterosexual attraction. Farrell, who had the capacity to play *against* as well as *to* height and other markers of dominance, authority and moral superiority, proved a highly expressive vehicle for Borzage's explorations of shifting and sometimes contradictory masculinities.[18] The screen magnetism of the photogenic Farrell drew on expressive performance skills, which used to advantage his beautiful face, eyes and body, as well as more naturalistic ones. He was able to portray highly charged emotions which suggested passion and desire as well as more tender, pure and 'spiritual' feelings and convey strength and protectiveness at the same time as vulnerability. Farrell was at his best when in partnership with Gaynor (and when directed by Borzage) and his men were inextricably informed and enabled by Gaynor's women. Her many talents are beyond the scope of this essay but she and Farrell established a remarkable chemistry on screen, producing a coupling as 'believable' as it was variously feisty, romantic, caring, companionate, erotic and passionately sublime. Who could ask for more?

Farrell, 'a solid draw among the susceptible young ladies who tear down the theaters where his pictures are shown', was hugely popular with female fans.[19] I registered something of this attraction when first watching the films. Indeed, my notes taken at the time include 'fabulous ... beautiful body' and 'scene full of eroticism – what heterosexual woman wouldn't want to go to bed with this man?'. Some of the pleasures of the films lie in the female gaze and the objectification of the male body. In a memorable scene from *Seventh Heaven*, which 'expresses Borzage's capacity to feel comfortable with female desire', Diane/Gaynor secretly watches Chico/Farrell undress shortly after they have met.[20] The viewer looks, with her, at the (unsuspecting and largely unknown) male object of the gaze. *The River* also offers illicity viewing, especially when the young river boy, Allen John/Farrell, is unconscious or sleeping. Of all the Borzage silent films this one most clearly foregrounds the direct objectification of female desire; indeed, the whole film hinges on it, from our first glimpse of Allen John's body floating naked in the water.

On first viewing the films I also noted how much the 'extremely even tempered'; 'wonderfully protective and caring' and 'at times, almost infuriatingly nice and optimistic' characters of Chico, Gino and Tim (in *Seventh Heaven, Street Angel* and *Lucky Star* respectively) remind me of my brother, especially in their amiability, proletarian straightforwardness and mixture of strengths and gentleness as well as in their ability to love and think the best of people. I was conscious also of other connections between Farrell and my handsome tall (6 feet 4 inches) brother – who is nine years older than me, inherited my father's height and athleticism as well as name and, since my father's death has indeed become something of a father figure for me. I was always aware of the impact of his looks on women (Fig 2); at school older girls asked if I thought he looked more like Tony Curtis or Dirk Bogarde and my sister-in-law claims she fell for him because he looked like Rock Hudson whose particular style of softened masculine strength recalls Farrell's.[21] Even so, I was not quite prepared for the fact that looks, height, characterisation and persona could work to produce such a strong personal 'recognition' or that Borzage's promise of characters that 'everybody recognizes and loves' would be experienced so literally.

When researching Farrell's career I found myself ruminating on the similarities between his character and his star image, which seem to have been remarkably close.[22] The trade press, magazines, and the studio publicity machine helped circulate and create particular constructions of Farrell, most notably as ideal romantic mate and sporting icon. His facility to make women go weak at the knees was soon recognized and immediately after *Seventh Heaven* his heart-throb qualities were exploited in *The Red Dancer of Moscow* (Raoul Walsh,

US, 1928), in which he starred opposite Dolores Del Rio and looked fetchingly exotic, and *Fazil* (Howard Hawkes, US, 1928), a belated attempt to cash in on the Valentino phenomenon in which he played an Arab chieftain.[23] At the same time as the circulation of these films and related publicity, which enhanced Farrell's standing as romantic hero and object of desire, there was constant press speculation about an off-screen romance between Farrell and Gaynor, firmly established as Hollywood's favourite lovers after *Seventh Heaven*. They epitomised the new companionate coupling which was establishing itself as the basis of marriage in early twentieth-century America. At a time when women in the USA had recently won the vote and increasing numbers were working outside the home at a variety of jobs, more traditional forms of courtship and marriage gave way to a new emphasis on sexual fulfilment and 'partnership and communication in the domestic sphere', as opposed to separate spheres for husband and wife.[24] Given the importance of these cultural changes and the fact that movie theatres themselves became favoured places for courting (a more modern concept than 'keeping company'[25]) it is likely that 'knowledge' of an off-screen romance informed movie readings of Farrell as ideal partner.

Although none of the films I discuss construct the male leads' masculinities through sport, sporting images were crucial in the

Fig 2 Family Snapshot. Myself and my mother watching my brother (centre back), family and friends, 1956.

construction of Farrell's persona and, like the supposed romance, are likely to have inflected cinematic readings of him. Several sporting publicity photographs show his body to such advantage that they must have heightened contemporary appreciation of his physical attractiveness, if not sexuality. But images of Farrell as sportsman were more than just an excuse to show him in suntan and T-shirts; they suggest a considerable athletic competence. In 'real life' Farrell was one of the best sportsmen in Hollywood, with the exception of sportsmen-turned-actors, such as Johnny Weissmuller. He was well known as a tennis player, yachtsman and horse-rider and shared a room with Weissmuller at the 1932 Olympics.[26] Magazine articles constantly referred to his sporting activities and fans knew that he lived at the Hollywood Athletic Club when not at his beach house in Malibu. A photograph of Farrell with American Davis Cup tennis champions makes them look wimpish by comparison and the accompanying publicity blurb notes that Farrell 'wields a mean racquet'. He also played with Fred Perry and other international tennis players and in 1934 was a co-founder of the famous Palm Springs Racquet Club.[27] In short, he brought something of the kudos of the sports star to the screen. He had starred in a couple of rugged action movies (*Old Ironsides*, (James Cruze, US, 1926), aka. GB *Sons of the Sea*, and *The Rough Riders*, (Victor Fleming, US, 1927), aka. GB *The Trumpet Calls*) before Borzage cast him in *Seventh Heaven* and, given the attention paid to his sporty and sport*ing* persona immediately after the release of that smash hit, readings of subsequent films must have been inflected by knowledge of it.[28]

The sports images are suggestive of an ideal partner or team mate who plays the game according to the rules and plays it well. They also signal health, strength, energy, action, virility, wholesomeness, love of the outdoors and bodily coordination. For me such images relate strongly to my brother and father and I have no doubt that they play an important part in my appreciation of Farrell. I have long been aware of the importance of sport for me as a marker of appropriate and attractive masculinity but it is one I find difficult to unravel beyond a certain point.[29] At one level it seems straightforward. My early life and culture were dominated by football (even more than the cinema). The two men I most loved and admired during my formative years were talented sportsmen. My brother played professional football when I was an impressionable pre-teen/teenager and some of his footballer friends teased me so often about waiting for me to grow up so that they could marry me that part of me believed it. In 1956, the same year as my brother left home to play professionally, I discovered rock and roll, 'boys' and that football was about more than off-side rules, 5-3-2 formations, baggy shorts, Jackie Milburn or even winning 'the cup'. I became a fan of certain good-looking young footballers in much the same way as I became a fan of certain young male film stars and performers. The first pin-up picture ever to grace my bedroom wall was a signed photograph of the delectable Jimmy Robson of Burnley FC ('To Pat with love from Jimmy' it read), and he was soon joined by Elvis Presley and Gene Vincent. For me, sports, masculinity, male pin-ups and Oedipal desire for the father, it would seem, were all mixed up together.

However, a rigidly gender differentiated Oedipal trajectory is not the only or most appropriate analysis of representations of masculinity in these films or my responses to them. Even in psychoanalytic terms, a pre-Oedipal perspective, with its emphasis on the maternal, proves as rewarding. Tom Gunning's analysis of the late silent Borzage romances resists 'the more common Freudian melodrama of renunciation of the mother and identification with the father' and, acknowledging E. Ann Kaplan's examination of women's melodramas from a pre-Oedipal point of view, suggests that the films 'evoke a return to a sheltering maternal world'.[30] But, it seems to me, the evocation of maternal reunion, bonding and protection is problematised when the maternal is also male – something to which I will return. One of the delights and fascinations of these Borzage films is their representations of the 'masculine' and the 'feminine' as 'bisexual'; as *shifting* and *adjustable* categories, experiences and identities within a continuum rather than as binary oppositions. I wish now to consider the interplay between 'masculine' and 'feminine', softness and strength, competence and lack, particularly in the representations of men as maternal and maimed and as played out in the films through Farrell's body and dress, and also to consider further evocations of my brother triggered by Borzage's representations of masculinity.

The River is remarkable for the degree to which it shows both the 'feminine' and the 'masculine' as erotic components of masculinity; the male object of (female) desire is shown in alluring feminised poses as well as in 'beefcake' ones. The former include Allen John/Farrell lying passively in bed naked to the waist and carried, Christ-like, by a 'giant mute' who is as devoted to him as Farrell is to Gaynor in other films and whose solid body emphasises the vulnerability of Farrell's. The feminisation of the younger man is reinforced by its reference to a pose previously reserved for Farrell carrying Gaynor. It is almost as if Brozage wants the viewer at that moment to read Farrell as Gaynor; to read a male body as a female one and to fuse and confuse conceptions and readings of what it is to be male.

In the more general manner of Borzage gender reversals, *The River* constantly contrasts the innocent, virginal and feminised man with the knowing and known woman who sets out to seduce him. But he is sometimes coded as a frenetically competent male provider, chopping wood as hysterically as Tim/Farrell makes and mends things in *Lucky Star* (see below). The very excess of such images suggests sublimation of desire and compensation for inadequacy – in *The River* because he is not fully *sexually* competent, in the latter because he is not fully *physically* competent. It destabilises the very competency depicted. In other words, Borzage depicts an excess of the conventional trappings of male competency as a *problem* for masculinity. Invoking the melodramatic device of flagging the obvious, the ingenue in *The River* chops down enormous fir trees in such a way as to suggest not only excess sexual energy but also self-destruction; what he chops down is the phallus. Like Eastwood in *Unforgiven*, Borzage represents a commonly acceptable masculinity and takes it to excess in order to suggest that there is something disturbing and neurotic about it, that it needs tempering by other ways of being.

Borzage played out the dialectics of softness and strength, the 'masculine' and the 'feminine', competence and incompetence, through the depiction of men as maternal (Farrell in *Lucky Star* and Charles 'Buck' Jones in the romantic drama *Lazybones*) and/or maimed (most notably Farrell in both *Seventh Heaven* and *Lucky Star*). The deliberate and inspired casting of the well known Western star, 'Buck' Jones, whose fans were used to him 'shootin' up the town' and to 'his usual wild and woolly Western he-man stuff',[31] gave added impact to what was such an unusual male characterisation that Borzage frequently invoked the comic mode in telling the story of the lovable laid back Lazybone who adopts a baby to save a woman from disgrace and suicide. It was not the first time a man adopted a baby in a Borzage film; the male hero had done so in *Billy Jim* (US, 1922), but he then formed a heterosexual couple and hence the child became part of a conventional family. It could be argued that the presence of Lazybones's mother constitutes a family but it was he who did the mothering of the child and her adoption cost him his chance of heterosexual coupling with his sweetheart, marked in the mise-en-scène by a shot where they stand over the baby as a couple. Male mothering is most obvious in *Lazybones* wherein its object is a baby girl but it is suggested in *Lucky Star* wherein the 'child' is one of Borzage's many young female characters who has just 'left girlhood behind … and crossed the verge of womanhood', a theme also explored in *Until They Get Me* (1917) and *Seventh Heaven*.[32] In both *Lazybones* and *Lucky Star* the 'good' and competent male mother is contrasted to a 'bad' female one and each invokes the *Tootsie/Mrs Doubtfire* factor, i.e. a man being a better 'woman' than a woman. Lazybones/Steve is shown to be immensely caring as he puts milk from a cow into a bottle and tenderly feeds the baby. When she is aged about five he is portrayed as very protective of her feelings, even to the extent of putting himself in a bad light; he comforts her when she is ostracised because of her illegitimacy, cuddles her closely and cries when and because she does. In a later scene in which he helps her cope with grief, however, his 'teacherly' role is parental rather than specifically maternal, although in the narrative sequence of the film it can be read as part of the ongoing process of mothering.

The shift away from a heavily maternal parent is necessary because the narrative shifts, after a sequence in which 'Uncle Steve'/Lazybones goes to war (presented in humorous mode with Steve, significantly, one of the few Borzage veterans *not* to be maimed in battle), to the incestuous desire of a male 'mother' for his female 'daughter'. The focus becomes the pain of the heterosexual older male unable to declare his love for his adopted daughter and then learning she loves someone her own age. The taboos of generation and 'familial' relations are portrayed poignantly and sympathetically in 'one of the most explicit presentations of the incest theme that Borzage was constantly drawn towards'.[33] This theme is less explicit but nonetheless powerful in *Lucky Star*, particularly at the moment of Tim/Farrell's desire: he has just washed Mary/Gaynor's hair and begun to undo her dress to wash her body when he learns her age. The already complex joys and fears of maternal union are rendered even more complex by the fact of the 'mother' being male and further problematised by the inclusion of equally complex incest fantasies involving a maternal man. Together they blur the boundaries of mother/father, male/female and offer male, female and hybrid figures with which to bond both emotionally and sexually. Each theme on its own would be powerful; together they might be overwhelming were it not for Borzage's exercise of restraint and his lightness of touch, eschewing the atmospherics of set and cinematography associated with the highly affective but less 'taboo' romances of *Street Angel* and *Seventh Heaven*.

Male mothering is potentially more disruptive in *Lucky Star* than it is in *Lazybones* because Tim/Farrell is coded from the outset as extremely competent in relation to things masculine. After he is crippled by injuries sustained in World War One he undertakes a wide range of intimate motherly activities from washing Mary/Gaynor's hair and tying it up with ribbon to teaching her to cook and correctly lay the table. He makes a handkerchief and teaches her to blow her nose on it and, significantly, helps her get ready for her first 'big' dance – a special occasion traditionally reserved for mother and daughter. While the transformation involved in Mary's passage from dirty urchin to attractive young woman (he exclaims 'Baa-baa you're a blonde' after washing her hair) contains some reference to the woman-centred Cinderella story, the 'education' involved and his teacherly treating of her as a child suggest the more male-centred Pygmalion narrative. Borzage thus fuses not only implications of gender and role but also popular gendered narratives dealing with rites of passage.

Tim is extremely competent as a 'mother', just as he is competent as a man early in the film when we see him shin up a telegraph pole, fight in what seems to be a just cause and assert his moral and physical authority over Mary by spanking her when he learns that she is a cheat. (The spanking references parental and adult authority in general rather than specifying the maternal and is marked by an erotic frisson which signals the heterosexual desire and coupling to come.) Significantly, it is not until he is crippled and confined to a wheelchair that he is represented as maternal. At first consideration this would seem to be little more than the castrated man reduced to being a woman. However, this is offset and disrupted by the sheer strength of the Farrell male persona, the emotional power of the war scenes, the impact and standing of Tim's character by that stage in the narrative, including his status as a war veteran, and the hysterical portrayal of him as competent in relation to making and mending things. The latter assures the viewer that his masculinity is not lost forever while, at the same time, suggesting that a preferred version is to be found in his learning that things emotional as well as physical can be mended and/or adapted. By the time the coupling is completed, as per convention at the end of the film, the woman does not need the former intensive mothering and, conveniently, once he is fully a man again he does not have to mother. The difference is that the viewer knows he has the capacity to behave like one when necessary and that they both have learned – each from the other – the companionate way of the new coupling.

Borzage uses the interplay between the 'masculine' and the 'feminine' in Farrell's body, body language and film costumes to add non-verbal dimensions to the caring and concerned romantic hero which work to suggest the vulnerability of masculinity and openness to emotions. The 'feminine' can, of course, serve as much to highlight and confirm the 'masculine' as to disrupt or render unstable gender representations but in these films the dialectic between elements of the 'feminine' and 'masculine' in the depiction of Farrell's body and dress, works to emphasise the 'female'. His body is frequently lit and photographed to suggest and accentuate a softness held in tension with its bulk and strength and the vulnerability of masculinity and male competence and the tempering of strength with softness are reinforced by the dress of the Farrell characters. His hard-wearing utilitarian clothes are softened in style, cut and fabric. Invariably informal, they often consist of casual trousers and work vests or shirts open at the neck, suggesting not only a lack of social smartness but also a psychological openness. When Chico in *Seventh Heaven* returns from the Front blinded, his heroism is marked not by military honours or glory but rather by his faithfulness, love and determination to be reunited with his Diane and by learning to truly 'see'. His uniform is crumpled and grubby; his shirt and great coat are both open at the neck, accentuating his openness to change wherein lies his redemption.

Borzage drew on the iconographies of 'manly' occupational dress which offer images of professional competence and mark the hero as the capable provider required for successful screen coupling.[34] In *Lucky Star* it is no coincidence that when Tim wears a cardigan – a garment never accepted in the world of work and so often a marker of the feminine, a man past his 'prime' or the domestic sphere – it is after he is maimed and unable to legitimately wear his former occupational dress. By contrast in the more overtly sexual *The River*, where Farrell plays someone without craft, social or sexual competence, the character of Allen John appears without any clothes at all. The occupational dress worn by Tim at the beginning of *Lucky Star* is so emphatically 'authentic' as to be almost excessive and, in the melodramatic mode, works precisely because it is so obvious. His ruggedly 'outdoor' telegraph rigger's outfit, complete with full kit, including an axe, signifies a well-equipped craft competence and masculinity, even before we see him shinning up a long telegraph pole. Once that and his moral authority is established, he can then be maimed; *de-masculinised* in order to be *feminised* and thereby *re-masculinised*.

If the competent man wears occupational uniform, then the wearing of military uniform, associated as it is with body armour, can be represented as the ultimate in male competence.[35] But Borzage chose not to do this; indeed, it is precisely when his proletarian heroes wear military uniform that they are maimed. When their armour is penetrated they are de-masculinised and simultaneously feminised when their body armour is penetrated. Although the theme of overcoming maiming was central to the final section of *Humoresque* (US, 1919/1920), I consider Borzage's earlier *Until They Get Me* (US, 1917) a clearer exposition of the dangers to men of an overt, rigid masculinity. In the latter, Kirby/Jack Curtis is symbolically castrated when Margy/Pauline Starke takes away his pistols. Like the wise woman she is, she restores them only when he has proved that he is a human being as well as a policeman. Again, it is his excessive adherence to an over-rigid definition of law and order, to 'masculine' values, that leads to his downfall as a man and prevents him from getting the woman he desires, or at least until he reconstitutes his approach to life. The breakdown of an over-determined masculinity or male armour, Borzage repeatedly suggests, is necessary for masculine redemption. The ideal man is one who is partly de-masculinised in order to be partly feminised; who is *deconstructed* to be *reconstructed*. Expressed thus it is not difficult to see the broad appeal of these films to women. The de- and re-constructed man offered a fantasy hero capable of being reshaped according to women's wishes. Wounding makes men more accessible to women's imagination.[36] Rozsika Parker has suggested that wounded men allow heroines to experience their unacceptable feelings of desire as maternal pity but there is little pathos in Borzage's heroines in the films discussed here, partly because the maiming tends to occur relatively late in the narrative and to be overcome.[37] Nor does the invaliding of the male necessarily transform the heroine into a mother figure as Parker suggests.[38] Parker also argues that in order for men to appear desirable they have to resemble the objects of beauty and desire in our society, namely women.[39] But Borzage's romantic heroes are definitely desirable *before* they are wounded and some are not wounded at all yet they arouse desire in the heroine and this viewer. Nevertheless, the fact that Mary/Gaynor in *Lucky Star* does not acknowledge her attraction to Tim/Farrell until *after* he is maimed suggests that, in certain cases, the nearer the hero gets to being a 'heroine' the easier it is not only for fictional women to empathise with them but also to desire them. At the very least, it would seem that wounding *facilitates* the expression of female desire.

Just as my earlier set of readings of the Farrell characters suggested a desire for the symbolic father, so also my arguments about the feminisation of the male suggest that part of my response might be a desire to return to the mother. I was certainly aware, when working through the points made earlier about my brother, of a need to differentiate him from my father who was inevitably a more patriarchal figure than my brother whose sweet easiness of being (as well as teasing and protectiveness) suffuse my memories of childhood. That my generalised memories and associations of my early years even begin to approximate to the plenitude I imagine to be that of the pre-Oedipal bonding with the mother, owes a great deal, I am sure, to my actual mother, who was plenitudinous in myriad ways, but I have long felt my brother plays some part in it. His *brothering* included *mothering* from the very beginning; when I was only a few weeks old he would take me from my cot and comfort me if I cried, even take me into his bed to sleep with him. Like Lazybones, his masculinity (or at least that of his late boyhood and early adolescence) did not preclude highly gendered 'feminine' work.

The degree to which my brother, through build, athleticism and overtly heterosexual persona, was/is relatively easily able to live out a masculinity that does not seem to be threatened by his being 'soft-hearted' and showing emotions, returns me to the characters played by Farrell and Jones and to the films under discussion. When views of coupling and marriage and expectations of men, especially younger men, were changing, one strategy for stabilising gender relations was to facilitate adjustment to those changes. At one level, Farrell and Jones were as safe vehicles as any to convey the message that men could be better partners and people by being more like women. Against this conservative interpretation of the films, as smoothing the way for slight changes in the culture of heterosexual coupling without seriously challenging gender relations or acceptable notions of appropriate sexuality for men and women, must be set the space that Borzage opened up for more radical explorations of sexuality and masculinity. Much more than would have been possible with less ambiguously heterosexual stars, Farrell and Jones assisted Borzage to explore more deeply than most other Hollywood directors in the late 1920s the nature of contemporary masculinity and sexuality.

The more I have tried to tease out my own reactions to the films and the characters, the more I realise how preliminary are our investigations of audience responses at the individual level. Given the intentions of Borzage, it is not surprising that the characters should remind me of someone I know or, in films which offer shifting positions on the 'masculine' and 'feminine', that, in psychoanalytical terms, my responses would seem to include the desire to return to the mother as well as desire for the father. Nor, given my interest in non-binary gender constructions and personal relationships which fuse the loving, the companionate/comradely, the sexual and the sublime, is it surprising that films which deal with the deconstruction and reconstruction of the masculinities of 'ordinary' men should have resonances for me. That they do and that they are such beautifully made and multi-layered films makes them a rare treat.

NOTES

1 I first saw them at the *Giornate del Cinema Muto* in Pordenone, Italy, 1992, and am grateful to the organisers of that very special festival as I am to the Research Committee, School of Arts, De Montfort University, for funding overseas travel in connection with this project. I am particularly grateful to Jim Cook who viewed and discussed the films with me in Italy and made valuable comments on this article. My thanks also to Christine Geraghty and Christine Gledhill for viewing and discussing Borzage movies with me and, last but by no means least to Janet Thumim and Beverley Skeggs for their valuable comments and encouragement.

2 Hervé Dumont, 'Jacob's Ladder, or Love and Adversity', *Griffithiana*, Number 46, December 1992, p89. Between 1920 and 1926 he made 25 films, with *Seventh Heaven*, his only film of 1927, proving one of the most successful films of the silent era (its first year's box office earnings were bettered only by *The Jazz Singer*). He won an *Academy Award* as Best Director in 1929 and again in 1931 (for *Best Girl*). A poll of 50 film makers in 1928 placed Borzage as the leading American film director and in the same year 200 critics voted him third most popular American director, after Hubert Brenon and King Vidor and before Raoul Walsh, Josef von

Sternberg, Victor Fleming, Erust Lubitsch and Charles Chaplin. He went on to direct 45 sound features but, although in 1962, the year of his death, he received from the Directors' Guild of America the D W Griffith award for his outstanding contribution to film directing, his reputation has suffered badly in the post-World War Two years. His work has only recently begun to attract something of the credit it deserves, despite some critical attention in the early 1970s. Suffice it to emphasize here that, at the time of the films discussed, he was one of the leading film directors of the day, equal second (with Raoul Walsh) only to John Ford in terms of salary. In 1926 Walsh and Borzage earned $1,500 per week in comparison to Ford's $1,750. I have no figures for the salary of Farrell at that date, when he was a relative newcomer to Hollywood, but by 1933 he could command $3,000 per week (see note 4). For further details on Borzage see Henry Agel and Michael Henry, 'Frank Borzage', *Anthologie du Cinéma*, Paris, 1973, pp. 243-291; John Belton, *The Hollywood Professionals. Howard Hawks, Frank Borzage, Edgar G Ulmer*, The Tantivy Press, London, 1974; Frederick Lamster, *Soul Made Great Through Love and Adversity. The Film Work of Frank Borzage*, The Scarecrow Press, London, 1981, and Hervé Dumont, *Frank Borzage – Sarastre à Hollywood*, Hazam, Paris, 1993. The latter is a major comprehensive study and I am grateful to Hervé for interesting discussions at Pordenore and subsequent correspondence. NB. There are no prints of the films I discuss available in Britain, although the NFT held a short Borzage season in the winter of 1993/94 (after the French Cinémathèque had organised a complete Borzage retrospective of about 70 films) and has held others in earlier years.

3 Jean Mitry, *Histoire du Cinéma*, Vol 3, Paris, 1973, p439, cited in Dumont, 'Jacob's Ladder', *op. cit.*, p95.

4 Kirtley Baskette, 'The New Charles Farrell', *Photoplay*, December 1933, p33.

5 Dumont, 'Jacob's Ladder', *op. cit.*, p89.

6 Opening titles, *Street Angel* (US, 1927), *op. cit.*

7 NB. I wish to emphasise the importance of specificity (historical and psychic) in the study of affectivity and film.

8 Born and raised in Salt Lake City, of Italian and Austrian origins on his father's side and Swiss and German on his mother's, Borzage first appeared on stage in about 1906 aged 13. See Davide Turconi, 'The Silent Films of Frank Borzage', *Griffithiana*. Number 46, December 1992, pp6-8 and Dumont's article and book (see note 2) for further details.

9 Peter Milne, 'Some Words from Frank Borzage', *Griffithiana*, No 46, December 1992, p132 (originally published in 1922). NB. Borzage added 'If this is true then all life is a joke and while some humorists hold to this idea, I am not one of those who believe it so'.

10 DeWitt Bodeen, 'Frances Marion Wrote the Scripts of Some of the Milestone Movies', *Films in Review*, February 1969, p83 cited in Turconi, *op. cit.*, p14. Marion, who wrote the script for *Humoresque* (1919/20) based on the popular short story by Fanny Hurst, urged that Borzage be appointed director because 'He had that unique and enviable combination in a director: good taste and the ability to play on the heartstrings'.

11 Milne, *op. cit.*, p132.

12 *Ibid*, p131. How far viewers identified with or recognised characters in Borzage films of the 1920s is difficult to estimate at this distance in time but the box office success of the films suggests that they enjoyed substantial male as well as female audiences.

13 Dumont, 'Jacob's Ladder', *op. cit.*, p98 and *Frank Borzage, passim*.

14 *Ibid*. p89.

15 Turconi, *op. cit.*, p5, note 2.

16 Grace Simpson, 'Charles the Unspoiled', *Picturegoer*, Volume 16, Number 96, December 1928, p60.

17 Dumont, 'Jacob's Ladder', p89.

18 Virginia Wright Wexman, *Creating The Couple. Love, Marriage and Hollywood Performance*, Princeton University Press, Princeton, NJ., 1993, pp27-28.

19 Leonard Hall, 'Charlie Has To Fight', *Photoplay*, Volume 40, Number 2, July 1933, p30.

20 Tom Gunning, 'Essays in Mad Love', *Sight and Sound*, January, 1993, p17. This is one of the best short articles on Borzage's silent films.

21 See Richard Dyer, 'Rock – The Last Guy You'd Have Figured?', in Pat Kirkham and Janet Thumim (eds), *You Tarzan: Masculinity, Movies and Men*, Lawrence & Wishart, London, 1993, pp27-34.

22 Richard Dyer in *Stars*, British Film Institute, London, 1979, pp145-149 notes that this is rarely the case. See Baskette, *op. cit.*; Hall, *op. cit.*; Simpson, *op. cit.*, Reginald Taviner, 'Charlie goes on His Own', *Photoplay*, Volume 43, Number 3, February 1933, pp45 & 90 and DeWitt Bodeen, *Charles Farrell, Films in Review*, October 1976, pp449-463, for evidence in support of my point.

23 Simpson, *op. cit.*, p62 and Bodeen, *op. cit.*, pp454-455.

24 Wexman, *op. cit.*, pp12-13.

25 *Ibid*.

26 Bodeen, *op. cit.*, p460.

27 *Ibid*., p462 and *Classic Film Collector*, Number 48, Autumn, 1975 (for a reprint of a piece on Farrell originally in *The News Tribune*).

28 Bodeen, *op. cit.*, pp452 and 463-464 (filmography).

29 The complications in understanding the significance of sport and masculinity for me (let alone speculating on what it might mean for women who are my contemporaries or those who watched Farrell's starring roles at the time the films were released) arise partly because I do not seem to use being a sportsman as a crucial marker

of masculinity in terms of sexual desire (which usually precedes my knowledge of sporting prowess – or otherwise). There are other seemingly significant strong similarities between the men with whom I have had important relationships, including being intellectual and/or creative, having few possessions, even less money and radical politics. However, in only two significant relationships (one when I was aged seventeen, the other almost thirty years later) has the man involved not been, at some stage in his life, good (i.e. more than competent) at sport. A problem for me in thinking through what I find attractive in sporting images is that in both these relationships that lack did not seem to matter – although the initial intensities simply may have temporarily compensated for the lack of whatever it is that 'the good sportsman' stands for for me. Although I have tried not to shy away from the connection between sport, parent/male sibling figures and sexuality, my predominant (conscious) response to the knowledge that a man in my life – and it is by no means restricted to lovers – is or has been a talented sportsman is one of reassurance. That also seems to relate to integrity, fairness and reliability – which immediately take me back to my brother and father. There is not time or space to pursue this discussion here but I would be fascinated to know of other women's reactions to film stars, film characters and 'real men' particularly, but not exclusively, as sportsmen.

30 Gunning, *op. cit.*, p18.
31 Tusconi, *op. cit.*, p30.
32 Inter-title, *Until They Get Me* (Frank Borzage, US, 1917).
33 Gunning, *op. cit.*, p19.
34 Wexman, *op. cit.*, p84.
35 See Klaus Theweleit (trans. Stephen Conway), *Male Fantasies*, Volumes 1 and 2, University of Minnesota Press, Minneapolis, 1987 and 1989 respectively, especially Volume 1, *Women, Floods, Bodies, History*, and Wexman, *op. cit.*, pp105-113.
36 Rozsika Parker, 'Images of Men', in Sarah Kent and Jacqueline Morreau (eds), *Women's Images of Men*, Writers and Readers Publishing, London, 1985, pp44-54, reprinted from *Spare Rib*, Number 99, October 1980.
37 *Ibid.*, p46.
38 *Ibid.*, p48.
39 *Ibid.*, p46.

Pedro Almodóvar's *Tie Me Up! Tie Me Down!*: The Mechanics of Masculinity

Rikki Morgan

'Learning mechanics is easier than learning male psychology. You can figure out a bike, but you can never figure out a man' – Pepa (Carmen Maura) in *Women on the Verge of a Nervous Breakdown*, (Almodóvar, Spain, 1987)

Tie Me Up! Tie Me Down! is the most provocative of Spanish director Pedro Almodóvar's controversial films. As Mandy Merck observed, the film seems 'virtually calculated to divide the critics between dutiful outrage and equally dutiful defence.'[1] The bare bones of the plot speak for themselves: on his release from a psychiatric institution, Ricky (Antonio Banderas) seeks out Marina (Victoria Abril), an ex-prostitute, porn-movie actress and recently reformed heroin addict, now starring in a horror B-movie, *Midnight Phantom*, directed by the wheelchair-bound Máximo Espejo (Francisco Rabal). When she ignores his overtures, Ricky takes her prisoner and ties her up in her apartment so that she can get to know him, fall in love, marry and have his children. There follows a curious mixture of tenderness and violence, romanticism and imposition in the course of which Marina becomes duly enamoured. When her sister Lola (Loles León) discovers her tied to the bed, she orchestrates an escape. After explanations and a cooling off period, however, Marina returns, reconciles Ricky with her sister and brings him into the bosom of her own family. The final shot sees the three of them driving off together into the sunset, singing.

113

By virtue – or vice – of locating its narrative within the excesses of misogyny, *Tie Me Up! Tie Me Down!* draws particular attention to the mechanics of masculinity and, by focusing on a blurring of the boundaries between such problematic concepts as 'madness' and 'normality', it shows these mechanisms at work in the complex and absurdly contradictory behaviour of a 'normal' madman who adopts 'madly' exaggerated patterns of masculinity to pursue conventional social 'norms'. No wonder the critics had trouble with this one! It is precisely because the film operates at the extremities of both misogyny and romance (and because the ideological foundations of these superficially antithetical notions share common assumptions about gender roles) that the film is able to activate its critical thrust through a discourse of the absurd. This article examines the way in which *Tie Me Up! Tie Me Down!* throws into stark critical relief some of the bases, expectations and results of the operation of rigid gender roles which survive and flourish through their anchorage within an ideologically controlled patriarchal social order.

The very idea of a 'romance based on bondage'[2] and the apparently pernicious implications of the 'happy ending' clearly account for the charges of misogyny which greeted the film's release in the anglophone press.[3] Almodóvar himself indignantly contested these condemnations, protesting his pro-feminism – as Carol Sarler points out, he is 'clearly proud of his feminist credentials and he parades them, at times a mite self-consciously'.[4] More to the point, however, Almodóvar has gained a reputation as a director whose films are characterised by their camp disdain for rigid gender binaries and their subversion of traditional institutions. Literalist readings of the film sit rather incongruously with this profile and with his aesthetic approach which is so notoriously characterised by an outrageously anarchic brand of black humour. The centrality of this black humour in his work reflects its prominence in Spanish popular culture and draws on and perpetuates the critical tradition of satire which abounds at many levels of cultural production in Spain from the roguish picaresque novels and satirical poetry of the seventeeth century 'Golden Age' to the surrealism, *esperpento* and *tremendismo* of this century and the continuing proliferation of popular satirical magazines.

The notions of romance and misogyny are nowhere more clearly exercised than in romantic melodrama and the slasher/horror movie with their respectively gendered identities as 'women's films' and the male genre *par excellence*.[5] Both genres are characterised by the conflictive relationships they explore between sexuality and/or violence and the social order and are central to the highly stylised generic mix which typifies Almodóvar's films. In *Tie Me Up! Tie Me Down!* the movement between the different generic conventions associated with these forms parallels and reinforces Ricky's moods and behaviour as he lurches wildly between romantic courtship, domestic banter and violence, all with the same narrative goal: conquest of Marina. Slippage between these two genres is also a feature of the film-within-the-film in which Marina again plays the female victim. *Midnight Phantom*, so someone remarks, is 'more like a love story than a horror story' and its director, Máximo Espejo, observes that 'sometimes they are confused'. Ricky is similarly confused about the difference between love and violation, but his confusion, as we shall see, clearly demonstrates the head-on collision of a series of conflicting messages emitted by social organisation.

Comedy, though generally a less regular bedfellow of horror and melodrama (because of its ability to weaken dramatic tension), is always an essential ingredient in Almodóvar's generic cocktails. It shares the visual and emotional excess of melodrama and horror and most typically takes the form of parody, taking otherwise dramatic situations into the realms of the absurd. In *Tie Me Up! Tie Me Down!* the generic mix creates a perversely idiosyncratic hybrid – a kind of 'domestic horrordrama' – within which elements of horror, comedy and romantic melodrama combine parodically to exaggerate the absurdities implicit in the principles and processes of patriarchal social conditioning.

The critical discourse of the film is first indicated by a subversion of the conventions of the horror genre. Familiar uses of non-diegetic music, lighting, editing and camera angles and the suggestive cross-references to *Psycho* (Hitchcock, US, 1960) and *Dressed to Kill* (De Palma, US, 1980), 'established by Ricki's ridiculous wig and his arrival after Marina has been masturbating in the bath,'[6] position the spectator to anticipate a probable rape or sexually-motivated killing, and to identify Ricky as a classic psychopath. Initially these expectations are borne out by Ricky's forced entry into her apartment and his physical violence. However, the anticipated sexual violation does not occur. Its absence has a disorientating effect on the spectator and opens up a narrative gap which is filled by a preposterously incongruous substitution: Ricky's desire for social integration and 'normal' family life. The misogynist objective is thus displaced onto a socially-acceptable one and the shift catches the spectator in an uncomfortable doublebind of complicity, ambiguously positioned between recognition of Ricky's goal as 'normal' but perception of his methods as 'abnormal'. It is from the mismatch between the 'logic' of the aims and the 'madness' of the methods that the black humour stems and the discourse of the absurd is activated. This mismatch is nowhere more apparent than in the sequence in which Ricky explains to an incredulous Marina his reasons for having forced his way into her apartment, knocked her unconscious and taken her captive. The shot is set up to encourage empathy with the bemused disbelief of Marina (in the foreground) as Ricky states his purpose (from a mendicant position in the background which contradicts his previously threatening representation): 'I tried to speak to you but you wouldn't let me, so I've had to kidnap you so that you can get to know me properly and then you'll fall in love with me. I'm 23 years old, I've got 50,000 pesetas and I'm alone in the world. I'll try to be a good husband to you and a good father to your children'. This disruption brings about a crucial shift in narrative emphasis, focusing attention on the power relations of gender and their reinforcement by the operation of social institutions. The spectator is both distanced from conventional generic expectations and drawn into the critical arena of absurdity.

A similar disruption is produced by a surprising lack of the kind of exploitative camerawork which would normally be *de rigueur* in the thriller or slasher movie. Kim Newman's review observes that 'Almodóvar surprisingly has refrained from exploiting the fetish in the way that a Hitchcock or an Argento might … rigorously refusing to give any erotic charge to the ropes and gags Ricky uses to keep Marina under control.[7] Marina's position both on the film set and as captive in her apartment offers opportunities for the 'male gaze'[8] and the scopophilic pleasures within which traditionally 'the woman displayed has functioned … as erotic object for the characters within the screen story, and as erotic object for the spectator within the auditorium'[9] and yet these and other potentially objectifying opportunities are not only frequently self-consciously denied, but the rejection of voyeuristic practices is explicitly foregrounded.[10]

Once Ricky has penetrated Marina's apartment, he relinquishes the earlier practice of voyeuristically-coded watching that the spectator has shared. As her captor, occupying a clearly dominant position of power over her, it is doubly surprising that Ricky is the instigator of these denials (for himself and the 'male gaze' of the spectator). When Marina tells Ricky to turn around while she changes, he immediately acquiesces, studiously avoids touching her intimately when tying and untying her and his involuntary arousal is a matter of embarrassment to him (he turns away from her to hide his erection and dismisses the idea of masturbation as embarrassingly crude and inappropriate). Another, more powerful, distancing mechanism occurs in the film-within-the-film which parallels and draws attention to the power relations of gender in the main plot. Máximo Espejo (whose very name, 'Ultimate Mirror', hints at Lacanian reflections) embodies and rehearses the whole concept of the 'male gaze', mirroring both directorial and spectatorial voyeurism from the confines of his wheelchair. He is repeatedly shown watching Marina on and off set in an emphatically sexually-coded manner. Rather than offering shared point-of-view shots, however, the camera positions the spectator to contemplate Máximo's voyeurism from a critical distance. Images of Marina's porn video performances are never contemplated directly by the spectator, they are always shots of Maximo watching and partially obscuring them. On the film set, his voyeurism is highlighted in shots such as the waist-level take from behind Marina and through her crooked arm, framing his look directed at her crotch. On the occasions when the spectator does share a point-of-view shot with Maximo, these are interrupted, as one particularly important instance demonstrates: as Máximo/the spectator stares at Marina's scantily-clad rear bending over on the film set, the contemplation is cut short when she places a cushion over her backside and spins around to reprimand him, discomfort the complicit spectator and disrupt the voyeuristic looking. On this occasion her comment addresses both the voyeuristic and the fetishistic modes of scopophilic looking,[11] by playing on the proximity in Spanish of 'mirar' (to look) and 'admirar' (to admire): 'No me mires así' 'No te miro, te admiro' 'Pues no me admires así' ('Don't look at me like that' 'I'm not looking at you, I'm admiring you' 'Well, don't admire me like that').

Like the disruption of generic conventions and expectations, the studied curtailment of voyeurism and the self-conscious focusing upon it open up a critical distance between the spectator and the visual text. The spectator is invited first to share the voyeuristic looking and subsequently, by a shift in point of view to the Marina character or through Ricky's moments of self-reproach, to identify with the reprobation of that same practice. The parallel which is drawn between spectatorship and voyeurism by alternating between the two main locations where Marina is the subject of the looking (the film set and the apartment-prison) introduces questions of gender and power into the relationship between the spectator and the images themselves and places the whole issue of looking at the centre of the film. This curtailment of scopophilic pleasures and the crucial replacement of the anticipated rape with Ricky's ambitions of social integration (marriage and family) pose the fundamental concerns of the film: the power relations of gender, their reinforcement by social institutions and the absurdity of prescribed gender norms. The disruptive strategies within the narrative and cinematic structures of the film are crucial to the positioning of the spectator in relation to these concerns and they mirror the initial frustration of Ricky's expectations of the patriarchal social order and enable the discourse of the absurd to operate.

The ambiguities and contradictions surrounding the notion of normality are also clearly at issue in *Tie Me Up! Tie Me Down!* and the function of the Ricky character might be understood as the kind of 'insurrection of subjugated knowledges' envisaged by Michel Foucault.[12] These 'subjugated knowledges' refer to discourses (such as that of the psychiatric patient) which have been 'disqualified' from the 'hierarchy of knowledges and sciences' by dominant epistemologies. Foucault argues that 'it is through the re-appearance of ... these disqualified knowledges that criticism performs its work'[13] and, indeed, the critical discourse of the 'madman' is a tradition in Spanish cultural production, reaching back to such mythical protagonists as Calderón de la Barca's Segismundo in *Life's a Dream* (1635) and Cervantes' *Don Quijote de la Mancha* (1605). Ricky's deluded 'logic' and the convergence of 'madness' and 'normality' in his reasoning have a critical function in that they cast the pursuit of socially accepted norms as madness: the discourse of the 'madman' thus reveals the 'madness' of 'normality'.

Obsessive and excessive patterns of behaviour are common traits of the bizarre characters that populate Almodóvar's films and his heterosexual men frequently demonstrate the most objectionable excesses of male chauvinism and misogyny. The obsessive sadism of Luci's policeman husband in *Pepi, Luci, Bom and Other Girls On the Heap* (Spain, 1980), Iván's callous detachment in *Women On the Verge of a Nervous Breakdown* (Spain, 1987), Gloria's husband's insensitive, *machismo* in *What*

Have I Done To Deserve This? (Spain, 1984) and the psychopathic tendencies of Diego Montes in *Matador* (Spain, 1986) are amongst the most obvious examples. Ricky's behaviour in *Tie Me Up! Tie Me Down!* constitutes a more complex case of 'neurotic masculinity' verging on hysteria. It is this hysterical behaviour, a gross exaggeration of the traits of dominant heterosexual masculinity, which delivers the film's transparently critical comment on the nature of 'normal' masculinity, since 'neurotic and normal behaviour differ in degree rather than in kind'![14] As Stephen Heath observes, 'the hysteric forces the "signifying matter" to confess and thereby constitutes a discourse'.[15]

The fact that Ricky equates the concept of 'normality' with the idea of the family is hardly surprising since the institution of the family is central to the functioning of capitalist society and to the maintenance of social order. Louis Althusser identified it (along with education and religion – also recurrent themes in Almodóvar's films) as one of the most powerful ideological state apparatuses, creating conditions for the reproduction of dominant ideology and thereby seeking to perpetuate existing social structures.[16] This power and influence stems from the family's ability to offer both comforting security and psychological and emotional support in exchange for conformity to its laws. Non-conformity can carry the penalty of withdrawal of affection and support and even ostracism. The family thus wields both the reward for conformity to dominant ideology and the punishment for rebellion. Small wonder that Almódovar has referred to the family as 'the greatest repressive organism' whilst recognising that 'psychologically, the family occupies an indispensible, inevitable and necessary place' – a duality which is a constant theme in his films.[17]

Ricky's family-forming aspirations can partially be understood as a desire for security, particularly in view of his social marginalisation hitherto. Marina is perceived as the key to this security and the instrument of his social integration. However, the patriarchal organisation of the family also promises a position of dominance to the adult male and this clearly determines the role he assumes and his patterns of behaviour towards Marina who must, again by definition of her female role, accept a submissive position.

Ricky's emergence into society as a 'normal' adult heterosexual male in itself suggests a parodic synthesis of Freudian notions of the male Oedipal crisis and the socialising function of the family. His relationship with the female *directora* of the psychiatric institution displays all the signs of an Oedipal attachment within which she represents both maternal protection and libidinal attraction, as her parting gift to him indicates: 50,000 pesetas 'for the moments of pleasure and madness you have given me'. However, he rapidly relinquishes the maternal comforts she offers, rejecting subordination to female authority and the 'castrating' experience of incarceration (an experience he will later impose on Marina) in exchange for the illusion of freedom and self-determination represented by integration into society. Despite the *directora*'s protestations, it is the *judge* – the supreme *masculine* authority of the Law – who declares Ricky normal and authorises his release. At the same time, however, the reliability of patriarchal authority is once more being called into question through its alignment with Ricky's 'madness'. Ricky clearly recognises and accepts the 'reality principle' of the society into which he is now emerging: the power base resides in the male figure and it is with patriarchal male authority that he must align himself by assuming the conventional heterosexual male role model.

The socially-constructed nature of this role and the notions of image and performance attaching to gender-specific patterns of behaviour are indicated by the emphasis placed on role playing in this film. Ricky significantly heads straight for the film set on which Marina herself is playing out the stereotypical role of the female victim in Máximo Espejo's horror movie. He prepares and equips himself for his own role of suitor-cum-violator in her dressing-room, donning the long-haired wig and demonstrating his ability to change character at will. The importance of role-playing is constantly reinforced by the re-enactment of rituals (such as Ricky's abbreviated 'courtship' of Marina: buying her a gaudy heart-shaped box of chocolates and performing handstands in the street to attract her attention and impress) and grotesque parodies of marital routines and bonds. A particularly obvious instance occurs as Ricky and Marina stand before the bathroom mirror while he attaches a false moustache and Marina is instructed to cover her bruises with make-up before they take to the street, significantly handcuffed together: 'I like the two of us to be together like this in the bathroom, like a married couple getting ready to go out'. The situation prompts further analogies with the Lacanian mirror stage and misrecognition of the reflected image as an ideal or super-ego and again draws attention to Ricky's image-led agenda and conduct. Men, as Paul Julian Smith remarks, 'are also tied up in this film, imprisoned by the bonds of heterosexual masculinity.'[18]

Steve Neale observes that 'Masculinity, as an ideal at least, is implicitly known',[19] and it is Ricky's apparently deluded, but actually merely hyperbolised, imitation of paradigms of these 'known ideals' that throws them into critical relief. Conventional notions of masculinity are in themselves contradictory, exerting opposing pressures on men to demonstrate such potentially conflicting characteristics as power and restraint, authority and protection, sexual prowess and moral superiority. These conflicts are constantly at play in Ricky's wild oscillations between violent imposition and his absurdly misguided gestures of 'gentleness' and 'consideration', all designed to secure Marina's conformity to a correspondingly 'considerate' and submissive female role model. His attentive gestures are never disengaged from the notion of violent imposition: witness, for example, his concern not to tie the ropes too tightly, avoiding touching her genitals as he adjusts her bonds, buying a more gentle sticking plaster to gag her, and his giving her the 'treat' of a different prison next door and making her breakfast in bed where she is tied up!

Ricky's understanding of his role is based on the concept of the adult male as protector and provider, hence the emphasis on being a good husband and father and offering financial 'security' in his opening gambit to Marina. This extends to his quixotically 'chivalrous' delusions of wanting to 'save' Marina (his latterday Dulcinea) from her previous life of prostitution and drug addiction ('I promised I'd get you off the streets and protect you') and thus enable her too to become 'normal' and conform to her designated role as wife and mother. He presents himself as both judge (of Marina's lifestyle) and saviour and, in his pursuit of 'normal' social integration for himself *and* Marina, invokes the reformist methods learnt from those state institutions in which he himself has been 'socialised', namely, incarceration and enforced conformity.

When Marina calls Ricky *'mamarracho'* (a figure of ridicule) and points out that she doesn't want to be protected ('I'll never fall in love with you, never! ... Who asked you to take me off the street and protect me? Who asked you to be my husband and the father of my children? Who asked for your 50,000 pesetas? Keep them and invest them in somebody else!'), her rejection hits at the very base of the myth and threatens to destabilise the 'patriarchal order' to which he aspires. Her outburst constitutes an attack on his honour (a prominent feature of traditional Spanish notions of masculinity), contemptuously dismissing his offer of protection as absurdly presumptious and reducing it to the level of a financial transaction. Furthermore, by challenging one of the foundations of male power, she poses the ultimate threat of castration.

Marina's disruptive potential and the precariousness of the patriarchal myth itself is further indicated by the fact that the very question of who is 'saving' whom is ambiguous throughout the film: Marina had already begun to take control of her own 'salvation' by moving upmarket from prostitution and porn movies to Máximo's horror B and overcoming her heroin addiction *before* Ricky appeared on the scene. Furthermore, when Ricky later describes his life's journey as a metro-line map on which Marina is the final stop, *she* is posited as *his* saviour, the embodiment of the male fantasy of the 'right woman' to tame his wild, aberrant spirit: 'On one of my escapes I met you and that changed my life. Since then I've only thought of you and, since my mind was occupied by thinking of you, I didn't do anything crazy and I became normal.'[20]

This ambiguity is reprised in the final sequence of the film which is offered as a kind of epilogue. This final sequence significantly takes place in Ricky's *pueblo* (his home village), drawing on its cultural significance as a symbol of roots, origins and pride in Spain. The village, however, and the 'family' model (an illusory memory of his dead parents) which Ricky wished to reproduce for himself through Marina, is now literally and figuratively in ruins. By implication, he is offered the opportunity to be 'reborn' into Marina's quite different, all-female family comprising Lola, their mother and Lola's daughter. The terms of Ricky's acceptance are established by Marina and Lola and the reconciliation has a strongly ceremonial tone as the formal introduction to Lola is followed by the return of previously stolen items and Ricky is duly interrogated as to his willingness to give up theft and work for a living. The women are, at least superficially, in charge as Ricky is relegated to the back seat of the car and driven into the future by Marina. This coda clearly attempts to turn around the whole concept of male domination and offer a vision of what Paul Julian Smith has referred to as 'a gender-separatist world in which woman is triumphant'.[21] The measure of the success of this attempt is apparent in the fact that most critics have totally ignored the final sequence or dismissed it as an 'awkward plot hiccough as everyone suddenly goes to the country'.[22]

Nevertheless, destabilising devices such as the ambiguity

surrounding the notion of 'saving' serve as reminders of the fragility of the masculine ideal and its need for constant reassertion and reinforcement. Ricky's androgenous appearance and his perverse combination of aggression and vulnerability have a similar effect, indicating the coexistence within the male psyche of both 'masculine' and 'feminine' traits – a duality which conventional constructions of masculinity seek to deny. The imperative suppression of the 'feminine' and assertion of the 'masculine' creates the psychological imbalance earlier referred to as 'neurotic masculinity'. Contrary to Freud's view that the extension of one-sex thoughts (from that stage in the child's early development in which it is unaware of sexual difference) for too long causes neurosis,[23] in Almodóvar's films, the opposite seems to be the case: it is the rigid definitions of the 'two-sex premise' that leads to the neurosis, demanding a conformity to discrete gender binaries which are essentially unattainable and whose pursuit is not only futile, but destructive for both men and women. A recurrent theme in Almodóvar's films is the appeal to a 'one-sex premise' within which conventionally gendered roles, characteristics and sexualities are fluid and where *alternative* relations and family formulations are frequently posited as more successful than the destructive perversity of traditional gender paradigms and the aberrent heterosexual relations they can produce.[24]

Ironically Ricky wins Marina's affection precisely when he displays the kind of weakness traditionally associated with the *feminine* and becomes the object of sadistic treatment himself. The coincidence of his physical defeat and mutilation with Marina's final acceptance recalls the 'theme of lost or doomed male narcissism' which Steve Neale (following Laura Mulvey) has observed in some westerns,[25] Ricky's amazed comment emphasises the *cost* of his final 'conquest' and, by implication, the cost of social integration and access to patriarchal power via acceptable masculinity: '*¡Joder! ¡Qué trabajo me ha costado!*'.[26] (Fucking hell, that was hard work!). Neale argues that the images of 'bodies splintered and torn apart' which precede the integration of some Western heroes into society through marriage 'can be viewed at one level at least as the image of narcissism in its moment of disintegration and destruction'.[27] This highlights yet another inherent contradiction in conventional notions of masculinity which create a 'tension between two points of attraction, the symbolic (social integration and marriage) and nostalgic narcissism'.[28]

The patriarchal order has created mechanisms for dealing with its own inherent contradictions and vulnerability, however. These are largely based on notions of male moral superiority and a corresponding female inferiority and, consequently, guilt. The appeal to such concepts is apparent in Ricky's reaction to Marina's attack on his masculinity. He claims the moral highground and judgmentally berates her for lack of gratitude (for his offerings of blackmarket drugs for her toothache, love and salvation) and for her disregard for his feelings! Accusations of selfishness and insensitivity are designed to activate the female guilt syndrome. The formula appears to work like clockwork and has a marked effect on her attitude (she is no longer concerned, for example, about removing her clothes in his presence). This sequence prefigures her change of heart and subsequent sexual reciprocation, which is also explained narratively in terms of guilt (because he is beaten up by drug-dealers when trying to obtain drugs for her) and maternalism (provoked by the sight of his battered body and his comment as she tends to his wounds: 'This reminds me of my parents. My mother used to shave my father in the patio at home. It's the only thing I remember about them'). Marina's own history (of loveless exploitation by men) makes her susceptible to what she recognises as a perversely crude, but compelling, demonstration of 'love' through a code of violence.

Whilst these characters mimic gender-specific roles into the realms of the absurd, the form of the film itself is also a mimickry of conventional cinematic codes and narrative structures. In his discussion of Almodóvar's position as a gay film-maker, Paul Julian Smith draws on Andrew Ross's definition of the camp aesthetic (so characteristic of Almodóvar's films) as a 'commentary on survival in a world dominated by the tastes, interests and definitions of others' and observes that this definition 'holds good for the films of Almodóvar in which marginal characters survive (like the director himself) by plundering dominant codes, dominant narratives.'[29]

Almodóvar's formula is clearly a pastiche of one of the ways in which classic narrative cinema (melodrama in particular) typically seeks to neutralise the 'castration threat' represented by the female figure through 'devaluation, punishment or saving of the guilty object'.[30] However, in the context of 'madness' within which the whole film is cast, the manifest absurdity and the exaggeration of the characters' formulaic conformity to their gender-specific roles of domination and submission renders the pastiche as irony. The *double* irony lies in the fact that these characters (marginalised by their gender-specific manifestations of 'anti-social' behaviour: violence and prostitution) are so clearly bound to the language and behaviour codes of the patriarchal system of authority responsible for their margina-lisation. Ricky can only articulate his desire through a code of aggression and imposition and Marina (conditioned by her history of drug dependency and exploitation by men) is only able to articulate her feelings through a code of submission, epitomised in the words 'Tie me up!', which she finally addresses to Ricky.

Delivering a critique of misogyny through a pastiche of its most traditionally exponent narratives and genres is, to put it mildly, playing with fire. The danger of satire and irony is that their critical edge is *implicit*. Detractors of *Tie Me Up! Tie Me Down!* will argue its implicit criticism of misogyny is insufficient to outweigh the lack of *explicit* criticism and that it fails to open up a critical distance sufficient to place the narrative unequivocally beyond literal readings. Whilst my analysis rejects this argument and attempts to demonstrate the operation of an openly critical discourse, *Tie Me Up! Tie Me Down!* remains a complex film, open to very differing readings. Although, in my view, it does not constitute a *condonement* of misogyny, its exposition of the mechanics of masculinity has the vindicating tone of an *apologia*, particularly in the subtextual proposition that men are as oppressed and victimised as women by the straightjacket of patriarchy. As such, the film demands a generosity of response which, whilst letting male spectators 'off the hook', may still be disturbingly compromising for women.

NOTES

1 Mandy Merck, 'Soap on a Rope', *City Limits*, 5 July 1990.
2 Dominic Wells, 'The Pain in Spain', *Time Out*, 4 Nov. 1992, p19.
3 Such condemnations were not a prominent feature of the critical response in Spain. See Paul Julian Smith, *Laws of Desire: Questions of Homosexuality in Spanish Writing and Film 1960-1990*, Oxford University Press, Oxford, 1992, p213.
4 Carol Sarler, 'Man in the Supporting Role', *The Times Saturday Review*, 21 March 1992, p6.
5 The notion of the slasher film as a particularly male genre is problematised in Carol Clover's extensive study, *Men, Women and Chainsaws: Gender in the Modern Horror Film*, BFI, London, 1992.
6 Merck, *op.cit.*
7 Kim Newman, *Monthly Film Bulletin*, Volume 57, Number 678, July 1990, p190.

8 See Ann E. Kaplan, 'Is the Gaze Male?', *Women and Film: Both Sides of the Camera*, Routledge, London, 1988.

9 Laura Mulvey, 'Visual Pleasure and Narrative Cinema', *Visual and Other Pleasures*, Macmillan, London, 1989, p19.

10 Paul Julian Smith has discussed Marina's notoriously 'erotic' bathtub sequence with the clockwork frogman and noted that the absence of an introductory establishing shot serves to 'disorient voyeurs, to disturb their fixed and dominant position.' Smith, *op.cit.*, p206.

11 Mulvey, *op.cit.*, p21.

12 Colin Gordon (ed), *Power/Knowledge: Selected Interviews & Other Writings 1972-1977 by Michel Foucault*, Pantheon, New York, 1980, p81.

13 *Ibid.*, p82.

14 J.A.C. Brown, *Freud and Post-Freudians*, Penguin, Harmondsworth, 1964, p9.

15 Stephen Heath, 'Difference', *The Sexual Subject: A Screen Reader in Sexuality*, Routledge, London, 1992, p51.

16 See Louis Althusser, 'Ideology and the State', *Lenin and Philosophy and Other Essays*, trans. Ben Brewster, New Light Books, London, 1971.

17 Almodóvar in interview, Paris, January, 1992.

18 Smith, *op.cit.*, p210.

19 Steve Neale, 'Masculinity as Spectacle', in *The Sexual Subject: A Screen Reader in Sexuality*, *op. cit.*, p286.

20 Marina's relationship with Máximo Espejo is similarly ambiguous. Whilst he apparently rescues her from a career in pornography and 'saves' her from the monster of *Midnight Phantom*, the making of the film is actually a 'therapeutic' process for him, as we learn from the *Fotogramas* magazine article Ricky reads on the bus. Marina is apparently instrumental in saving Máximo from facing his own mortality through the film since, as his wife tells Lola, 'The problem is that he doesn't want to finish the film because he knows it'll be the last one … It's his way of fighting death.'

21 Smith, *op.cit.*, pp210-211. On this same subject, Almodóvar has claimed that 'It's the triumph of matriarchy, in the best sense of the word. The young man is looking for love and family, but in the last act it's the woman who decides yes or no. She and her sister set the conditions …' (Almodóvar quoted in Marcia Pally, 'The Politics of Passion: Pedro Almodóvar and the Camp Esthetic', *Cinéaste*, 18 January 1990, pp32-35.

22 Newman, *op.cit.*

23 Clover, *op.cit.*, p15.

24 This is a major focus in Almodóvar's *Matador* which I have explored in 'Pedro Almodóvar's *Matador*: Degenderising Gender?', *Journal of Gender Studies*, Volume 1, Number 3, May 1992.

25 Neale, *op.cit.*, p283.

26 My emphasis.

27 Neale, *op.cit.*, p283. See also Mulvey. 'Afterthoughts on "Visual Pleasure and Narrative Cinema" inspired by *Duel in the Sun*', *Framework*, Summer 1981, Numbers 15-17, pp12-15.

28 Mulvey quoted in Neale, *ibid.*, p282.

29 Smith, *op.cit.*, p212.

30 Mulvey, Visual Pleasure', *op. cit.*, p21.

Empire, Identity and Place: Masculinities in *Greystoke: The Legend of Tarzan*

Griselda Pollock

PROLOGUE

The pre-title sequence of Ferid Boughedir's documentary on twenty years of African cinema, *Camera d'Afrique* (France, 1983), quoting Med Hondo's *Les Biches Negres*, serves as the preamble to my analysis of the pre-title sequence of Hugh Hudson's *Greystoke: The Legend of Tarzan* (US, 1984). Hondo's film opens with a procession of women and children across the landscape carrying calabashes or modern aluminium buckets with equal grace. They pass by a bright yellow JCB and a large truck with a tank – for water or oil – on its back before joining a seated assembly of people of all ages, resting under the shade of a few trees in this dry, bright and used landscape. From this representation of both community and work, technology and craft, we cut to a half length figure, placed against a background of huge film posters. Behind the man's head we can read the words *Sophia Loren – Technicolor – Anthony Quinn* in bold letters. The man, an African, speaks in French, directly addressing the audience: 'You have come to see a film. In Africa we also love the cinema ... But what does cinema signify to the people of Africa, of the Third World?' In an ironically jovial discussion, the speaker implicates the presence of film and its exhibition technologies in Africa in relation to colonial penetration and economic exploitation of the continent. The cinema, originating in Europe and America, is historically a way of the first world being in and 'worlding' Africa and defining Africa to Africans.[2] As he speaks about this equal industrial and ideological colonisation the camera moves back to allow us a glimpse of a neighbouring poster. It shows a woman in abbreviated skins for a

128

costume. We read the words *Johnny Weiss* ... and finally, the careful and primed spectator will notice the huge slashed blood red letters of the word *TARZAN*, glimpsed before a close up of the African mouthing the word C-I-N-E-M-A.

Hudson's *Greystoke* dared to recycle in the 1980s 'the Legend of Tarzan', arguably an irredeemably racist trope from the era of high imperialism derived from Edgar Rice Burroughs' novel *Tarzan of the Apes* (1912) which had inspired a whole series of egregiously racist films during the 1930s starring, most famously, Johnny Weissmuller. This film is critical of its source as it distances us from the 'old order' variously embodied in a number of key male characters. The distancing takes place, however, through separating 'Tarzan' from the colonial, social Darwinist world of its origins, representing him not as its ultimate expression but as a divided and contradicted figure seeking to find his own integrity as a man in the aftermath of its decline. This Tarzan is closer to films about children found in the wild such as *L'Enfant Sauvage* (Truffaut, France, 1969) and *The Enigma of Kaspar Hauser* (Herzog, Germany, 1974). But the imaginary field of this contemporary struggle for understanding humanity through its origins, heredity and environment is the appropriated spaces of a mythical Africa which is even less inhabited and less historical than that over which Johnny Weissmuller's inarticulate, musclebound Tarzan lorded it. The very gesture that updates 'Tarzan' as a hero for our times none the less exposes a specifically *post*-colonial racism. Contrary to authorial intentions claimed on its behalf, *Greystoke* (Hugh Hudson, US, 1984)[1] realises a specific relation between a representation of a masculine quest and the colonial imaginary which is as structural in the 1980s as in the early 1900s. It is this which qualifies the question of 'man's search for identity' (Hugh Hudson speaking of his film) as a matter of a whiteness that is all the more telling for never imagining that it needed to be addressed.

Action movies of the kind associated with heroic actors like Quinn supplemented by lusciously desirable and often distressed heroines played by Loren schematically stand for a western regime of sexual difference in the western cinema so precisely characterised by Laura Mulvey – the masculine subject as figure in the landscape, the narrative's agent in space and time: the woman as icon and object of gaze, possession and punishment.[3] But the Loren/Quinn movie in technicolor is also an implicit colonial gesture; the oblique reference to Tarzan is also powerfully significant of the horrific mis-representation of Africa coded in the Burroughs novel and its offshoot Tarzan movies that is at once a total *worlding* and appropriation of Africa in cinematic representation for the West's imaginary as its field of adventure and self discovery. Significant too is the fact that the only image allowed in this sequence is that of Maureen O'Sullivan as Jane, costumed in total defiance of traditional African dress – which is woven cotton, richly dyed and patterned and worn in skin-protecting full-length swathes.[4] Ragged and partial covering with wild animal skins is eloquent of the West's denial of African technology and craft production, let alone trade, while at the same time it makes the body thus clothed bespeak the masculine subject of which Jane is always a complementary sign, Tarzan, man the hunter. It also casts the whole mise-en-scène and thus Africa itself back into pre-history.[5] The worlding of Africa thus also occurs through this inscription onto its landscape, emptied of all specific and local social and kinship systems, but over-inscribed with a western regime of sexual difference. In this movement the countries and people of Africa disappear behind the mythic signifier of [European] Woman. Africa both ceases to be a social and cultural entity while it is also appropriated as a 'virgin territory' and 'dark continent', that is it is feminised – awaiting the white man's mastery and determination.[6] Finally, since the film will also erase 'woman', (Jane), Africa suffers a multiple negation.

TIME AND THE OTHER

It would be possible to read *Greystoke* as a self-conscious return to the Tarzan myth whose aim is to revise the gross colonial ideology of the original in order to draw out from the story universal issues around the question of man's identity.

> It's the *themes* that interest me. Man's origin and continuous search for that origin. The haphazard nature of our birth. Tarzan-Clayton is born into what we call a noble family. But he doesn't live in that environment, he lives in an environment in which he has to struggle like the man in the street has to struggle. The place he's into is no different from being born in Notting Hill Gate or the South Bronx – a ghetto.[7] And he's got to fight to survive.
>
> And then the white man comes in, and in his arrogance, D'Arnot … makes the great error of saying 'You don't belong here' … And so he persuades him, he corrupts him, he's like the serpent in the Garden of Eden. And Tarzan is brought back from the jungle and plonked down in the 'civilised world'. And what

happens is very tragic really. For he's very intelligent, very sensitive, and he realises that it's not the place for him. And the penalty he pays for not conforming ... is that his surrogate ape father is killed. And that finally drives him back to the jungle. The real power of the story is that he won't conform, he's his own man. He's not going to be put into a mould and told to obey the rules. Same as the characters in *Chariots*, in fact.[8].

This film undermines and contradicts the statements made on its behalf.[9] The film received much more critical attention in the French press than in Britain or America and was treated as an auteur film. Interviews with Hugh Hudson reveal a director with a developed literary conception of the meanings carried by his story. Warner Brothers, the producers may have anticipated an action picture in the mould of *Raiders of the Lost Ark* (Spielberg, US, 1981). What they got was a meticulous costume drama with more affinity with Truffaut's philosophical reconstruction of Jean Itard's experiment with Victor, the wild boy of Aveyron, in *L'Enfant Sauvage*: asking questions like, what makes humans human – language, morality or something innate? Can a child brought up apart from human society ever be fully socialised? Is there human nature or is being human, by definition, the process of socialisation via language?

Hudson's statement is exemplary of such concerns, the question of individuality and social conformity, the Oedipal issues around the family and identity, and questions of paradise and the 'castration' of civilisation through language:

> *Cinematographe*: Once he has left paradise, he can never return?
> *Hugh Hudson*: It's finished. Once one learns language, there is no more paradise. D'Arnot is the serpent in the Garden of Eden. From the moment Tarzan, who was in a state of pure innocence, receives words, he is lost. On the one hand he cannot do anything without language. It is the ambiguity of history: D'Arnot comes and gives Tarzan the apple. Once the apple is bitten, it is the end, but it is also the beginning. It is knowledge and all that comes with knowledge. The problem of identity. The dilemma of Tarzan is that of all men. We are in a terrible void. No one has roots any more. We do not know how to communicate, everything has become electronic ... At the end, Tarzan appears to be saying to the world: 'I am like you, I do not know anymore what to do ... I am a lost soul. I acquired knowledge and self-consciousness and I kept my instincts and I do not know what to do. The serpent appeared in my garden and now, I am lost ...[10]

These statements reveal a confusion between a general theme – *man* and *his* search for origins and identity,[11] and a superficial sociological application which turns out to be as uncritical, if more disguisedly racist, as the overtly imperialist story by Rice Burroughs which the film presents itself as an updated revision of. In both cases the socio-economic experience and environment of bourgeois white men's cultural and social others become an imaginary landscape in which white men can explore mythically their quite specific dilemmas around identity while misrecognising their own cultural specificity through the naturalisation process achieved by the mytheme of white man in the 'jungle' or 'paradise' – in fact another's landscape which is projected back in time as the mythic prehistory or sub-history of the West. The film raises the issues, therefore, of empire, identity and place.[12]

In Eurocentric western culture such questions get posed exclusively in the masculine and through a masculinity that is 'white under erasure' by virtue of being signified through its relation to an equally universalised white *under erasure* feminine other. In the new version, *Greystoke*, the feminine other is almost displaced by the opposition: the human versus the animal. Man the hunter and his embodied prey, woman, displacing Africa itself, which is the trope of the Rice Burroughs' novels, is updated by the existential self-exploration of the masculine subject. This involves a reversed journey to the heart of [western] 'civilisation' accompanied by scientists and soldiers across a series of spaces which equally dramatise masculine mastery – not over woman, but over his own nature projected onto a landscape and embodied in the animal. Through the application of contemporary primatology and its studies of 'man's nearest relatives', the primates become an embodiment of 'human nature' in its wild, or pre- or sub-social state. In so far as Africa is the site of Tarzan's 'jungle paradise' and his apes, i.e. man in a primal habitat, the Africans can only be erased or worse, elided, with this base, uncivilised, evolutionarily lower prehuman nature. This happens in *Greystoke* not through colonial application of social Darwinism, as in Burroughs' novel, but through a liberal intent to avoid social specificity and dramatise only the 'themes'. The inattention derives from the imperialism implicit in the notion of universalism.

For those unfamiliar with this film a short synopsis is in order at this point. The film tells the story of the accident by which the infant son, 'Johnnie' [Tarzan figure], of a Scottish nobleman Lord John Clayton and his wife Lady Alice, themselves shipwrecked on the coast of Africa, comes to live amongst a community of apes – a cross between chimps and gorillas – in equatorial West Africa. He is discovered by the survivor of a scientific mission sent by the British Museum, a Belgian, Capitaine Philippe D'Arnot. D'Arnot is nursed back to life by Tarzan/Johnnie after being wounded and pursued by local people who are represented as almost without language and who are portrayed as cannibals. D'Arnot teaches his wild man to shave, to speak (French and English), to experience via the mirror of imagery his difference from the animals around him and to understand the concept of the Oedipal family and descent. There is no space for comparison with black-skinned humans – the opposition is white/black: human/ape. 'When did you last see a white ape?' asks D'Arnot. The presence of hairless but dark-skinned tool-making and using, speaking bipeds i.e. other humans in the same forest is simply erased. They exist only as dangerous aliens in their own world. Taken back to the ancestral estate in Scotland, Greystoke, Johnnie (he is never called Tarzan in this film except in the titles when Christopher Lambert is introduced as *John Clayton, Tarzan, Lord of the Apes*) is claimed by his grandfather, the ageing Earl of Greystoke (Ralph Richardson) and becomes involved with his grandfather's ward, a young American woman called Jane (Andie McDowell) who teaches him to dance and conjugate Latin verbs. Grandad dies. Jane and Johnnie have sex and become engaged.[13] The climax of the movie takes place in the Natural History Museum when 'Johnnie', now Earl of Greystoke, opens a new gallery dedicated to the principles of Charles Darwin, full of stuffed and mutilated animals – a scene of concentrated death and destruction which overpowers the social (human?) veneer the Earl has acquired, driving him outside to a laboratory in which he discovers in a cage his 'ape-father', the silverback known as Greybeard. Liberating him, they romp together into Kensington Gardens where the chief scientist Sir Evelyn Blount (John Wells) orders the shooting of the escaped gorilla. In a cry of rage and despair, 'Johnnie' cradles the dead creature wailing to the assembled onlookers, '*il est mon père*', and then 'he was my father'. In the chaos of grief and confusion following this episode Johnnie decides he must 'go back'. His decision is supported by Jane who says 'I want him to be whole' and the film returns from the darkened mansion of death and desolation in Scotland to the lush vegetation of Equatorial West Africa, where, clothed in colonial whites, D'Arnot and Jane painfully bid farewell to the half-naked Johnnie who leaps and bounds and hoots his way back to his gorilla community, while the soundtrack carries D'Arnot's voice saying that he hopes one day the world will turn to make it possible for the two of them, Jane and Johnnie to be together in this place.

This 'difficult' ending reveals the distance between the Weissmuller/O'Sullivan Tarzan movies and *Greystoke*. Clad somewhat skimpily, the Jane of the 1930s–40s found no problem being the little housewife in Tarzan's inventively mechanised jungle home just upriver from the local trading post. Everything in *Greystoke* leads to the point at which Africa cannot be the site of a heterosexual union of Europeans 'gone native'. Its spaces are not colonised territories and appear hardly inhabited at all; they signify in fact temporality – and the timescale is the history of the masculine subject.

The landscape carries the connotations of the different temporalities and registers of the masculine subject caught between maternal and paternal regimes of identification and subjectivity acquired only through the loss and repression of a part of the subject's own history. In order to explain why the film ends with a spatial return that is a temporal regression to masculine narcissism, I shall have to start at the beginning.

TIME AS PLACE: AFRICA/SCOTLAND

The film's opening sets up its two key spaces 'Equatorial West Africa' and 'Scotland' and it would be easy to identify them as representations of a founding binary of western culture: Nature (Africa)/Culture (Britain – itself represented by aristocratic rural Scotland and metropolitan scientific London). In fact this thematic, which is present, is profoundly reconfigured through the actual construction of the film's rhyming use of place and articulation of identity across its spaces. Before proceeding to demonstrate this, however, it is firstly necessary to consider how marginal is the opposition man/woman as a variant of the binary nature/culture. What is really significant about this version of the Tarzan story is the peripheral position of 'Jane'. The film is not articulated through the relation of Tarzan to a feminine other.[14] Its treatment of masculinity is interesting precisely because it foregrounds what the final heterosexual union veils – the complex negotiations with competing masculine others and the continuing power of the realm of the Pre-Oedipal mother.[15]

The ramification of this shift puts 'Tarzan' in a different frame and suggests that we have to ask of this film: what status does the figure of Tarzan almost without Jane have in such a radical reworking of the legend?[16] I would suggest that the film becomes a specific dramatisation of a contemporary masculinity and its crises in which Hudson's notions of 'man's search for his origins' and the 'struggle for survival' in 'an environment' in order to be his own man actually indexes to more than banal existentialism and social Darwinism. It bespeaks a fantasy of masculine narcissism in which the phallus is imagined to be possessable. This involves a series of complex imaginary moves in relation to the maternal body and the genealogy of the father but without Woman (the symbolic representation of the phallus which the masculine subject will in fact pretend to repossess, hence the impossibility of a sustained adult sexual union).

In her analysis of the divided (or duplicated) hero in some westerns, Laura Mulvey has argued that some action films which structurally depend upon an emblematic use of landscape, figure and housing play to a phallic narcissism in which one fantasy of the male subject receives embodiment in the form of a hero who resists submission to the castrating law of the father, foregoes love and never enters domesticity or social position.[17] The interest of *Greystoke The Legend of Tarzan* lies in the implicit presence of this structure of the narcissistic hero.[18]

Tarzan is now not the action hero, master of the jungle, Lord of the Apes, but a regressing idealisation of masculine narcissism who cannot submit to the law of society, sexuality and marriage. The figure thus constructed has extremely contemporary ramifications as a combination of sundry politics of wholeness and escapist organic restoration of an ideal, safe world: environmentalism, animal rights, and liberal individualism which were both the product of Thatcherism and its liberal but muted and impotent reaction.

With the death of the old order, represented as a paternalist aristrocracy by the aged Earl (Ralph Richardson) who owns all he surveys (a landscape of equal depopulation figured only by animals he trains and rides) and the emergence of the new bureaucratic and scientific order represented by Sir Evelyn Blount (John Wells) who lords it over a mausoleum of dead and dissected animals, there seems to be no place to be 'whole', as if, by stretching the analogy, the current social and ideological order is too constricting or impossible for the realisation of a young self-seeking but responsible masculinity. The son revolts against rather than contests for the father's mastery. Unlike *The Mosquito Coast* or even *Crocodile Dundee*, which have important resonances with this legendary material, the opposition is never between urban jungle where people are the problem and another simpler way of life, a kind of 'back to basics', however complex and dangerous it turns out to be. *Greystoke* is not constructed on that axis.

There are, therefore, two threads to track through the film from its significant opening. The first is the paradoxical position of Johnnie as a negated Tarzan, as a figure who defies castration and exits from the Symbolic- which can be traced through the application of structural analysis of the narrative as myth. The second is the extended array of masculinities represented in the film from which the one that is desired but remains impossible is retrieved by the final scene with Johnnie reversing the temporal sequence of his accession to human subjectivity – language, family and sexuality – and escaping back into the dense green womb of a primordial Africa where lie the bones of both his mothers. (Hudson describes his opening as 'the jungle – the Earth, Paradise, Mother Earth …'[19])

IN THE BEGINNING …

The film opens by juxtaposing two tableaux.[20]

The first scene is indicated by a title: Equatorial West Africa, 1885. Despite the dating, putting the action right in the middle of what is called 'The Scramble for Africa', the scene we see is, in effect, the beginning of the world. Coded by a huge panoramic shot of an uninhabited landscape we see the world before time.[21] A volcano threatens and a streak of lurid red snakes across the horizon. Birds call as we hear the rumble of thunder. Cut to a high crane shot of a single ape, locked in the dense greenery, raising and beating a huge stick – in a manner reminiscent of the great scene of discovering tool use in Kubrick's *2001* as well as true to National Geographic Natural History Films showing recent research on chimp behaviour and their use of clubs as threatening gestures.[22] Visually, acoustically and by action, this scene suggests a primordial moment, a genesis, Africa as the place before time, before history, a space on which time and history are not yet inscribed.

There is, however, a population of primates. Through modern understanding of their behaviour and assumed hierarchies, which appear to mirror some aspects of western ideology, there emerges the possibility of narrative, which does imply time and history. Narrative is precipitated by an event that can set the two in motion in this otherwise timeless space. The 'event' is the anger and violence of the great silverback, Greybeard, who, maddened by the sudden storm that ravages the peace of this primordial state of timelessness, chases a young mother ape, Kala, with her tiny babe clinging desperately to her damp fur. She has to make a huge leap to escape Greybeard, and in doing so her baby falls to its death. History begins with loss – an image which manifests the latent structures of subjectivity itself and creates the very gap into which the human child will later be inserted. This creates a narrative function for the human child other than as hero: restitution for her loss. The mourning ape mother's cry screams out across the landscape that becomes now also an acoustically marked environment that has moved beyond noise to a primary but powerful articulation that is communication and expression.

A second panorama fills the screen. A gentle yellow morning sunlight bathes a huge mansion nestling in the rolling hills of cultivated landscape artistically framed via Claude and Constable. The title printed over a rich brown ploughed field reads 'Scotland Ten Months Earlier.'[23] This is the space of history and a way of controlling time: tradition, accumulated narratives and a succession of deaths and substitutions. There is control over the landscape, agriculture. Architecture protects the living beings from the excesses of nature which poured down and maddened the primates of the cinematically earlier and chronologically later scene just discussed.

Then action interrupts the stillness as a man on a horse and a man in a two-horse phaeton come thundering through the landscape racing each other as they urge on their galloping steeds. Humans and animals are juxtaposed in a landscape in ways in which control over the animals and the managed worked land become 'landscape' laid out for mastery through possession rather than labour and mutually reinforce the meaning of the men who control both animal and land.

The titles roll over this landscape to the sounds of Elgar's First Symphony with all its heavy overtones of British Empire and heritage. Where there was birdsong and thunder, there is orchestral music (Edwardian English). Where there was animal hooting and growling, there is language (upper-class English). This dialogue that now comes across on the soundtrack reveals that the younger man, a son, is going and so is his wife Alice. Their destination is not stated, apart from it being 'no place for her'. It is on the one hand, 'over there', the other place, the destination since the fifteenth century of western man's imaginary tropical journey.[24] But, on the other, the viewer will quickly assume that 'there' is the place we have just been, ten months later! The other space is evoked within this landscape, introducing the film's problematic not as alternating spaces of difference, but interpenetrated and traversed spaces.

Departure scenes follow as the young couple take their leave for a journey to the Tropics. As they leave, it begins to rain and the music suddenly becomes disturbed – warning us as well as underlining the visual image of the elderly Earl's grave foreboding. He is left in solitary melancholy possession of the screen, behind a rain washed pane of glass. A sudden dissonance jars on the music track.

It would be easy at this point to set these two opening scenes up as simply Nature/Culture. Undoubtedly they lend themselves to this and lean upon its possibility. But the film is more complexly inscribed around the question of time, and relies on the relay between the two spaces rather than on their pure opposition. For what follows the setting in place of the Greystoke mansion is not entry into it, but rather a scene outside it, another kind of confrontation with nature and in relation to animals which signifies measures of human control over the animal and masculine self-production in that relation to landscape as its setting. The film sets up for the viewer not only the sequence of scenes but a pattern of memory. This opening scene of the old Earl and his son will repeat with Johnnie/Tarzan in his father's place, forging a link between the two masculinities, via dynasty and identification, that transcends the difference of the spaces; while the Earl's son, will soon be found in another confrontation with animals which he loses at the cost of his life, a scene that his own son will re-enact victoriously to establish himself as the dominant male, Lord of the Apes in the same 'African' space. Thus the opening two set-ups establish corresponding, if alternating spaces of masculinity rather than the simple opposition of nature/culture that a superficial reader might immediately mistake.

Music forms the bond which allows us to bridge space. For the next scene is a shipwreck off the coast of Africa. The same dissonant notes play across the scene of wreckage and death. Scotland is deposited in Africa where all of it will die save the baby that is to be born there. For Lady Alice Clayton gives birth to a son and dies of malaria shortly after. Lord Clayton dies soon after in a struggle with Greybeard when the apes finally penetrate the tree house that he has built from the ship's wreckage. The silverback has been followed into the cabin by the grieving ape mother, still carrying the corpse of the infant who fell from her grasp during the mighty storm with which the film opened and with which the film has only just caught up, fifteen minutes into the movie. She hears the human infant boy's cry and drops her dead baby to claim and comfort this human one. Thus Scotland, represented as a family/dynasty, experiences death and lack: the Earl has lost both his son and daughter-in-law. Scotland produces a child which is taken over to make good the loss in the animal family of Africa which was the narrative-precipitating event of the first scene – the beginning of the world, of time and of the story.

The child – the Tarzan figure – functions as a token that circulates between two spaces which it not only joins together but in some way incorporates as the problematic of identity. His meaning is loss and restitution for others. The child/boy/man can move between the two spaces but at whatever pole he rests he will know only loss because the drama is established fundamentally not as Nature and Culture but Oedipally, that is the structuring framework is composed of two families; two systems.[25] The loss which the first scene narrates, produces a childless mother who can be restored to her motherhood only by creating another loss to a family signified fundamentally only as a male genealogy. Two families are put into conflict in a way which overdetermines the impossible identity of the child, whose narrative will in all its contingency narrate the predicament of the masculine subject *per se* forced to pass from a maternal space within which he experiences unity and later a fantasy of total omnipotence to the paternal law at the price of submission to the 'castration' of language and the law of the Father.

As a hybrid of sorts, 'Tarzan' must mediate and negotiate aspects of a male human dilemma about its own status. Nature (a feminised originary maternal space including an archaic father figure) could be inside him as the child raised in it, and he could represent man dominant in a natural habitat without being nature (i.e. the mother). The relation of this human figure to the nearest relatives amongst the animals, the communal and communicating apes, becomes the crucial siting of the story of a fantasy of escape from patriarchal into phallic masculinity, rather than the backdrop to the colonial project of the original Tarzan narrative which was the installation and naturalisation of an imperial masculinity.

I am forced into making this somewhat unusual distinction. Of course, patriarchal masculinity is orchestrated around the phallus. But in a culturally applied psychoanalytic reading of this film, I am suggesting that we can use the term phallic as in the 'phallic phase', a period prior to the resolution of Oedipal complex and the submission to 'castration' (to which masculinity must submit even if it is fantastically disavowed through the figure of the Woman as Other and lacking). The phallic phase involves fantasies by means of which the male child believes either that it can be all that the mother desires, i.e. the phallus, or believes that the mother is phallic, as it were all-powerful, and believes through the state of primary narcissism that he has the phallus, i.e. is omnipotent.[26] These fantasies are all highly defensive against the continuing drip drip of loss, separation and emptying out which is the trajectory of the subject to speaking, sexed subjectivity. So I use the term patriarchal masculinity to refer to submission to the law, and phallic masculinity to signal the continuing pre-Oedipal regressive masculine fantasy, what Laura Mulvey calls Oedipal nostalgia, 'an internal oscillation of desire, which lies dormant, waiting to be "pleasured" in stories of this kind'.[27]

In this revision of the myth, Tarzan functions as a mediating figure, the trickster, that can by 'the accident of his childhood' experience both places, families, worlds which have been set up as not so much absolute oppositions with the implication of progression from one to the other, or mastery by the one over the other, but as poles of oscillation of desire which, none the less, imply a temporality – time before history and the time of tradition, which is hegemonic imperial and patriarchal history. They set the terms and parameters of his being, externalising aspects of its possibility, being at the same time signifiers of his 'nature', i.e. human nature. It is this term with its contradictory ideological burden rather than the pair nature/culture which this film seems to dramatise in a contemporary form. Is the nature of a man conflicted or a matter of oppositions that might have to be sublimated? Is the nature of a man a matter of a past or a future and how will the one be reconciled with the other? Can it be imaginarily enjoyed by its refusal? Faced with the decline of a political order premised on masculine dynasties, and supplanted by science and technology and its apparatchiks, does masculine fantasy regress to boyhood stories with their servicing of those infantile fantasies of a phallic omnipotence? Does not the idea of wanting to be 'whole' signify implicitly the refusal of the castration, the subject realised only in splitting, division and loss of the real to the symbolic?

GROWING UP AND GOING BACK

The meaning of Tarzan in this film is set, therefore, by his entry into it as a child, which was Hudson's and Austin's specific reorganisation of the original script by Robert Towne. Such a beginning could merely suggest that the subsequent narrative will chronicle his development 'to manhood' – the thematic of a kind of historical biopic. But that temporal drive is mediated by the other aspect of this entry as infant. For he is the desired but lost object of two incompatible family systems, two clans, two dynasties. The one in Africa and somehow outside time and thus beyond society turns the space of Africa into the figuration of one kind of pre-historic (and pre-Oedipal) community with a specific kind of egoistic individual realisation within it; the other in Scotland makes that space signify the constraints and demands of social conformity, submission to history and to the law of the Father to whose place the endless line of male offspring of an aristocratic dynasty literally accede, each in turning bearing the same name, Earl of Greystoke, and having to bear the burden of that 'place in society' whatever their individual impulse may be.

This is articulated in the chaotic scenes that precede the ending of the film when Johnnie has wept over the dead silverback, calling him 'my father'. Sir Evelyn Blount argues that Johnnie must overcome the accident of his childhood and 'take his place in society', confirming the social system by embodying the name, the tradition, the law of history. Johnnie's reply is that part of him is the Earl of Greystoke and part of him is *wild*. The term twists with different meanings: wild as in wild animal – *fauve* in French, or wild as in wild card, something that upsets the apple cart and throws the system out by its unexpected character. One could also read this as: part of me has acceded to the Symbolic and literally accepted the Name of the Father, masculinity as the temporary occupancy of the Father's place; while part of me remains a child, pre-symbolic, pre-Oedipal with fantasies of narcissistic omnipotence intact – not borrowing the place of the unattainable Paternal Phallus, but believing through the rituals of primate battles for dominance that I have the phallus, and I refuse to accept castration and your law. That is very wild, and it is usually only imagined in the *Wild* West.

In the Rice Burroughs original, the function of growing up 'wild' is to prove that the natural aristocracy or superiority of the white race – eugenicist heredity – will win out whatever the environment. In *Greystoke*, that childhood is raised to a symbolic function as the permanent alternative to castration and Symbolic masculinity. It is in the play of the two families, two identities, two possible places for his 'manhood' which is set up by the film's spatial alternation between Africa and Scotland that raises the possibility for the film to stage the temporal contradictions of masculinity. The film, like many a western, thus opens the route to regression as if it is the final heroic affirmation of masculinity. Misrecognised as an existential choice of personal freedom and individual integrity, the figure of Tarzan as Johnnie reclaims the narcissistic dream of phallic omnipotence by refusing to submit to the law of the father and by winding the clock of subjective development *backwards*.

From the point at which D'Arnot took on the task of teaching 'Tarzan' language, 'Johnnie' was on a journey towards socialisation that would clothe him, marry him off and, locate him in society. What he experiences in the course of this entry into society is sexuality and death – the castration against which he revolts. Significantly in the hysteria of his grief after the shooting of Greybeard, Johnnie rides around the castle grounds whipping the horses before the carriage he is wildly driving through the rain, (an interesting compounding of images of his father/grandfather racing horses and his silverback father going wild in a thunderstorm) shrieking 'Mother – Father – Family', the words D'Arnot would chant to him to insist upon his humanity. The final scene of the film shows the grown man going back – 'I'm going back' he declares when he comes into the castle after the horse driving scene just mentioned.[28] Back to a place is also back in time. The spatial journey offers us a literal level on which to graft the metaphoric rejection of the Symbolic. The end of the film's narrative is most ambiguous because it does not end where narratives should, with heterosexual union. That is baulked as Johnnie/Tarzan abandons language, and reclaims his hooting; abandons bipedalism to bound over the hillside and leaves behind D'Arnot and Jane as the bereaved figures representing Mother – Father – Family as he reverses time and reclaims both his childhood and his utter omnipotence as Lord of the Apes rather than as the 'castrated' and therefore human Earl of Greystoke.

What of his sexuality now? The literal minded viewer may legitimately worry that the film has not dealt with this aspect, now that he has been initiated by Jane. I do not think that the scriptwriters thought this through. But my reading of which fantasy the film is 'pleasuring' might suggest this solution.

Sexuality is a construct composed out of component drives that are only focused on genital activity by the Oedipal trauma. Thus the film also offers the escape from sexuality as another effect, indeed, price of the acquisition of subjectivity. Tarzan might simply be imagined to revert to the polymorphous perversity of infancy. Unravel the wedding of the drives through the castration complex and 'sexuality' is also undone. Who needs it if one imagines one has, or even is, the phallus?

Theoretically, of course, no one has or ever is the phallus which is, we are told, merely a signifier – a means to organise meaning around lack. Its paradoxical capacity to signify power lies precisely in its inaccessibility as the nothing which stands therefore for the lost everything. I am using the imagery here to signify fantasies arising in the imaginary phase in which initial negotiations of the fate of being lacking operate unchecked by reality and by social convention. Thus the story of women being found to be castrated must be read as a later legend by means of which the lack that all subjects, masculine as well as feminine experience, is projected retrospectively by masculine subject away from themselves. Thus men acquire masculinity Oedipally through the replacement of one fantasy – that they are the phallus or have it, infantile notions of omnipotence – by another, namely that by accepting the 'castration' of the law they will accede to the Father's place, 'assuming' a phallic position while never having it or being it through relations to sexual others, male or female. I am suggesting that under certain historical circumstances the narcissistic fantasy based in and on the boy's own body and its phallic pleasures finds expression in a range of cultural forms ... *Boys' Own Adventures* so to speak. This film, *Greystoke*, straddles two key moments in which such adventure stories became culturally pervasive in the colonial West and yet which would appear to be in opposition: late Edwardian Imperialism and Thatcherite Modern Toryism. What intrigues me is the relation between that latter cultural and political context and the emergence of the possibility of using a trope from the former moment to articulate the dilemmas of the 1980s. Because of the impossible task the film was set, it could never be a box office hit: as a narrative it could achieve no resolution because the film literally ends by going backwards. If the film breaks down as a narrative, it is none the less, available for a different kind of reading that comes closer to the way Freud would construct his case studies; a kind of layering of memory, fantasy and retrospectively imposed signifiers. This film can be read chapter by chapter, tableau by tableau, following the pattern of accumulating rhymes. This produces an archaeological figuration of the fiction that is the subject in masculinity. The film text's structuring of the contradictions it posed, and those it exposed, make *Greystoke* an important site for examining the return of the masculine repressed, as it were, and the relations between cultural stories, legends and myths and their continuing potential to stage culturally particular, politically specific, yet psychically persistent dramas of the subject. What remains disturbing, however, for all the disruption of Oedipal narrativity, is that the condition for this dramatisation is still the dehumanisation of Africa. This is what makes the Tarzan legend ultimately an irredeemable figure that attests to a colonial foundation in contemporary psychic structures and fantasies.

NOTES

1 Prod. Warner Bros. Starring Christopher Lambert, Ian Holm, Ralph Richardson, James Fox, John Wells and Andie McDowell.

2 The term 'worlding' derives from the work of Gayatri Spivak, especially 'The Rani of Sirmur', *History and Theory*, 1985, pp247-272.

3 Laura Mulvey, 'Visual Pleasure and Narrative Cinema', *Visual and Other Pleasures*, Macmillan, London 1989.

4 I am indebted to conversations with Joanne B. Eichler on dress and textiles in West Africa. See *Dress and Gender: Making and Meaning*, edited by Ruth Barnes and Joanne Eichler, Berg Publishers, Providence, R.I., 1993.

5 Remember Raquel Welch in a skin bikini in *2 Million Years BC*.

6 For a detailed analysis of the meaning of 'Africa' in western discourse since antiquity see Christopher Miller, *Blank Darkness: Africanist Discourse in French*, University of Chicago Press, Chicago, 1985.

7 In this context we cannot avoid the implication that certain urban areas are like a 'jungle' and that the nature of this jungle is related to the nature of the people living there: Notting Hill and South Bronx are culturally black neighbourhoods. This is the kind of inattention to the implications of statements made in the register of the 'man in the street' which characterises the liberal text with a specific kind of unexamined racist structure.

8 Harlan Kennedy, 'Interview with Hugh Hudson: *Greystoke*', *Films*, May 1984, p22.

9 The film originated in a script written by Robert Towne who wanted to direct it. His original script begins with a scene in a trading post and the revelation of the almost super human strength

of the mature Tarzan accompanied by D'Arnot. It begins at the derelict outposts of colonial civilisation and Tarzan's adult encounter with it. The radically revised script in fact filmed produced a radically different agenda as expressed repeatedly by Hudson in these interviews.

10 'Enfants Sauvages: Entretiens avec Hugh Hudson' *Cinematographe*, 1984, p8.

11 The automatic use of a generic masculine for human explorations of origins and identity has been cleverly disputed in its own mythic territory by Elaine Morgan in *The Descent of Woman*, Souvenir Press, London 1972. She challenges the masculine bias of evolutionary anthropology through a feminist reading of theories of the acquatic ape.

12 These are the themes of a major film, *Territories*, produced by Sankofa in 1985, which posed the questions on the streets of Notting Hill Gate and articulated them across gender and sexuality so signally unexplored and unimagined, though certainly still present in *Greystoke*.

13 I want to acknowledge the work of Amanda Phillips as a M A student on the M A in the Social History of Art, who first analysed the extraordinary character of the love scene in this film and identified the dislocated position of Jane and thus woman in the narrative. She wrote a paper on this topic for a seminar on the film.

14 I should point out that the word Tarzan is never used in this film. The main character is known as Johnnie, John, Lord Clayton or Lord Greystoke – for the film does not make Rice Burroughs' mistake of imagining the animals as speakers with their own language; Tarzan means white ape in the language of the apes in the original book. I refer to this character in this way to signify the continuing operation of the myth thus named in the original book and dispersed in popular culture through this signifier.

15 In the first Rice Burroughs novel, Jane is shipwrecked on the coast of Africa with her father while hunting for treasure which will release her from a promise to marry the American man to whom her father is in debt. Tarzan spies upon her and eventually has to rescue her from assault by his arch ape rival Kerchak. His 'gentlemanly behaviour and honouring of her virtue' during this rescue and sojourn in the jungle is used to prove his innate aristocracy in contrast to the 'black brute' he overcomes to save Jane. On her return to America with her father, Tarzan resolves to follow her to Baltimore ... even though, there he does not declare himself the real Lord Greystoke and leaves her to marry his cousin who currently bears the title. He does return to Africa to carry on the adventures which make Rice Burroughs wealthy. The core of this drama is his sexuality and its management in relation to a feminine object.

16 Jane Porter does of course occur in the film, at Greystoke, but everything about these scenes indicate their lack of intensity and ideological investment.

17 Laura Mulvey, 'Afterthoughts on "Visual Pleasure and Narrative Cinema" Inspired by *Duel in the Sun …*' *Framework* 15/16 1981 and reprinted in *Visual and Other Pleasures, op. cit.*, pp29-37. In *The Man who Shot Liberty Valance* the story is told in flashback by Ranse Stoddart (James Stewart) who is now a married man and a respected Senator (society, law, rule of the father etc.). He recalls his rivalry for his wife Hallie with Tom Donniphon (John Wayne) who in fact did kill the rampaging criminal Liberty Valance while making it appear that Ranse was the hero. Tom never marries and remains an outsider to society. He dies and the film's story is occasioned by the mourning at his funeral.

18 'This narrative structure is based on an opposition between two irreconcilables. The two paths cannot cross. On one side there is the encapsulation of power, phallic attributes, in an individual who has to bow himself out of history. On the other, an individual impotence rewarded by politics and financial power, which in the long run, in fact, becomes history. Here the function of "marriage" is as crucial as it is in the folk tale. It plays the same part in creating narrative resolution, but is even more important in that "marriage" is an integral attribute of the upholder of the law. In this sense Hallie's choice between the two men is predetermined. Hallie equals princess equals Oedipal resolution rewarded, equals repression of narcissistic sexuality in marriage. *Ibid.*, (*Framework*), p14.

19 *Films*, May 1984, p23.

20 In an interview on the release of the film in 1984 Hugh Hudson complained bitterly that his artistic conception of the film as a whole had to be sacrificed to the necessities of exhibition programming. Thus a considerable amount of the film had to be edited down to allow more playing times per day at the cinema. The video release of *Greystoke* restored the film to Hudson's original full-length cut. This includes a long pre-title and title sequence, which, with the final scene, will be the topic of this Chapter.

21 Thomas Pakenham, *The Scramble for Africa 1876-1912*, Weidenfeld and Nicholson, London, 1991, chronicles the campaigns of European imperial ambitions which carved up the African continent.

22 The film makers studied in particular the work of Jane Goodall on chimp behaviour in Tanzania while also using Dianne Fossey material on mountain gorillas. The key National Geographic documentary is *Monkeys, Apes and Man*, 1971.

23 I will come back to this extraordinary inversion of film time in due course.

24 See Cleo McNelly, 'Natives, Women and Claude Lévi-Strauss: A Reading of *Tristes Tropiques* as Myth', *Massachussetts Review*, 16, 1975, pp7-29.

25 Although each 'family' has a male and female parent at some point within it, they are marked as different: Africa as family is initially

only Mother (Kala) and Child and Scotland as Father (the Earl) and Son. Greybeard's reappearance as *'mon pére'* in the later stages becomes a signifier of a fraternity of identity. This suggests the maternal family versus the paternal family – i.e. Pre-Oedipal and Oedipal.

26 Male trauma is based on the culturally defined discovery of maternal lack – her castration, which appears in the film when Kala is brutally murdered with a spear in her chest. On her death, when Tarzan has mothered her as she mothered him when he was wounded in a fight, he cries out in grief, echoing her earlier screams, but the cry rises on the soundtrack to become a full masculine roar – acoustically marking his passage into masculinity over her castrated/murdered body.

27 Mulvey, *op.cit.*, p15.

28 (Note the same lack of specified destination as in the opening scene when Lord Clayton states to the Earl 'I've decided to go.')

'Too Straight a Drive to the Tollbooth': Masculinity, Mortality and Al Pacino

Susannah Radstone

In *Sea of Love* (Harold Becker, US, 1989), Al Pacino/Frank is a New York cop with a drink problem, a divorce and a mid-life crisis. Hardly a recipe, one might think, for female fascination. Yet for me, now, there is something compelling about Pacino – and particularly about Pacino's authoritative portrayal here of a man whose authority is on the wane. Female fascination with losers is anything but new and Pacino's status as star confirms his powers of attraction for a wide audience of cinema-goers. Yet we all have our *particular* preferences for male and female stars – preferences which film theory's generalisations concerning spectatorship and identification have so far only partially elucidated.[1] Can my own preference for Pacino tell us anything about the appeal of particular stars to specific audiences? And what can my training in the rational pursuit of (feminist) knowledge contribute to this quest? For while there are phases – and even fashions – in the production of feminist knowledge, there is certainly more than one story that I could tell about the feelings Pacino evokes in and for me. While our scholarship, then, is shaped by the contingencies we call history, and while our autobiographies shift on the sands of memory, association and contingency, fascination or desire always exceeds its object, refusing both constraint and satisfaction. How then, to tell its story? One place to begin – a routinised beginning, after all, and one that excludes other beginnings and other possible contexts – would be with *one* context within which I experience my fascination, that of my own feminist study of masculinity and cinema. Though scholarship cannot deliver the 'truth' about fascination, this essay hopes to show

how scholarship and fascination trace each others' paths through history, memory and desire.

Within the context of my academic work, Frank/Pacino emerges as representative of contemporary masculinity's vicissitudes. Haunted by intimations of mortality, he hunts down a serial killer whose male victims – found face-down, naked, with bullets through the brain – have all advertised in the lonely-hearts columns. The film's title refers to an old 'single', *Sea of Love*, which is always found playing at the murder site. Frank and his colleagues are convinced that the killer is a woman and they set a trap by advertising in verse, as had the murder victims. He and his new colleague-cum-buddy Sherman/John Goodman, take turns dating and waiting on table, fingerprinting their 'dates'' wine-glasses. Suspense rises when Frank dates for real one of these assignees, Helen, played in suitably ambiguous and feisty fashion by (the wonderful) Ellen Barkin.[2] The steamy sex scenes which follow permit much play on the deathly connotations of sex. The film's dénouement, however, reveals that the cops' assumption that the killer is a woman, their association of death with Woman, is erroneous as the killer turns out to be Helen's abandoned husband whose inability to live with the knowledge of his ex-wife's continuing sexual life leads him to murder her partners. Paradoxically, Frank's redemption relies on his (clearly overdetermined) 'error'. In a fight to the death with the killer, who now wants to kill *him*, Frank proves himself as man and cop, gives up drink, and, with the threat of deathly sex defeated, gets his girl. In a tidy doubling that confirms the coherence of Pacino's star-image,[3] Frank's come-back was also Pacino's. For, having defeated a rumoured over-familiarity with the bottle, *Sea of Love* signalled Pacino's own return to form.[4]

My interest in Pacino in general and in *Sea of Love* in particular appears to be sparked less by the dénouement and the come-back, however, and more by what is for me most memorable of the performance and most compelling in the Pacino image – a certain fragility, a particular quality of fear, an edgy sense of collapse staved off, all underlined by Pacino's emphatic shortness which the camera does nothing to mask.[5] Increasingly, indeed, Pacino's screen roles have played up this smallness, together with the qualities of fragility and vulnerability. In *Scent Of A Woman* (Martin Brest, US, 1992) he plays a blind former military officer, while in his more recent British release, *Carlito's Way* (Brian De Palma, UK, 1993), the minor hoodlum he plays tells his story retrospectively from the point of death, leaving us wondering not if, but how exactly, he comes to meet his death.[6] No recuperative dénouement there. In the earlier *Sea of Love*, which *does* restore Frank to a perhaps chastened version of his former self, the unravelling of the plot slips from my mind. I remember, rather, the scene where Frank returns to his flat to find his father – a diminutively frail figure and an ex-cop made yet more frail by his own confrontation with mortality in the shape of his ex-partner's death. I remember Frank's sheer terror as he thinks he sees a gun in Helen's handbag, while she's undressing.[7] I remember Frank, leaning over the body of murder victim number one to shake hands with and confide to Gruber, a colleague and his ex-wife Denice's new husband, that while he and Denice were married: 'I was never going to die', but now, he says, he's feeling 'kinda mortal all of a sudden.' And I can't forget a following scene – from which this article's title comes – in which Frank anxiously recounts to his ex-wife his thoughts during a confrontation with what he – in typically fallible fashion – mistakenly took to be a threatening gunman: 'I'm staring down the barrel of a gun and these are my exact thoughts. I don't love nobody ... I'm going to die someday. This is it. Gotta love somebody. Otherwise it's too straight a drive to the tollbooth.' I'm struck here not just by Frank/Pacino's acknowledgements of his needs but by his sheer loquacity – a far cry from the emotional and linguistic reticence of the 'strong, silent' male hero.[8] 'Talk to me', the invocation to speech, is virtually *Sea Of Love*'s refrain – a refrain shared by and responded to by the film's male and female characters, though with varied intonation and effect.

My fascination with this film in particular and with Pacino more generally seems to be prompted by two themes – Frank/Pacino's repeated acknowledgements of the limits of self-sufficiency ('gotta love somebody') and the play on Frank/Pacino's fallibility, vulnerability, fragility – all recall a quote from *Hamlet* (to which I'll return) 'the thousand natural shocks that flesh is heir to'. Together, these themes point to Frank/Pacino's – and the film's concern with mortality's threat, in a focus which Helen/Barkin finds excessive: 'This town is like one big city of the dead for you, hah?', she comments.

My interest is thus apparently sparked off by the spectacle of patriarchal masculinity divesting itself of much of its sustaining apparatus. Frank/Pacino's plea for love – his acknowledgement of his need for another – together with his awareness of the passing of time and its effects on the body[9] seem to inch him (and us?) away from patriarchal masculinity's denials of both emotional and corporeal lacks and inch him (and us?) towards an acknowledgement of masculinity's 'symbolic castration'.[10] What appears to be happening here is a sliding of white US masculinity[11] towards the patriarchal construction of its other, femininity, along with, to be sure, a degree of confusion concerning who possesses and who lacks the phallus: hence the fear of (and perhaps the desire for) the potentially phallic (gun-toting) Helen/Barkin.

Sea Of Love's brotherhood of cops engage in a series of nostalgic and totemic rituals. Early in the film a nostalgic establishment shot of 'dated' New York city hoardings sets the scene for a sequence in which Frank and his team trap a large group of criminals in a hall by issuing fake invitations to meet the Yankees. But the Yankees never come and instead, warrants are issued. Later, Frank and Sherman's first meeting takes place at a huge police convention where promotions are handed out. This scene of apparent plenitude, celebration and 'old style' brotherhood is shot through, however, by scenes of fighting as Frank's playful demonstration of martial arts escalates into an attack on his ex-wife's husband, Gruber. It appears that the centre is not holding. The Yankee totems fail to appear and violence fills the void. The film's nostalgic gestures towards a lost way of life (and towards older cop movies?) suggest, meanwhile, that something of the past has been lost.

Sea Of Love's fascination with male murder victims, together with its nostalgic, totemic rituals recall *Totem and Taboo*[12], Freud's story of the brothers' murder of the primal Father. The film emerges as shot through with desire for this murdered primal Father. According to Freud, the brothers' parricide sought to end the primal Father's strictures concerning endogamy,[13] together with their forced subordination to his rule. The brothers' hope for a homecoming to unbridled desire free from the father's law, however, repressed one side of their own filial feelings. Remorse was not something the brothers had bargained for. Primitive society's totemic and sacrificial rituals were understood by Freud as representative of both the brothers' parricidal and their affectionate feelings towards their murdered father.[14] Freud tells this story of parricide, of remorse and of filial ambivalence to explain the emergence of patriarchy as he knew it. According to this story, the totemic representation of the murdered father and of the sons' remorse and longing was eventually supplanted by gods, which Freud understands as father surrogates, which took a more human shape.[15]

Freud's explanation for this shift from totem worship to the worship of gods (and then, in many religions, to monotheism) emphasises the sons' identification with and unfulfillable longing for the Father. The brothers all shared a wish to be like the murdered father, but this wish to attain individual supreme power was an impossible one, given their fraternal pact. 'For the future', argues Freud, 'no one could or might ever again attain the father's supreme power, even though that was what all of them had striven for.'[16] Thus, Freud continues, gradually the brothers' bitterness towards the father was superceded by a longing for him. Over time, an ideal emerged, moulded in the image of the primal Father's unlimited powers. Gradually society restored the father to his place. But a gap still remained between the patriarchal father and the primal Father: 'and the gulf between the new fathers of a family and the unrestricted primal Father of the horde was wide enough to guarantee the continuance of the religious craving, the persistence of an unappeased longing for the father.'[17] *Totem and Taboo* emerges here, then, as an account of patriarchal masculinity's psychic foundations in an impossible nostalgic identification with an idealised image of the father.[18] On this account, Frank's handshake with Gruber over the body of murder victim number one might be read as a re-enactment of those rituals through which the exiled brothers commemorated their parricide *and* sought redemption *from* the father. The film's insistent nostalgia, which binds the act of murder to the longing produced by old 'singles' evokes, too, a masculine association between violence and irredeemable loss.

Feminist film theory has routinised the analysis of the classical cinematic tropes through which mainstream cinema has sought to fulfill this impossible nostalgic desire for and identification with this idealised figure. It traces a series of manoeuvres in which femininity emerges as the loser.[19] More recently, the costs for *masculinity* of these procedures have been itemised by Steve Neale, amongst others. In his Lacanian-influenced analysis of *Chariots of Fire* (Hugh Hudson, UK, 1981), Neale argues that the cinematic system works to sustain an identification with the second rather than the third stage of the Oedipal process.[20] Following Colin McCabe, Neale suggests that in the second stage, the father is misrecognised as a full presence, as 'the phallus incarnate', rather than a being who, like the son, must find his place 'within an organisation of desire that he does not control.'[21] Neale's reading of *Chariots Of Fire* rests on McCabe's insistence that this third stage:

remains for us, caught in a patriarchal society, only a partially realised possibility. *All the efforts of society are devoted to encouraging as complete a regression to the second stage as is conformable with sanity.* (emphasis added)[22]

Neale's reading builds on McCabe's formulation by proposing that male homosexuality as well as women and female desire are repressed in the achievement of a stable masculine identity within phallic authority.[23]

I might now propose that *Sea Of Love* represents a move from the second to the third stage of the Oedipal process – the achievement of which McCabe saw as only ever a 'partially realised possibility' in patriarchal society. On this account, Frank/Pacino's insistent intimations of mortality become masculinity relinquishing its identification with 'the phallus incarnate', and, one might add, inviolate. When an exhausted and inebriated Frank/Pacino returns to the scene of victim number one's murder – an apartment of morgue-like chill and grey – he lays himself down on the bed, exactly filling the space previously occupied by the corpse. Here, identification appears to be with the body of *Totem and Taboo*'s murdered father, rather than with the idealised all-powerful father of patriarchy's imaginary. Perhaps this signifies an acknowledgement of the illusory status of the father of the Oedipal second stage? At another point, Frank returns home to discover his aged and frail ex-cop father rendered yet weaker by an encounter with mortality in the shape of his ex-partner's death. Frank's father stays on while Frank hosts a boozy evening during which he and his colleagues try to write a rhyming advertisement. Frank responds to the darkest of these poems: 'I'm sitting across from Mortitia Adams here!' The scene's ending, in which Frank half-carries his father's tiny figure to bed apparently does little to revivify patriarchy's idealised father, perhaps confirming, rather, the father's position under rather than outside the law, and particularly the law of 'natural history'.[24] Neale's reading of *Chariots Of Fire* emphasised that the patriarchal maintenance of the second stage of the Oedipal process depended on the repression not only of women, but of male homosexual desire,[25] since the representation of either marks a break with an identification with the idealised father's self-sufficiency. Frank/Pacino's repeated insistence that he *lacks* 'somebody' might be read therefore as a break with such narcissistic self-sufficiency. The film's repetitive allusions to male homosexual desire might also be read in this way.[26] Though

Freud believed that *sublimated* homosexual feeling was an important factor in binding groups together,[27], the bond between *Sea Of Love*'s 'brothers' appears at times to be forged through the acknowledgement, rather than the sublimation, of homosexual desire and the veil lifts: Frank's conversations with colleagues are peppered with homosexual allusions whose function appears closer to titillation than to pejoration.[28] For instance, when Frank and his new buddy-cum-partner Sherman team up to set a trap for the killer, their enactment of heterosexual promiscuity – the cops date five or six women in an evening – is underlain by a play on homosexuality. Frank offers his flat to Sherman/Goodman (who is too tired to drive home – yet another instance here of the sheer susceptibility of the male) and Sherman responds by asking if they are going to sleep together. Frank's laconic and only possibly ironic response of 'Sure, why not?' draws what looks like a delighted grin from Sherman. The film's evident focus on homosexuality, however, lends itself uneasily to a reading that proposes a move from the second to the third stage of the Oedipal process because *Sea Of Love*'s 'homosexuality', which at times inscribes mutual desire between men, at others inscribes desire for the 'phallic woman'. One of Frank's 'dates', who sees through his assumed identity as a printer, accuses him of having cops' eyes and walks away from the ambush with the defiant 'You're a printer, I've got a dick.' This remark provides the pretext for a jokey conversation between Frank and Sherman in which Sherman asks Frank: 'think you could go for a babe with a dick?' This sequence, including Frank's response – that it would depend on the personality – suggests a variety of readings. Frank's encounter with the woman who 'sees through' his disguise together with the play on homosexuality generated by her challenge could be read as further evidence of *Sea Of Love*'s exposure of masculinity's symbolic castration: the woman sees through him and the men acknowledge a desire which threatens patriarchal masculinity. But it could also be read otherwise since the defiance with which the woman delivers her 'you're a printer, I gotta dick' is, arguably, undermined by the statement's ultimate re-phallicisation of Frank/Pacino: the one who, we are reminded, still has the law and the phallus on his side. Furthermore, although her remark appears to motivate male homosexual play, it is worth considering that the play she motivates is between a man and 'a babe with a dick' – a phallic woman. The cops' fantasies about the killer – the 'shooter' – as well as their 'homosexual' fantasies emerge here, then, as ambivalent fantasies of and about the phallic woman. These undercurrents lend weight to, rather than challenge, my argument that *Sea Of Love* evidences contemporary masculinity's uncertain identification with the idealised phallic father of the Oedipal second stage. They also suggest that masculinity's contemporary instabilities may be prompting a further move away from, rather than towards the Oedipal third stage. The fantasy of the phallic woman, 'the shooter', is overdetermined. With the loss of the phallic father comes not progression to the third stage of Oedipal development but *regression* to an earlier pre-Oedipal stage presided over by fantasies of an all-powerful, terrifying phallic mother. This phallic woman can then take the blame for the killing: she represents, therefore, both a projective denial of that much regretted parricide and an acknowledgement of the father's death. If such is the case, my previous reading of *Sea Of Love*'s relinquishment of masculinity's identification with an idealised and self-sufficient phallic father appears over-optimistic, for the return, in representation, of the phallic mother – replete with threat as *Sea Of Love* so amply demonstrates – holds no necessary promise for feminism.

The readings of *Sea Of Love* that I have so far proposed have their context in wider debates about contemporary representations of masculinity, mainly in feminist and postmodernist theory, which have addressed whether or not masculinity is 'in crisis'.[29] Widely documented changes in the economy such as the technologisation and/or feminisation of labour, together with the shift from manufacturing to service industries will, inevitably, have an effect on masculinity. However, the divergent views on the place of such major changes within wider social and cultural trends have produced varied readings of contemporary masculinity. Indeed, not everyone would concur with the initial positing of a crisis. *Sea Of Love* can be read as evidencing not so much a crisis in masculinity, but as part of a ubiquitous and routine *testing* of masculinity by means of which patriarchal masculinity continues to maintain itself.[30] Such work inevitably entails both the discovery of and the mending of 'cracks' in masculinity. But cracks do not necessarily imply collapse. In the main, feminist, postmodernist and psychoanalytic theorists are positing a change at the heart of contemporary masculinity, though there is little consensus regarding either the determinants of this change or its likely outcome. Thus Lynne Segal's feminist reading of contemporary masculinity stresses the determining force of feminist theory and practice in producing what she guardedly welcomes as 'slow motion' change.[31] On the other hand, Craig Owens's postmodernist thesis associates what he calls postmodernism's loss of 'master narratives'[32] with the waning of patriarchy's alignment of masculinity with mastery and posits, therefore, a compatibility between feminism and postmodernism.

Owen's optimistic (from a feminist viewpoint) reading of contemporary cultural changes has recently been challenged from a number of different feminist positions located within several disciplines. Within feminist film theory, Barbara Creed has challenged Owens' proposition that postmodernism's impact will necessarily be compatible with feminist aims. Creed agrees with Owens that visual culture is suffused by '[a] multiplicity of signs of mastery; a mourning of loss; images of the phallic woman'[33] – signs which have emerged in my own reading of *Sea Of Love* – but she does not see these signs as portents of the dawning of a new feminist age. She also points out that Owen's mistranslation of Lyotard's *grands recits* as 'narratives of mastery' leads him to conflate Lyotard's assumption of a crisis in the status of knowledge with an assumed 'crisis in the representation of man as "subject" within the signifying practices of Western patriarchal societies',[34] accusing Owens of *subsuming* feminism within postmodernism. Creed's analysis of the current crisis as the loss of the *paternal metaphor*, or the paternal signifier,[35] leads her to conclude (contra Owens) via the analysis of a number of sci-fi horror films that although the films she analyses are suffused with both the mourning of loss and with the theme of 'becoming woman', or what Alice Jardine calls gynesis,[36] the 'woman' represented may well signify patriarchy's ambivalent encounter with its unknown spaces through strategies which do little to dissociate the feminine *from* horror. Thus Creed reaches her conclusion that 'the crisis of the master narratives may not necessarily benefit women.'[37] I have already proposed that *Sea Of Love* feminises Frank/Pacino, acknowledges the death of the father and raises up the spectre of the phallic woman. If we follow Creed, we might read these signs as 'gynesis, as written by men, [which] could well prove to be a "new ruse of reason." '[38] In other words Frank's 'feminisation' may signify not an acknowledgement of the loss of the primacy of the paternal signifier, but an attempt by reason to penetrate, or to colonise its own 'unknown', which it has always coded as feminine: as we have seen, this is a dangerous enterprise that involves an identificatory encounter with the phallic mother.

Creed's essay raises the question of whether or not

contemporary masculinity is (finally) coming to terms with its own loss, its own lack, its symbolic castration or whether, rather, what looks like an acknowledgement of loss is, in fact, a defence *against* loss. Juliana Schiesari's *The Gendering of Melancholia*[39] – a work of feminist literary theory – takes up this theme and argues firmly for the latter position. According to Schiesari, the rhetoric of loss and of mourning (for the lost phallus) through which contemporary masculinity arguably speaks itself, forms part of a melancholic tradition through which the masculine subject has 'appropriated a femininity he can never possess, all the while characterising that difference, that lack, as a monstrous, threatening femininity.'[40] In her argument that 'mourn(ing) the phallus may be a way to maintain its centrality'[41], Schiesari draws on Petrach, Tasso, and most notably, Shakespeare, particularly *Hamlet*, whose return, here, brings us back to Pacino and *Sea Of Love*. For Schiesari, Hamlet epitomises the melancholic hero, whose fascination with loss (of the father) and with mortality has its place within a 'politics of lack' which attributes 'value to some subjects who lack but not to others who appear equally "lacking".'[42] Towards the end of *The Gendering Of Melancholia*. Schiesari rounds on Barthes and Eagleton for their misplaced celebratory identifications with Hamlet as postmodernist 'lacking' or 'feminised' hero.[43] '[T]he name of Hamlet is not surprisingly invoked by a number of recent postmodernists' argues Schiesari, before honing her attack: 'More than just a clinical case, more than just depressed, the melancholic thinker has an accredited lack ... one that supposedly speaks for all of us. The question remains, though,' she concludes, 'of *who* can continue to appropriate the notion of lack in such a way as to phallicize its implications.'[44]

Having announced my fascination with Pacino and with *Sea Of Love*, I have tried to reach some understanding of this fascination by placing the star and the film within the context of my own current scholarly preoccupations. Initially, this path led me to emphasise the film's apparent moves away from patriarchal masculinity, thereby recuperating my pleasure within feminist terms. My latter remarks, however, have destabilised that 'progressive' reading of *Sea Of Love* and in so doing, have left me with a 'guilty' pleasure. The question of *Sea Of Love*'s overall relation to patriarchal masculinity is clearly a vexed one, since the film arguably both critiques *and* mourns the loss of masculinity grounded in an identification with the primal Father.[45] Yet – under the sway, perhaps, of an over-zealous conscience – I have moved between condemning or justifying my pleasure in a film which I have constructed alternately as progressive and reactionary, thereby producing arguably reductive readings of the film, while avoiding difficult and yet potentially productive questions about memory, about identification and about context. So far, then, my rehearsals of my own most pressing scholarly questions have moved between a self-punishing alignment of my pleasure with the politically incorrect, and a regrettably priggish alignment of that same pleasure with political correctness. Pam Cook's rigorously honest discussion of her own pleasure in *Raging Bull*[46] suggests that a move beyond these positions *might* be possible. Cook's essay explicitly confronts what she calls 'the[se] more difficult and painful aspects of our desires in relation to our politics' before taking issue with feminist readings of *Raging Bull* which 'saw in its explicit representation of violence as a masculine social disease a radical critique of masculinity.'[47] In place of such readings Cook proposes, rather, that the film's putting of masculinity into crisis, together with its tragic form, invites us to *mourn* rather than to celebrate the loss of that masculinity represented by the young, powerful fighter Jake La Motta/ Robert De Niro. Cook's analysis of her pleasure in *Raging Bull* fully acknowledges the imbrication of her own desire with the film's desire, as she sees it, for the lost phallus. But Cook's reading does simultaneously move to recoup this 'unruly' desire as at least *partially* politically progressive since she argues that Jake's violence and energy, which are the source of his drive for success and his resistance to exploitation, represent, in displaced (and individualised) form, the energy, resistance and victimisation of the Italian-American immigrant community. Thus, to an extent, Cook seems to justify her pleasure in and desire for La Motta/Jake as that of a 'political woman's'[48] complex fascination with a virile working-class hero. The strength of her argument, however, resides elsewhere. Firstly, she reads La Motta not just in relation to an *abstract* 'lost phallus', but also in relation to the representation of a series of historically specific losses experienced by American-Italian immigrants. Secondly, she acknowledges unflinchingly the more 'unacceptable' aspects of her pleasure and identification: her sadistic pleasure in watching La Motta/De Niro 'lose it', as well as her mourning for the lost phallus. However, although La Motta's loss is understood as representing, in displaced form, the losses of an historically specific identity and community, Cook's *own* pleasures are understood as those of either an undifferentiated, or, once, a 'political' woman. This leaves unanswered questions about the *specific* appeal of male stars and performances to *particular* female audiences. Can any more be understood about my own fascination with Frank/Pacino and *Sea Of Love*?

I am further struck, now, by similarities between *Sea Of Love* and *Raging Bull*, which both concern themselves with nostalgia for a 'lost' masculinity of the past and with a central protagonist whose masculinity is seen to fall short of this impossible ideal. But perhaps the similarities go further. In *Sea Of Love*, Pacino's Italian looks remain diegetically 'redundant' but in both films, masculine 'crisis' is allied to 'Italianness'. Cook argues that *Raging Bull* displaces the fury and victimisation of the entire Italian-American community into the individualised story of La Motta/De Niro, but she says little about her pleasure in De Niro/La Motta's 'Italianness'. I wonder to what extent *my* pleasure in Pacino/Frank is tied to the film's siting of masculine crisis in an Italianate body? And I remember stories my father told me of a West End Jewish boy growing up on the streets of Soho and being fed by the Italians at their restaurants' back doors. Stories, too, about Jews passing for Italian and surviving the war. I realise that for me the boundary between 'Italianness' and 'Jewishness' is permeable and that my fascination with Pacino and with *Sea Of Love* can be traced, in part, from a scholarly fascination with representations of the abstract 'loss' of the primal Father, or phallus, to a constellation of memories – or fantasies – of a more concrete, specific and personal nature: in particular those of my raging and failing father's expulsion from the home, and his consequent loss to me. For me, then, Pacino evokes a series of affects associated with Jewishness, failure, loss and my father. Affects that move between triumph over a failing father and sorrow at his loss. Which is not to say that *Sea Of Love*'s nostalgia *is* my nostalgia, but rather that Pacino's looks, together with the film's narrative preoccupations with masculine crisis and the son's relation to the primal Father mesh with my own daughterly concerns.[49] Clearly I am pointing to a complex process. The diminutive, failing Pacino/Frank certainly reminds me of my own father. My fascination, then is surely in part that of the Oedipal daughter. But it seems that I also find a point of narcissistic identification with Frank/Pacino. To a degree, I align my own wish for a more perfect father with the film's desire for a redeemed masculinity. But perhaps the subject of my narcissistic identification has not yet been exhausted: perhaps, indeed, I also make a more typically *feminine* identification with Frank/Pacino's 'falling short'.[50] Femininity's narcissism has been described, after all, as 'damaged', since women can never live up to the ideal of femininity circulated throughout the cultural domain.[51] And if one response to damaged narcissism is to recoup its pain as (feminine) masochistic pleasure, that same damaged narcissism can also lead to sadism, which triumphs at another's pain. Here, then, I seem to insert my own daughterly and more typically feminine responses into the film's address. I am touching on broad questions about the relations between daughterly spectatorship and representations of ethnically differentiated masculinity. Recent theorisations of the ways in which ethnicity plays against the patriarchal construction of masculinity, point to the gradations of masculine power and powerlessness that ethnicity effects.[52] Perhaps, then, the narcissistic aspects of my fascination with Frank/Pacino are enabled less by spectatorial 'cross-dressing'[53] and more by the 'feminisation' of masculinity that ethnicity and, in my own reading of Sea Of Love, 'Jewishness' produces? Thus, my sadistic pleasure in Frank/Pacino's losses vies with my joy at his comeback. And though I *could* move now to align these pleasures with a 'politically correct' 'cross-ethnic' identification with struggle and victimisation – I'd rather propose that such feminist 'housework' would merely tidy up the messier issues of fathers and daughters and the *daughter*'s longing for her father.

When Richard Dyer strove to analyse the appeal of Judy Garland to a gay audience he stressed, amongst other traits, her capacity to 'come back': through the oft-reported pain, the drugs and the drink, she sang of and promised triumph to an audience who recognised their own struggles in hers.[54] Dyer does not countenance that a degree of sadism, of pleasure in Garland's pain, might vie with these celebrations, making her comebacks yet more poignant, perhaps. Freud's dictums concerning the remorse that follows upon triumph are borne out, however, by my own fascination with Frank/Pacino's 'failings' – a fascination that is undeniably tied to both triumph and mourning. Like Garland, Pacino rises from the flames, promising, perhaps, that fathers – and my father – will too.

With thanks to Lily Todd for suggesting that I might enjoy Sea Of Love, to Ann Scott for sharing her thoughts on the film and to Amal Treacher for discussing and encouraging the development of this essay.

NOTES

1 For analyses of stars and their appeal to cinemagoers see: Richard Dyer, *Stars*, British Film Institute, London, 1979; Richard Dyer, *Heavenly Bodies: Film Stars and Society*, Macmillan, Basingstoke, 1987; Christine Gledhill (ed.), *Stardom: Industry of Desire*, Routledge, London, 1991. Jackie Stacey, *Star Gazing: Hollywood Cinema and Female Spectatorship*, Routledge, London, 1993, opens up one avenue for investigating the specific appeal of particular stars by combining ethnographic research with theories of spectatorship.

2 This essay's particular focus on Pacino precludes more than the acknowledgement of *Sea Of Love*'s reworking of the *femme fatale*. For one brief discussion of this topic see Nickolas Pappas, 'A Sea Of Love Among Men', *Film Criticism*, Volume 14, Number 3, Spring 1990, pp14-26. Pappas' discussion focuses in the main on *Sea Of Love*'s homosexuality and its address to a male spectator. The question of the film's sexual politics in relation to its representation of Woman and its address to a female spectator has yet to be more fully explored.

3 Richard Dyer points to the variable fit between star-image and character, and argues that a very close fit between the two, such as I am proposing here, occurs only relatively infrequently; see Dyer, 1979, *op.cit.*, pp145-9.

4 Critical opinion appears to have unanimously heralded Pacino's performance in *Sea Of Love* as a come-back; see, for instance, Laurent Vachaud, *Positif* Number 348, February 1990, p60; *Screen International*, No. 722, 16 September 1989, p6; *Variety*, 13 September 1989, p18; Brian Case, in *Time Out*, Number 1014, 24 January 1990, p30, whose jubilant 'welcome back, Al', seems to have spoken for everybody.

5 Classical Hollywood strategies for 'adding' height to shorter male stars have included low-angle shots and raised floors – though it should be remembered that such strategies do not inevitably align *power* with the figure in the shot. See David Bordwell and Kristin Thompson, *Film Art: An Introduction*, Third Edition, McGraw Hill, New York, 1990, p177.

In mainstream cinema, the 'small guy' and the 'sidekick' have been mainstays against whom the hero has been 'measured'. For one analysis of the identificatory processes between such characters and the male spectator see Ian Green, 'Malefunction', *Screen*, Volume 25 Numbers 4-5, July-October 1984, pp36-48. What is striking about *Sea Of Love* – and about the smallness of Pacino – is that the film offers us no more typically heroic figure against whom to measure him (though tall, Sherman/John Goodman's sheer flabbiness distances him from the classical male hero). The diminutive Frank/Pacino emerges, then as the 'measure' of masculinity.

6 Laurent Vachaud argues that Pacino's roles share an impulse for self-destruction which can 'destroy a life's work at a stroke.' Vachaud, 1990, *op.cit.*, p61, (translation mine).

7 *Sea Of Love*'s connotative associating of sex with death has been read by at least one critic in relation to cultural anxieties about AIDS; see Anne Billson, *Monthly Film Bulletin*, Volume 57, Number 674, March 1990, p77.

8 Steve Neale has associated silence or the absence of language with the narcissism of patriarchal masculinity's identification with an ideal ego, and argues that language acquisition produces 'symbolic castration'; see Steve Neale, 'Masculinity As Spectacle', *Screen*, Volume 24, Number 6, November-December 1983, p7.

9 In his essay 'The Storyteller', Walter Benjamin nostalgically contrasts lost forms of oral storytelling with the rise of the novel. Benjamin's essay mourns the loss of the storyteller's particular authority which he associates with the knowledge of death and with the authority lent by natural history; see Walter Benjamin, *Illuminations: Essays and Reflections*, Hannah Arendt, (ed), Schocken, New York, 1968, pp83-109. Benjamin's essay lends itself to a re-reading in relation to the theories of masculinity I rehearse in this essay, but his nostalgically evoked 'storyteller' should not, perhaps, be conflated with 'chastened' or non-patriarchal masculinity since this would conflate the capacity to acknowledge death with the capacity to embrace *difference*.

10 Here I use the term 'symbolic castration' to refer to the Lacanian-inspired understanding of the experience of entering into culture and language as an experience of loss, in relation to narcissism's fantasies of self-sufficiency. The acquisition of language and subjectivity entails the acknowledgement of the separation of the name of the father from its bearer but under patriarchy, the father's and hence the son's 'symbolic castration', once acknowledged, is constantly disavowed through processes of projection and denial. This essay now goes on to ask whether *Sea Of Love* undoes these processes.

11 Here I specify 'white US masculinity', since the distribution of 'feminine' and 'masculine' attributes between male and female stars has been shown to vary between national cinemas. For an analysis that foregrounds the difference between classical Hollywood's and French cinema's male stars, see Ginette Vincendeau, 'Gérard Depardieu: the axiom of contemporary French cinema', *Screen*, Volume 34 Number 4, Winter 1993, pp343-361, especially pp356 onwards.

12 Sigmund Freud, *Totem and Taboo*, Routledge, London, 1960 (first published 1913).

13 Marrying within, rather than outside, one's own tribe.

14 See especially Freud, 1960, *op.cit.*, p143.

15 *Ibid.*, p148.

16 *Ibid.*

17 *Ibid.*, p149.

18 Steve Neale notes the nostalgic tone with which mainstream cinema mourns the loss of masculine narcissism; see Neale, 1983, *op.cit.*, pp9-10. In the main, psychoanalysis, and particularly Lacan has dwelt upon femininity's imbrication with nostalgia; see Jane Gallop, *Reading Lacan*, Cornell University Press, Ithaca and London, 1985, pp145-6; see also Susannah Radstone, 'Remembering Ourselves: Memory, Writing and the Female Self', in Penny Florence and Deidre Reynolds, (eds), *Feminist Subjects: Multi Media*, Manchester University Press, Manchester, 1994.

19 See Laura Mulvey, 'Visual Pleasure and Narrative Cinema', *Screen* Vol. 16 No. 3 1975, pp6-18.

20 Neale refers here to McCabe's Lacanian-inspired summary of Freud's tracing of the three stages of Oedipal development; see Steve Neale, 1982, *op.cit.*, esp. pp49-50. In the first stage, the male child is dependent upon the mother and strives to be what she wants. In the second stage, the child recognises sexual difference and imagines himself to be the phallus that she lacks, before acknowledging that the mother's desire is for the father who is imagined as 'the phallus incarnate'. In the third stage, the little boy would acknowledge his father's limitations – the father would then be perceived as *himself* lacking.

21 Neale, 1982, *op.cit.*, p50.

22 Colin McCabe quoted in Neale, 1982, *op.cit.*, p5; (emphasis mine).

23 *Ibid.*, p52. In a later essay, Neale writes that ' ... male homosexuality is constantly present as undercurrent, as a potentially troubling aspect of many films and genres, but one that is dealt with obliquely, symptomatically, and that has to be repressed.' Neale, 1983, *op.cit.*, p15.)

24 See note 9 above.

25 ' ... the achievement of an Oedipal resolution in accordance with the principles of a patriarchal society is dependent upon a repression not only of women and of female desire, but also of male homosexual desire.' Neale, 1982, *op.cit.*, p52.

26 Pappas, 1990, *op.cit.*, dwells on *Sea of Love*'s arguable homosexuality. Pappas associates this homosexuality with male narcissism and fear of women – a reading of the film's sexual politics which I find reductive.

27 See Sigmund Freud, 'Leonardo da Vinci and a Memory of his Childhood', *Standard Edition of the Complete Psychological Works of Sigmund Freud*, James Strachey, (ed), Hogarth Press, London, 1953-73, pp59-137; first published 1910.

28 As Neale, 1983, *op.cit.*, has argued, homosexuality figures as a troubling undercurrent in many films and genres, and particularly, perhaps, in those films and genres which exclude women from their narratives. Typically, the repression of homosexuality has been associated with violence between male characters, as well as with its pejorative denial. Certain films, particularly male buddy movies,

blur the boundary, however, between pejoration and titillation. My point is that *Sea Of Love* seems to shift the play off between these terms heavily towards titillation.

29 My quote refers to the title of Pam Cook's essay: 'Masculinity in Crisis', *Screen*, Volume 23 Numbers 3-4, September/October 1982, pp38-46 from which I draw in the latter sections of this essay. Several discussions of contemporary masculinity's arguable crisis have informed this essay: Steven Frosh, *Sexual Difference: Masculinity and Psychoanalysis*, Routledge, London, 1994, analyses contemporary masculinity from a psychoanalytic viewpoint informed by both Lacanian and Kleinian perspectives. Lynne Segal's *Slow Motion: Changing Masculinities, Changing Men*, Virago, London, 1990, is a feminist analysis of contemporary masculinity informed by both sociological and psychoanalytic theory. Alice Jardine's *Gynesis: Configurations of Woman and Modernity*, Cornell University Press, Ithaca, 1985, analyses masculinity's apparent contemporary 'feminisation' in the context of debates concerning feminism and postmodernism.

30 Neale, 1983, *op.cit.*, p6. Here, Neale argues that the power and omnipotence of the classical male hero is generally tested and qualified.

31 See particularly Segal, 1990, *op.cit.*, 'Beyond Gender Hierarchy: Can Men Change?', chapter 10, pp272-319.

32 Craig Owens, 'The Discourse of Others: Feminists and Postmodernism', in Hal Foster, (ed), *Postmodern Culture*, Pluto, London, 1985, p65.

33 Barbara Creed, 'From Here To Modernity: Feminism and Postmodernism', *Screen*, Volume 28, Number 2, 1987, p51.

34 *Ibid.*

35 *Ibid.*, p52. Creed is here following Alice Jardine's argument: Jardine, 1985, *op.cit.*, p67. Jardine's point is that we should approach the current crisis not as a crisis in male authority, but as the loss of the paternal signifier, which has, up until its loss, *stabilised meaning* and legitimated knowledge.

36 Jardine coins the term 'gynesis' to refer to what she regards as a new 'ruse of reason' in which (principally French) writers and theorists have reincorporated and reconceptualised the non-knowledges of Enlightenment master narratives. Jardine points out that such spaces have always been coded 'as feminine, as woman.' Jardine, 1985, *op.cit.*, pp22-25.

37 Creed, 1987, *op.cit.*, p66.

38 *Ibid.*, p67, quoting Jardine, 1985, *op.cit.*, p22.

39 Juliana Schiesari, *The Gendering of Melancholia: Feminism, Psychoanalysis and the Symbolics of Loss in Renaissance Literature*, Cornell University Press, Ithaca, 1992.

40 *Ibid.*, p213.

41 *Ibid.*, p265.

42 *Ibid.*, pix.

43 *Ibid.*, p236 onwards.

44 *Ibid.*, p265.

45 This raises the question of whether the film invites identification with its mourning for the primal Father as well as with its arguable critique of such an identification. Ian Green critiques Neale, 1983, *op.cit.*, for his implication that identification excludes critique; see Ian Green, 'Malefunction', in *Screen*, Volume 25 Numbers 4-5, July-October 1984, p41. I would agree with Green's comment that 'this is a stark division to make' (*Ibid*), though in the context of my reading of *Sea Of Love*, this remains assertive and requires further textual substantiation.

46 Cook, 1982, *op.cit.*

47 *Ibid.*, p39.

48 *Ibid.*, p42.

49 Though feminist film criticism has focused on the cinematic representation of father/daughter relationships, (see, for instance, Ginette Vincendeau, 'Family Plots: the fathers and daughters of French cinema', *Sight and Sound*, Volume 3, Issue 11, March 1992, pp14-17, few analyses have foregrounded the question of daughterly spectatorship in relation to fathers, (or indeed mothers).

50 Neale points to the sense of inadequacy screen 'ideal egos' may prompt in both male and female spectators; Neale, 1983, *op.cit.*, p8. Ian Green, however, draws attention to the triumphant, self-pitying identifications 'that some men make with the "little men" of film', who stalk male stars; Green, 1984, *op.cit.*, p43.

51 See, for instance, Ros Coward, 'The Look', in Ros Coward, *Female Desire: Women's Sexuality Today*, Paladin, London, 1984, pp75-82.

52 Steven Frosh, follows Segal, 1990, *op.cit.*, in calling for an exploration of the emergence and experience of different masculinities: 'Recognition of "different masculinities" means, for instance, acknowledgement of the specificity of experiences of men who are black or white, homosexual, bisexual or heterosexual, Jewish or Gentile – powerless or powerful.' Frosh, 1994, *op.cit.*, p92.

53 See Laura Mulvey, 1975, *op.cit.*

54 Richard Dyer, 1987, *op.cit.*, pp141-194.

Oscar Micheaux's Multifaceted Portrayals of the African–American Male: The *Good*, The *Bad*, and The *Ugly*

Charlene Regester

The African–American, Oscar Micheaux (1884–1951), a pioneer in film-making, rightfully occupies an honourable place in the history of American culture, and more specifically, in the history of black art forms within that culture. Struggling against incredible odds, he rose to prominence as a writer and film-maker. Micheaux completed seven novels, most of which were published by his own company established to circumvent the obstacles created by white publishers reluctant to publish works by black writers. Most importantly, for the purposes of this essay, he produced nearly fifty films between 1918 and 1948.

Micheaux remains a legendary figure in African–American cinema. During an era in which black film-makers were rare and barely survived, let alone challenged the establishment, he dared to produce films that portrayed black life from his own perspective – one in direct contrast to that provided by Hollywood. Micheaux addressed issues such as interracial relationships, intra-racial prejudice, incestuous relationships, lynching, racial unrest, the intimidatory tactics of anti-black groups such as, the Ku Klux Klan (in a period when such groups enjoyed free reign, if not tacit approval) that were not only controversial within white society but also problematic for members of his own race.

Although Micheaux became one of the more prolific black film-makers of inter-war years, the basis for his success was laid by the efforts of fellow black film-makers and would-be film-makers in earlier years. William Foster of Chicago, Illinois established the Will Foster Moving Picture Company around 1910 and produced several all-black cast films,[1] while Noble and George P. Johnson founded the Lincoln Motion Picture Company in Los Angeles, California, in 1916 and went on to produce a number of quality African–American films.[2] Peter P. Jones experimented with film-making in 1914,[3] Hunter C. Haynes organised the Hunter C. Haynes Photo Play Co. around the same time,[4] Sidney P. Dones was associated with the Democracy Film Corporation in Los Angeles in 1920,[5] Leigh Whipper formed the Renaissance Film Company in 1921, which specialised in the production of black newsreels,[6] and Virgil Williams started the Royal Gardens Studio and Motion Picture Production Company in about 1919.[7]

Some of these early African–American film-makers paved the way for Micheaux, but some also competed with him. It should be noted, however, that for the most part, other black film-makers presented considerably less competition than did white film-makers because black audiences were attracted to the relatively slick productions of the well financed white film companies. Even in the category of ethnic films, it was white men such as Robert Levy of the Real Film Corporation, and Richard E. Norman, Sr. of the Norman Film Manufacturing Company who capitalised on the profits generated by black audiences who wanted to witness black images on the screen.[8]

One of the great and lasting contributions of Micheaux's films resulted from his determination to reshape the portrayal of the black male. Most white Hollywood productions stereotyped black males as mentally inept, indigent, non-threatening and laughter-provoking characters – the 'Stepin Fetchits' of American society. Stepin Fetchit was the stage and screen name of the African–American actor, Lincoln Theodore Monroe Andrew Perry, who played roles that demeaned and distorted African–Americans. Stepin Fetchit was not only the name he adopted but it also became a tag for stereotyping the self-degrading caricaturing roles in which many black males were depicted[9] and, as such, was often used in motion pictures to provide comic relief for white audiences. These despicable portrayals included drawling speech, slow and lazy movements as well as scatter-brained and shiftless demeanour. Fetchit, according to film critic Donald Bogle, was the epitome of the 'coon' stereotype who in his display of 'coon antics' reinforced the comforting notion among whites that black males were satisfied with the exploitation, degradation, and secondary status to which they were relegated in American society.[10] At the same time and in stark contrast, white film-makers also perpetuated a myth of black supermacho qualities as ones to be both resented and feared by whites, and more specifically, by white women.[11]

Taken in the context of the American racial scene of the 1920s and 1930s, Micheaux's challenging of this grotesque stereotype of the African–American male within one of America's fastest growing industries was bold and audacious. Add to that his confrontational stand within his own racial group, offering not just a 'good' black male to counter the Hollywood image, but rather a portrayal of 'real' black males, some 'good', some bad, some a little of each, and Micheaux stands out as a man who dared to challenge one-dimensional portrayals of the African–American male.

Even as Micheaux expressed his concern regarding the denial to blacks of power, prestige, social, economic, and political status in American society and cinema, he frequently conveyed his discontent with his fellow blacks, accusing them of not assuming responsibility for their own fate in life. He argued that African–Americans must strive to elevate themselves, a point of view for which he was harshly criticised because it seemed that he did not sufficiently acknowledge the fact that discriminatory practices which limited opportunities for African–Americans were an integral part of American society. Micheaux, however, contended that blacks must persist in their struggle to ameliorate themselves in spite of the many obstacles and disadvantages they faced. In Micheaux's semi-autobiographical book *The Conquest* (1913), he stated, 'My persistent declarations [were] that there were not enough competent colored people to grasp the many opportunities that presented themselves, and that if white people could possess such nice homes, wealth, and luxuries, so in time, could the colored people.'[12] Buying into the American myth that anyone can make it, he added, 'One of the greatest tasks of my life has been to convince a certain class of my racial acquaintances that a colored man can be anything.'[13] Micheaux has been accused of being preoccupied with middle-class values, frequently a sub-theme in his films – an attitude which brought him into disfavour with many of his own race. It was felt that he was insensitive to the plight of many African–Americans during an era when they found few employment opportunities in the urban centres to which they had migrated in the early 1900s, when they were faced with race riots and lynchings, when they were either denied entrance into the military or forced to assume secondary military status.[14] Micheaux did not see these as insurmountable obstacles, believing that after viewing middle-class lifestyles and positive values, cinema audiences would endorse and emulate them and thereby, strive harder to 'improve' themselves.

Micheaux was a firm believer in teaching by example. In another semi-autobiography, *The Homesteader* (1917), he stated, ' "It is not that I care so much for the fruits of my labor; but if I could actually succeed, it would mean so much to the credit of a multitude of others ... Others who need the example.' " ... His race needed examples; they needed instances of successes.'[15]

Masculinity has a very different meaning for black males than it has for non-black ones although black manhood is inextricably tied to white manhood or masculinity, particularly in a society where black men have remained virtually powerless and their position, power, and status have often been dictated by the dominant power structures of white men. The gendered subjectivity and identity of the African–American male is marked by his historical as well as his social experience. Various attempts have been made to define the masculinity of black males; Leonard Kriegel, for example, in 1979 asserted, 'It all seems so clear – the black man declaring himself a man, his positioning himself beyond the boundaries of white America, his growing contempt for the styles of masculine reality that white Americans have apparently embraced, his struggling to achieve a sense of realistic terms and possible new ventures in which his manhood, as he defines it, becomes the gauge by which others measure their own adequacy as men.'[16] Richard Majors and Janet Billson, argued that African–American men have defined their manhood based on criteria defined by white males which includes serving as breadwinner, provider, procreator, and protector. They contend that, unfortuntely, black males have not had consistent access to the same opportunities and thereby, exert their manhood to achieve 'success' within such a framework.[17] Robert Staples, by contrast, viewed the black male as in conflict with the normative definition of masculinity and noted that few black males had been able to achieve in the same manner as white males. According to Staples, masculinity for the white male has often implied a certain autonomy over or control of his environment;

something which has remained virtually non-existent for the black male.[18]

To define black masculinity requires examining blacks as they relate to the social, political, and economic forces of control within the dominant society. For the purposes of this discussion, black masculinity needs to include a desire for power, which has historically been denied; a desire to express their sexuality in a positive manner, which has been denied or subverted (i.e. being reduced to purely sexual beings or being associated with violence) to pacify white males' insecurities and fears regarding their own sexuality; and a desire to exert control in an environment beyond their control. Black masculinity, according to Kobena Mercer and Isaac Julien, is a 'subordinated' masculinity that has surfaced, been popularised, and perpetuated by motion pictures.[19] Masculinity for black males also has another dimension, particularly when virtually powerless black males internalise views regarding manhood as defined by white male standards and their masculinity manifests itself in the development of 'macho' attitudes. According to Mercer and Julien, 'macho' attitudes refers to those assumed by black males who project themselves as being tough, in control, and independent:

> 'Macho' may be regarded as a form of misdirected or 'negative' resistance, as it is shaped by the challenge to the hegemony of the socially dominant white male, yet it assumes a form which is in turn oppressive to black women, children and indeed, to black men themselves, as it can entail self-destructive acts and attitudes.[20]

The representations on (white) Hollywood screens of black masculinity portray 'the rise to fame of the black man through the use of his body in sports; the hysterical treatment of the mulatto, the product of a mingling of blood [in one] who lives out in ... his body the racial confusions of a society; the importance of the rape motif, power relations between the races realised through power relations between bodies, black men overpowering white women's bodies in rape, white men overpowering black men's bodies in castration and lynching.'[21] Consistent with these views, in an examination of the African–American screen image, Mark Reid has argued that the general perception was that 'The mass audience could not accept black sexuality unless it was portrayed in a violent or primitive manner.'[22]

Among the earliest black males to appear on the motion

structural similarities between the two genres. Linked by common ideologies of gender, romantic comedy and melodrama are, after all, the primary narrative forms available for telling the stories of women's lives; both can be considered feminised in their address to women and in their traditionally marginalised critical status. What is more surprising, however – and disturbing – is the increasing use of melodrama to tell the story of *men's* lives and *male* suffering – and to tell it straight. Underlying the seemingly innocuous fantasies of these recent comedies is another, darker scenario that recasts the story of the struggle for women's rights into a melodrama of male victims and female villains. This scenario not only recuperates areas of culture traditionally associated with femininity to use *against* women, but, as a conceptual structure, it also extends well beyond the local cineplex.

To understand this current turn in romantic comedy, it is helpful to recall briefly the romantic comedy of the classical Hollywood period, which was organised around a couple defined by 'equality' or even female dominance.[1] In such films as *Bringing Up Baby* (Howard Hawks, US, 1938), *Ball of Fire* (Howard Hawks, US, 1941) and *The Lady Eve* (Preston Sturges, US, 1941), male authority is something to be mocked, and masculinity the subject of laughter rather than pathos. As spectators, we are rarely asked to sympathise with whatever humiliation, chastisement or suffering the male hero endures, because it is usually so well-deserved, a necessary step toward the more fluid, more fully realised sexuality he – and the couple – ultimately achieve.[2] In contrast, the post-classical comedy has increasingly privileged the subjectivity of its male heroes over that of its heroines, appropriating female suffering – and the feminised genre of melodrama – in the service of a beleaguered and victimised masculinity.

The origins of this shift lie, I believe, in the widespread assault to structures of masculine authority that occurred in the 1960s – the Civil Rights movement, the revival of feminism, the Vietnam War, the Pill, Stonewall and the demand for gay rights, Watergate, inflation – all of which rattled institutions built on racial and sexual privilege to such an extent that masculinity could no longer serve as a safe subject for comedy. As a result, romantic comedy began to display a greater uneasiness about romance itself, evolving in the 1970s into what Frank Krutnik has described as the 'nervous romance', a romantic comedy that pushes toward melodramatic conclusions, combining nostalgia for a time of 'simpler' romance with a wariness about the possibilities of the heterosexual couple.[3] This wariness has hardly dissipated in the 1990s, when *Sleepless in Seattle* can defer not only sexual intimacy between the romantic couple, as in the classical comedies, but virtually any contact at all until the final moments of the film. The nervous romance is exemplified by such films as *Annie Hall* and *Manhattan* (Woody Allen, US, 1977 and 1979) and *Starting Over* (Alan Pakula, US, 1979), and perhaps no figure stands as a more telling example of the infusion of male melodrama into romantic comedy than Woody Allen. If certain elements of Allen's persona (intellectual, introspective, Jewish, East Coast, urban) have limited the scope of his popularity, the essence of that persona still taps into broader cultural anxieties about romance and masculinity itself; the neuroses he has examined so relentlessly in his work, from *Annie Hall* and *Manhattan* through *Husbands and Wives* (US, 1992), merely exaggerate more commonly held fears about the impact on men of changes in the status of women.

At first glance, Allen's feminised persona appears to represent just the kind of liberation from a repressive masculinity classical romantic comedy valued. However, the melodramatised male raises troubling issues regarding gender. As Juliana Schiesari argues in her study of the historical gendering of melancholy, the melodramatised male, or what she describes as '*homo melancholicus*, the melancholic *man*', stands both in reaction to and complicity with patriarchy.[4] He appropriates a suffering or loss more commonly associated with the feminine, then recuperates that loss into a 'privileged position within literary, philosophical and artistic canons'.[5] Whereas in a woman melancholy is coded as *disabling* and pathological, in men it 'enables' the transformation of apparent loss into male power 'in the guise of moral conscience, artistic creativity, or heightened sensitivity'.[6] The apparent feminisation of the sensitive male does not undo sexual difference, then, but reauthorises male power by denying women 'the very specificity of their being'.[7] In other words, his sensitivity more often reflects an attentiveness to his own needs than to those of women.

Such a male appropriation of femininity, feminised genres, and feminism itself has become especially pernicious in the late 1980s and early 1990s, a period that has occasionally been described as 'post feminist', as if gender inequity had finally been eradicated. In *Feminism Without Women*, Tania Modleski cites Stanley Cavell as an example of a critic who appears to be engaging positively with feminist concerns but may in fact be doing just the opposite. Cavell's work on melodrama, she writes, is motivated by the desire to 'preserve' philosophy as he knows it' by assimilating the issues raised by melodrama and feminism into the 'feminine' mind of a male philosopher: 'In poetically invoking the male philosopher's "melancholy inexpressiveness", Cavell solicits our recognition of the male as the superior candidate for our feeling of pathos, the melodramatic sentiment par excellence.'[8]

Similarly, Woody Allen and the other melodramatised males of the post-classical romantic comedy use their feminisation to bolster their own authority, which they then invoke to 'instruct' women about relationships, romance and femininity itself. Allen's feminisation is different from that of the male leads in *Bringing Up Baby, Ball of Fire* and *Lady Eve* because it occurs at the expense of women; the subjectivity of his male heroes monopolises his films. In Rob Reiner's *When Harry Met Sally ...* (US, 1989), a remake of Allen's *Annie Hall*, it is Harry/Billy Crystal, not Sally, who shares his thoughts with the audience through the film's only voice-over. Moreover, while popularising sympathetic representations of Jewish culture, Allen (and Crystal) limit that sympathy to men; it is not Jewish women who are shown to be the object of the Jewish man's desire, but Gentiles, played by Diane Keaton, Mariel Hemingway, Mia Farrow, and Meg Ryan.

In these films as well as others, such as *Broadcast News* (James Brooks, US, 1987), *Green Card* and *Frankie and Johnny* (Penny Marshall, US, 1991), men educate women, not the reverse. Compare, for example, Hopsy's sermons to the Lady Eve about the nature of love and forgiveness, or Peter Warne/Clark Gable's speeches in *It Happened One Night* (Frank Capra, US, 1934) about what he is looking for in a woman, with similar examples from post-classical romantic comedies. Whereas the hero of the classical romantic comedy is treated with an affectionate irony for his presumptiousness and naiveté, little irony surrounds the melodramatised male of the post-classical comedy. If he suffers, we understand and sympathise, for he is not neurotic, merely sensitive. If she suffers, she is simply neurotic – like the hard-driven TV producer in *Broadcast News*, or the order-obsessed woman who loves her garden in *Green Card*, or the alienated waitress in *Frankie and Johnny*. Each of these heroines resists her male suitor less out of her inherent independence or recognition of his need to change than out of something wounded or undeveloped in *her* – qualities which allow the hero to demonstrate his greater wisdom, charm, or sensitivity.

Pretty Woman presents an especially instructive example of the influence of melodrama on the post-classical romantic comedy because it so faithfully adheres to the conventions of classical romantic comedy, yet to such different ends, and because of its enormous popularity. The only film to exceed its box office in 1990 was Jerry Zucker's *Ghost*, which went to even more extraordinary lengths to melodramatise its male hero.

Beginning with a montage of shots of money changing hands (first plastic 'gold' coins in a magic act at an upper-class party, then real money in a drug transaction on the street), *Pretty Woman* displays a preoccupation with money and social class that is unusual in the post-classical romantic comedy. In this way it recalls the comedies of the classical period, which played the conflicts of romantic love against those of social class. In films such as *It Happened One Night* and *My Man Godfrey*, class fuels narrative conflict by exaggerating the obstacles between the heterosexual couple and heightening the stakes in their conflict. At the same time, the inevitable formation of the couple across class boundaries obscures or mediates real differences and divisions between social classes.

The erosion of an overt discourse concerning class in post-war America has undoubtedly influenced the shape of the post-classical comedy. Yet while that discourse has disappeared, class-related social tensions hardly have, especially during the 1980s, when government policy fostered runaway corporate greed and widened the gap between rich and poor. By returning to the class issues that initially shaped the genre during the Depression of the 1930s, *Pretty Woman* accomplishes much of the ideological work of the earlier films, using the couple to cover up class differences. Indeed, the increasing feminisation of poverty gives added weight to the film's use of the Cinderella fairy tale. At the same time, however, the film's use of melodrama limits its exploitation of the genre's potential regarding gender. *Pretty Woman* ties masculinity with economic prowess. Furthermore instead of mobilising laughter to question both, it props them up by eliciting sympathy for the victimised male.

Throughout, *Pretty Woman* displays an awareness of its relation to classical romantic comedy. A shot of Carole Lombard's star on Hollywood Boulevard brings to mind her performances in such romantic comedies as *Twentieth Century* (Howard Hawks, US, 1934) and *Nothing Sacred* (William Wellman, US, 1937), while Ralph Bellamy's name on the credits recalls his perennial role in the earlier films as doltish rival to the romantic male lead. *Pretty Woman*, like its antecedents, derives both comedy and conflict from the wide social and temperamental gap between its romantic leads. Edward is an enormously wealthy corporate tycoon who, like the male heroes of the classical comedies, hides his real emotional needs behind an obsession with work. Vivian is a small-town girl turned small-time prostitute. While vastly separated by wealth, Edward and Vivian share similar attitudes towards money: neither jokes about it and both 'screw people' for it. After a chance meeting, Edward hires Vivian to attend social events with him for a week because his lawyer has warned him that he needs to convey a friendlier image. By the end of the week, Vivian has shed her trampy-looking appearance to become an elegant companion for Edward, Edward has decided that he will no longer break apart vulnerable companies but rebuild them, and the two have fallen in love. Vivian won't settle for anything less than marriage, and after some hesitation, Edward agrees.

In several ways, the film's characterisation of Edward recalls the heroes of the classical romantic comedy. He is stiff, subdued, serious. He can't drive a car with a gear lever, she can. He's afraid of heights, most significantly, of course, emotional ones. Yet the film does not ironise his character or poke fun at the stereotypes of masculinity he embodies. Instead, by taking him, his pain and his power so seriously, it melodramatises him. We learn that Edward's ambition is fueled by anger at his wealthy father, who abandoned him as a child: the first company Edward took over was his father's. He tells Vivian that he was so emotionally wounded by his father that he needed $10,000 of therapy before he could express his anger. Even then, he could not bring himself to be with his father when he died only a month or so earlier.

The film's most significant use of melodrama is not its sentimentalised treatment of Edward's pain, however, but its substitution of moral judgments for comedic ones. The flaws in Edward's masculinity – his obsession with a cruel and sterile kind of work – express themselves through something that is not foolish but powerful, dangerous, and therefore evil. By associating those flaws with aspects of capitalism gone wrong – aspects readily correctible with romantic love – the film affirms that capitalism itself is ultimately right. *Pretty Woman* distinguishes between two kinds of capitalism: the bad, destructive kind that only 'makes money' – plastic coins – and the good kind that 'makes *things*'. Edward has made his fortune the evil 1980s way by preying on weak companies. Yet the film foists those evils onto its most odious characters, Edward's father and his unregenerate lawyer Phil, whose status as a melodramatic villain rather than a comic buffoon is confirmed when he humiliates then violently attacks Vivian. The rape is thwarted only by Edward's last-minute rescue. Edward, on the other hand, becomes the capitalist with a human face, and a handsome one at that. When he decides to go into partnership with the righteous but vulnerable shipbuilder played by Ralph Bellamy (to build destroyers, in an irony that is appropriate but probably unintended), he gains a new, good father.

By setting its Cinderella story against the backdrop of a melodrama of good and evil businessmen, *Pretty Woman* conveys overwhelmingly reassuring messages about class. First, Vivian's transformation shows that the signs of class – upper or lower – are as easily taken up or discarded as a borrowed credit card. After one week with Edward's card, Vivian seems born to wear the casual upper-class attire of designer blazer and jeans we see her in at the end of the film.[9] And Edward's transformation shows that after one week with the right woman, even the most heartless of businessmen can be redeemed. Yet Edward's reform exacts no cost to the couple, especially no financial cost. *Pretty Woman* diverges from the classical comedies in that it unabashedly trumpets the pleasures of being rich as ends in themselves. For example, the lovers travel by private jet to see a performance of *La Traviata*, an opera about a love affair between a courtesan and an aristocrat. The film borrows one scene in the sequence directly from *Moonstruck* (Norman Jewison, US, 1987), when the performance moves Vivian (in a gown even more brilliantly red than Cher's/Loretta's) to tears.[10] Yet, while opera is infused formally and thematically throughout *Moonstruck* to reveal the lovers' capacity for passion and to comment on the forms that passion takes, in *Pretty Woman* the trip to the opera provides an opportunity to display how elegantly Vivian wears jewels, how readily she acquires the taste of high culture, and how extravagantly but tastefully Edward spends his money. With its loving depictions of the life Edward can provide Vivian, *Pretty Woman* eroticises money more than true love.

When Edward tells Vivian at the end of the film that he is the prince rescuing the princess, she immediately replies that she is rescuing him right back. This exchange appears to suggest a redistribution of power between the sexes comparable to what occurred in the classical comedies. However, Edward's masculine authority remains intact. *Pretty Woman* affirms a masculinity defined as the ability to make money, and in this film, money can be evil but never foolish. The same is true of masculinity. Edward becomes a 'nurturing' businessman, but the film has too much respect for his economic prowess, and the masculinity so closely bound to it, to allow him to play the fool.

Unlike *Green Card* and *Broadcast News*, *Pretty Woman* does not lay the obstacles to the couple's union in the female character's 'neurotic' desire to be independent. Instead, its conflict is conventionally Oedipal; Edward's father is the real villain, and Vivian's desire for marriage places her squarely in the realm of the traditional woman. However, bolder examples abound in contemporary culture of melodrama being used to elicit sympathy for men by portraying them as victims – especially of *women*, or of the movement to separate men (especially white, professional men) from their disproportionate hold on social and cultural power. During the late 1980s, a period of vigorous backlash against feminism, films such as *Fatal Attraction* (Adrian Lyne, US, 1987) and *Misery* (Rob Reiner, US, 1990) have taken the melodramatised male well beyond the confines of comedy into genres where he can be terrorised and literally tortured by powerful women who also happen to be insane.

Two recent and highly publicised 'real life' cases have demonstrated even more distressingly the social currency of the structure I have described above. In 1992-93, Woody Allen's relation to a melodramatised masculinity spilled over from cinema to personal life, when his affair with a stepdaughter was made public – an affair which echoed the May-December romances Allen has examined in such films as *Manhattan* and *Husbands and Wives*. His long-term lover Mia Farrow then accused him of incest with another, younger daughter. Throughout the lengthy and angry battle in the media and courts that followed, Allen couched his case in terms of melodrama, presenting himself as an innocent victim of a woman driven mad by jealousy. Allen's strategy was similar to the one used a year earlier in the fall of 1991, when Clarence Thomas answered Anita Hill's charges of sexual harassment in televised hearings before the US Senate on his nomination to the Supreme Court. Again, Thomas shifted sympathy away from Hill by portraying himself as an indignant and outraged victim of a feminist and racist conspiracy. (Both Hill and Thomas are black.) In an inspired stroke of media savvy, Thomas capitalised on television's affinity for melodrama by staging an impassioned performance of his victimisation at the hands of a spurned woman who would stop at nothing to punish him for rejecting her. In contrast, Hill's reasoned and dignified restraint enabled her detractors to characterise her as prudish and cold, manipulative and unfeminine at the same time.

As these examples – and indeed, the history of cinema – suggest, melodrama is a powerful and appealing form. It is powerful precisely because it is so appealing, because its tug at our heart strings and its over-simplified moral universe are often so hard to resist. Melodrama has long appealed to women because it so movingly narrates the sufferings we have endured in patriarchal culture. Yet in the 1990s – when political correctness has become the target of ridicule and a Men's Movement seeks, amongst other things, to 'heal' men wounded by feminism – we must be especially wary whenever melodrama, a friendly and familiar form to women, is used in ways unfriendly to us.

NOTES

1 This article is excerpted from my book *The Unruly Woman: Gender and the Genres of Laughter* (University of Texas Press, 1995), where I argue these issues at greater length, especially in Chapter Seven, 'Masculinity and Melodrama in Postclassical Romantic Comedy'.

2 See Andrew Britton, 'Cary Grant: Comedy and Male Desire' in *CineAction* 3-4, 1986, pp37-49, for an excellent analysis of the 'chastisement' of men in the classical romantic comedy.

3 This uneasiness was already evident in two popular and highly acclaimed films of the 1960s, *The Apartment* (Billy Wilder, US, 1960), which rewrites the sex comedy around the weakness and vulnerability of the organisation man; and *The Graduate* (Mike Nichols, US, 1967), which focuses on the victimisation of a young male hero by a predatory older woman. See Frank Krutnik, ' "The Faint Aroma of Performing Seals": The "Nervous" Romance and the Comedy of the Sexes' in *Velvet Light Trap* 26, 1990, pp57-72; Steve Neale, 'The Big Romance or Something Wild?: Romantic Comedy Today', *Screen*, Volume 33, Number 3, 1992, pp284-299; Steve Neale and Frank Krutnik, *Popular Film and Television Comedy*, Routledge, New York, 1990, for more on romantic comedy.

4 Citing the witchcraft trials of the seventeenth century, Juliana Schiesari argues in *The Gendering of Melancholia: Feminism, Psychoanalysis, and the Symbolics of Loss in Renaissance Literature*, Cornell University Press, Ithaca, 1992, that 'sensitive manhood' has increased as a popular style of masculinity during periods defined by 'the brutal suppression of any or all forms of femininity

understood as excessive or threatening' (p21).

5 *Ibid.*, p11.

6 *Ibid.*, p14.

7 *Ibid.*, p31.

8 Tania Modleski, *Feminism Without Women: Culture and Criticism in a 'Postfeminist' Age*, Routledge, New York, 1991.

9 It is important that the myth invoked is that of Cinderella, not Pygmalion, which forms the basis of the musical *My Fair Lady* (George Cukor, US, 1964). In contrast to *Pretty Woman, My Fair Lady* details the laborious and painful efforts required to conceal the signs of the romantic heroine's working-class background. Even in *Born Yesterday* (Cukor, US, 1950), Billie must work hard to pass herself off as middle-class.

10 In the classical romantic comedy, men who suffer 'melodramatically' are ironised by being placed in a comic framework (e.g. Hopsy's misery on the train with the Lady Eve). The same is true in *Moonstruck*, which makes heavy use of melodrama but remains faithful to the spirit of classical comedy. The film plays on the suffering of its male characters for comic effect by showing it to be the consequence of self-delusion and the cause of unnecessary pain to others, especially women. Nicholas Cage's scene in the bakery, when he recounts the story of how he lost his hand, is a brilliant and hilarious example of male melodrama played as high comedy.

'I Don't Know Whether To Look At Him Or Read Him': *Cape Fear* and Male Scarification

Helen Stoddart

Scarification of one kind or another has always been an important component, across many western cultures, of classical male mythological narratives. Oedipus had his feet pierced together by his father, an action which should have led to his death but, in fact, the resulting swelling became the symptomatic source, not only of his name, but his final ability to establish his real parentage.[1] Likewise the Fisher King, in the medieval romance *Percival* who, having been pierced through both thighs by a javelin during battle, is in too much pain to ride a horse and distracts himself by fishing. Adonis was killed by a boar wound, Odysseus merely scarred by one, though the scar was also incorporated into his name.[2] The castration imagery is obvious, but what is equally interesting is that the name given in each case comes not from the wounding incident itself, but from the body's reaction to it – to the way that it carries the scar. This is echoed in Ray Bradbury's *Illustrated Man* (London 1952) and *Something Wicked this Way Comes* (London 1963); the illustrated men constantly dispute that their picture-marked bodies are tattooed, because these would merely constitute arbitrary, externally motivated signs. Instead, the implication is that the body's marks are illustrations of interiority – revelations of the carrier's psychic identity. All this is not to say, of course, that women do not also bear important scars, but what I want to focus on here is the role bodily scarification has (particularly tattoos as self-imposed scars) within formations of masculinity.

More specifically, through a reading of Martin Scorsese's *Cape Fear* (US, 1991), I hope to explore what these might reveal about the star image of Robert De Niro.

The process of the wounding of men has been a persistent source of cinematic spectacle and plays a crucial part in defining a kind of machismo-driven heroism, particularly in action adventure films. 'Super heroes' like Stallone in the *Rambo* films are both destructive to others and suffer masochistically:

> The protagonist, almost entirely cut off from others, endures the most hideous forms of manipulation and pain, reaches into the primordial levels of the self, and emerges as a hero with powers sufficient to fight the system to the point of catastrophe.[3]

Even in the more self-conscious adventure pictures, *Die Hard* (John McTiernan, US, 1988) and *Die Hard II* (Renny Harlin, US, 1992), Bruce Willis is both fighting to save society and fighting against legitimate forms of power and authority within it, and this task is perpetually equivalent to his walking barefoot across broken glass. Though at the beginning of *Die Hard* his vest may be pristine white, his body is marked with a scar on his shoulder and an adjacent tattoo.[4] The scars are the early signals of McClane's ability to endure and experience pain. The tattoo is also the self-conscious register (and an increasingly commonplace one) of a tough sadomasochism which functions to indicate the price of this heroic strength – his status as an outsider, his being 'cut off from others' (especially his wife) as well as his emotional inadequacy.

There is something paradoxical, however, about the use of tattoos in contemporary cinema. Ted Polhemus, writing in 1975, claimed that:

> Scarification and tattooing – the permanent body arts are aggressively conservative, and *un*fashionable, for typically they are the bodily expression of small social enclaves which are being swallowed up in the overall wave of social change and in what seems to be a general trend towards social impermanence. Fashion, a phenomenon of Western consumer economies, is aimed at no fixed point, but rather at the process of change itself.[5]

The adorning of a tattoo is, in these terms, a tactical defence or rebellion against the tide of fashion, mostly on the part of socially marginalised, eccentric, criminal or self-exiled groups and individuals because of its permanence. However, for this and other reasons it has now become a badge of fashion itself –

as have the permanent body arts in general, including body piercing. Not only is much current fashion photography littered with bodies sporting discreetly placed tattoos[6] but a large number of voguish contemporary films employ tattoos as part of a bodily mise-en-scène to indicate a character's dangerous or unpredictable and outlaw potential – for example Michael Madsen in *Reservoir Dogs* (Quentin Tarantino, US, 1993), Brad Pitt in *Kalifornia* (Dominic Sena, US, 1993) and Christian Slater in *True Romance* (Tony Scott, US, 1993).

There is a certain congruence between the kinds of character types conventionally identified by the tattoo and Robert De Niro's star image which is generally defined by his association with rebellious, sadomasochistic, psychopathic or generally mis-fitting characters. His body, perhaps more than any other in contemporary cinema, has been focused on as an important carrier of meaning in itself. Yet while certain male Hollywood stars such as Cruise, Redford, Costner and even Van Damme are constructed as attractive bodies, that is as objects of romantic desire and attraction for women, with De Niro it is his acting technique itself which is fetishised in press coverage. His 'star image' has become determined not only by the focus on his 'Method' approach to acting through which he is driven 'role by role to transform himself physically into the substance of the signified',[7] but also, as in the case of *Raging Bull* (Scorsese, US, 1980) by the anecdotes surrounding the sometimes masochistic lengths he has gone to in bringing about these transformations.[8] Indeed, there seems to be a connection between the very 'male' 'Method' style of acting, with its emphasis on the portrayal of violent and emotionally disturbed states through significant bodily gestures or movements, and the way scars and/or tattoos can be read as illustrations of interiority. This would seem to be borne out by some of the most significant tattooed performances in cinema, namely, Rod Steiger in *The Illustrated Man* (Jack Smight, US, 1969), and, more recently, Harvey Keitel in *The Piano* (Jane Campion, Australia, 1993).

When there is cinematic fascination with De Niro's naked body, however, there often seems to be a problem with objectifying it as unproblematically sexually attractive. The focus is either on its pain or on its violent potential, sometimes both, as in *Cape Fear*. In instances of the former this may be framed in terms which Steve Neale and others have argued are 'marks both of the repression involved and of a means by which the male body can be disqualified ... as [an] object of erotic contemplation and desire.'[9] A recent case in point would be

Backdraft (Ron Howard, US, 1991) in which Brian McCaffrey/ William Baldwin covertly watches through an office window as Donald Rimgale/De Niro changes shirts for work and reveals a large area of his back to be covered in burnt scar tissue. However, the scar also serves here to authenticate Rimgale as a real fire-fighter and as a rebellious outsider amongst the corrupt bureaucrats with whom he works. More spectacularly, in the boxing sequences of *Raging Bull*, although the camera teasingly pans down La Motta's torso in slow motion, the water which streams down his skin from a sponge is mixed with the blood from his facial injuries. In each case the potentially erotic gaze at the body is problematised, though not necessarily negated, by the lurid traces of physical suffering.

In *Cape Fear*, De Niro's body is at its most naked and vulnerable during the scene in which Lieutenant Elgart/Robert Mitchum brings Max Cady/De Niro in to be identified by Sam Bowden/Nick Nolte as the man who has been harassing him. Significantly, this scene is preceded by an exchange between the two men in which Cady emphasises his own acquisition of femininity. He associates this, however, with suffering, describing being in the place of a woman whilst in jail when he was 'held down and sodomised'. All this led him, he claims, to get in touch with 'the soft nurturing side of myself – the feminine side'. This association which he makes with the feminine is reinforced in the full body strip-search scene through the martyred but reproachful look on Cady's face, indicating the humiliation which his visual objectification clearly causes him. At the same time, whilst Cady occupies what, in Laura Mulvey's terms, is the female place cinematically in being the object of a collective male gaze within the film in a sustained moment of spectacle, this is complicated by Lieutenant Elgart's bemused 'I don't know whether to look at him or read him'. His tattoo-decorated body makes him both text and spectacle, ornament and action, passive and active object of the gaze.[10] The balance between each of these two terms is also reflected in the images drawn in the tattoos themselves. On his back he has a set of scales which measure 'truth' (a bible) against 'justice' (a knife) as well as a picture of a clown carrying both a smoking gun and a bible. It is clear from the first image of him in the film that Cady's body has itself become a text. Within a shot of a row of bookshelves in Cady's prison cell, he lifts himself up on a set of cross bars, thus completely obscuring our view of the books and replacing it with his heavily inscribed body. When asked by the prison guards as he leaves if he wants to take his books with him, he replies, 'Already read 'em.' He *is* his books. It is their intelligence (mainly biblical) in the form of tattoos which makes his body spectacular. As he embodies what he takes to be their message, he is also the active reinforcement of their contents. He both demands to be looked at and yet he escapes decipherment because he cannot be fixed simply as the object of the men's gaze.

Cady's tattoos are, of course, ambiguous in other ways because, whilst decorative, they also advertise violent destruction in their biblical proclamations of purging and vengeance. At the same time, in themselves they signify the recipient's suffering and passivity in having had his skin penetrated, 'opened-up' and beautified/decorated. The confused silence which Cady's ornate body brings on his spectators is exacerbated cinematically by the use of circular tracking shots and two-way mirrors, which make it nearly impossible to discern at any given moment who is looking at whom and whose point of view the spectator is being given. At one point all three characters are simultaneously visible on the glass which is meant to be there to separate lookers from looked-at. Nonetheless, Cady still manages to make eye contact with Bowden to return his gaze.

All this is certainly not to argue, as does Pam Cook, that Cady is 'an avenging angel acting on behalf of victimised women' because he 'reflects back at them their own rage and pain' as a result of their humiliation.[11] This film seems to me to have very little to say about women but is, on the contrary, much more concerned with relations of male doubling, a subject germane to the search scene described above. The feminine aspects of Cady's character and representation are more interesting for their part in male/male relationships than in their conections to women in the film. Between Cady and Bowden there is a dynamic of both destruction and desire, very much akin to that identified by Eve Sedgwick in nineteenth-century literature as male homosocial desire.[12] Such paranoid plots involve a mutual and murderous chase between two men, one good and one bad. The 'good' male eventually discovers himself to be mentally transparent before the dark, shadow self who has gained access to his unconscious and therefore he finds it increasingly difficult to distingush himself from the latter. An exemplary text within Sedgwick's thesis is Mary Shelley's *Frankenstein* (1818) and there are clear echoes of this narrative in *Cape Fear* in the way that Bowden is undoubtedly identified (within the law) as the engineer of his own destruction. Cady is also a creature who is 'born again', embittered by exile and who has learnt a language (the law) in his imprisonment with which he can challenge and reproach his negligent custodian. More particularly, women exist in these male paranoid narratives only insofar as they may be mobilised as the conduits of male/male fear and desire and this seems precisely to be the function of all three of the central women in *Cape Fear* whom Cady sexually violates to make Bowden suffer.

The shot in which the two men, Cady and Bowden are reflected back onto the same piece of glass dramatises both the war between them and their intimate connection. Mitchum's character, Elgart, is, of course, also identified with and implicated in the visual objectification of Cady on the level of a meta-textual joke. Not only did he play Cady in the original film version of *Cape Fear* (J. Lee Thompson, US, 1962), he also played the crazy tattooed preacher in *Night of the Hunter* (Charles Laughton, US, 1955) the character from whom De Niro reportedly took the idea of using tattoos. Both men, therefore, see themselves in Cady, a fact not only re-emphasised in his use of mirrored sun-glasses but also in sinister, near uncanny, plot repetitions. The most startling of these involves Lori Davis/Ileanna Douglas, Bowden's colleague and potential lover, who is first seen losing in a game of racquet ball with him. In coaching her, he holds her wrist, swings it forward and advises her twice, 'You gotta snap your wrist', thus pre-echoing the horrific scene (immediately following the body search) in which Cady literally snaps Lori's wrist as he sexually assaults her and bites a chunk out of the cheek which we have previously seen next to Bowden's as he moves her arm forward on court. When Cady attacks her he asks, 'Did he hurt you like this, that married guy? Or did he hurt you like this?' The message is clear; that Cady has access to Bowden's unconscious desires and that he has become their dark vehicle. The doubling theme is also underscored by the cinematographic technique of switching suddenly from a colour picture to its own negative image. In these shots the Bowdens are reduced to deathly, skeletal figures, thus emphasising their death-in-life existence and their reserves of self-destruction.

All this is to argue that, far from rendering Cady altogether feminine, the tattoos are a more important facet of a male/male fascination in which the feminine plays a part, but the female only an intermediary role. The problem with Cook's argument about Cady/De Niro as the 'avenger' of victimised women is that she jumps too readily from feminine to female. That is, she equates Cady's (self-) association of suffering and femininity with the experience of those gendered female. Indeed, as Cady himself admits when Bowden's wife Leigh/Jessica Lange expresses her repulsion at him, 'All that prison life made me coarse. Guess I'm covered in too many tattoos.' In this instance the tattoos distance him from, rather than bring him closer to, the middle-class women in the film.

In the same conversation, however, Cady laments that he had nothing else to do in prison but 'desecrate' his flesh and here lies the contradictory nature of his tattoos. Whilst in their content they signify Cady's religious commitment, in themselves they constitute a profane diversion of the flesh in that they stand in contravention of the Old Testament injunction on tattoos ('You are not to gash your bodies when someone dies, and you are not to tattoo yourselves.' Leviticus, 19: 28). This is only the first of many contradictions embodied by Cady, of whom it is very difficult to make sense. His devotion to Nietzsche and Stalin does not square well with his religious fundamentalism but neither does his evangelical promotion of Henry Miller. Cady is a confused and confusing figure whose tattoos function anarchically as a statement of violent reaction against a diseased social order rather as a pure commitment to Christian ethics. Like Travis Bickle in *Taxi Driver* (Martin Scorsese, US, 1975) who reverts to a more primitive Mohican style to become an urban warrior with a mission, Cady's bodily decorations represent an attempt to throw himself into reverse gear against the flow of a society which he believes to be moving too quickly and in the wrong direction. As such, these two characters, though they are both visually stigmatised social outsiders battling against corruption, are also, in line with Polhemus's classification of tattooing, 'aggressively conservative' outsiders and, as such, unpleasant symptoms of the order which produced them.

Finally, the connections I have been making between the social function of tattoos and the star image of De Niro must also, given the textual examples I have been using, be qualified in terms of their connection with Scorsese's auteurial preoccupations. Clearly *Cape Fear* is a further dramatisation of a theme in which Paul Schrader has been equally involved, as he indicates here in a discussion of *Raging Bull*:

> But there's obviously a pseudo-religious masochism to it – regeneration by blood, ritual beating – and that aspect of it certainly appealed to both Marty and me. ... redemption through

physical pain, like the Stations of the Cross, one torment after another. Not redemption by having a view of salvations or by grace, but just redemption by death an suffering, which is the darker side of the Christian message.[13]

The excesses of Max Cady's character may seem self-parodic and, at times, ridiculous yet, for this very reason, they are interesting in that they throw into extreme relief some of Scorsese's directorial fixations and the characteristics and performance techniques which have become associated with the De Niro star image. Rather than, in Steve Neale's terms 'disqualifying' De Niro's body as an object of 'erotic contemplation and desire', Cady's tattoos render it a vehicle for a complex series of desires. As I have hoped to show, they function both to reinforce the sadomasochistic associations carried by De Niro's body and to make a spectacle out of it; one which fascinates, confuses and thereby threatens the male on-lookers who hold him in their gaze.

NOTES

1 Marie Belmary, *Psychoanalysing Psychoanalysis: Freud and the Hidden Fault of the Father*, trans. Ned Lukacher, Johns Hopkins University Press, London, 1982 (1979), pp8-11. Belmary argues that Oedipus's wound represents the mark, not of his 'true identity' but of the sins of his father Laius who was cursed by Pelops for having abducted his son, Chrysippus, and forbidden to have children. Oedipus is named, not after the piercing itself, but his body's *response* to this. The sign of his wound therefore is a *symptomatic* rather than a symbolic one.

2 'It is interesting that when the Romans translated *The Odyssey*, they gave Odysseus the name Ulixes, which some believe to be a union of *oulas*, wound, and *ischea*, thigh. Ulysses' name then, becomes, literally, thigh wound.' Robert Bly, *Iron John*, Element Books, Longmead, Dorset, 1991, p215.

3 William Warner, 'Rambo and the Popular Pleasures of Pain', *Cultural Studies*, Lawrence Grossberg and Cary Nelson (eds), Routledge, New York, 1992, p675.

4 'The visible signifier of the sailor, the tattoo, must have had a powerful attraction for those who also wanted to be free ... from the normal constraints of society. Hence the adoption by all sorts of groups to signify unconstraint. The tattoo as a group signifier has thus been adopted by criminals and the 'criminal classes' ... to specifically denote self exclusion from society and its laws and norms. But it has also been adopted by other groups who stand outside society for other, less radical reasons.' David Curry,

'Decorating the Body Politic', *New Formations*, Summer, 1993, p72.

5 Ted Polhemus, 'Social Bodies' in Jonathan Benthall and Ted Polhemus (eds), *The Body as a Means of Expression*, Allen Lane, London, 1975, p32.

6 Admittedly many of these are washable, impermanent tattoos, a fact which, of course, reinforces Polhemus's argument.

7 Barry King, 'Articulating Stardom', *Stardom*, Christine Gledhill (ed), Routledge, London, 1991, pp176-77.

8 Shelley Winters, for example, 'He doesn't act, he *becomes*. The things that he does with his body are truly frightening: he can blush or get as white as a sheet in a second, and he could force his hair to curl on command if he wanted to.' Cited in 'The Godfather', *Premiere*, (UK Edition), October, 1993, p68.

9 Steve Neale, 'Masculinity as Spectacle: Reflections on Men and Mainstream Cinema', *Screen*, Volume 24, Number 6, 1983, pp2-16. See also Neale's point of reference, Paul Willemen, 'Anthony Mann: Looking at the Male', *Framework*, Numbers 15-17, pp16–20.

10 As David Curry notes, the tattoo is 'an artifice with two basic components: it both beautifies and gives a message.' Curry, *op.cit.*, p69.

11 Pam Cook, 'Scorsese's Masquerade', *Sight and Sound*, April, 1992, p15.

12 See Eve Sedgwick, *Between Men: English Literature and Male Homosocial Desire*, Columbia University Press, New York, 1985. Angela McRobbie also makes a fleeting allusion to the film's Gothic literary themes in her letter 'Sexual Violence', *Sight and Sound*, March, 1992, p63.

13 Paul Schrader, in Kevin Jackson (ed), *Schrader on Schrader & Other Writings*, Faber and Faber, London, 1990, pp132-133.

Burt's Neck: Masculine Corporeality and Estrangement

Gillian Swanson

In 1860, Italy was thrown into political and social upheaval by a man called Garibaldi. He sought to unify Italy into a modern nation freeing it from domination by a decadent aristocracy.

Caught in this turmoil was a proud Sicilian prince known as The Leopard. This is his story and that of his family, his way of life and his credo.

> Things will have to change
> in order that they remain the same.

        *   *   *   *

We were the leopards, the lions. Those who take our place will be jackals and sheep. The whole lot of us – leopards, lions, jackals, sheep – will continue to think of ourselves as the salt of the earth.

THE SPECTATOR AND THE WRITER

My interest in Burt Lancaster is not simply a critical one; it is an interest borne from attachment. From the perspective of such an interest, Burt Lancaster's body presents a kind of paradox: how is it that women can develop forms of passionate attachment to male bodies and images of male bodies, and how may such an attachment, centring on a body so dramatically masculine, be understood outside those accounts of identification and subjectivity which polarise masculinity and femininity? The attachment I describe accompanies an identification formed from affiliation and familiarity – the intimacy of recognising an object already known – and so cannot be accounted for by the pleasures of identifying with 'the masculine' as a moment of *escape* from the 'constraints' of femininity.[1] For my attachment to Burt's body is more to do with a recognition of some nostalgia, one concerning an imaginary loss: of solidity, of an encompassing and voluptuous corporeality. It is my speculation that the figuring of masculinity may present a *dissolving* corporeality that I want to examine in this piece. Could Burt's broad bull-neck, the most muscular and unmalleable of necks, represent a *failure* of signification 'in the masculine', rather than an affirmation of perpetual stability and centrality? The sexual instabilities implied by such a question suggested that the masculinity I wished to describe might not be so straightforwardly distinguished from those instabilities attributed to femininity.

While the failure of signification 'in the masculine' may be too easily described in terms of the feminine, perhaps there is something that allows me to single out Burt as one of those liminal figures masked – or made – by the very groundedness of his physique? But I find no way to reduce these discontinuous movements of estrangement and recognition to a term as encompassing as masculinity's opposite, any more than I can find a way to reduce my own identifications to an endless restatement of the feminine. As masculinity becomes unravelled and unstable in its representations, the co-ordinates of its definition are as dispersed, its meanings as elusive, as the tracing of its corporeal forms upon shifting landscapes. In such categorical uncertainty, when the contours of masculinity are themselves in question, no other term will do to translate its undecidability: the feminine provides a too easy fix with which to bind disrupted masculinities to the stable definitions envisioned by models of sexual difference and exchange; these terms can neither mirror nor reciprocate each other's foreignness. It is from this recognition that I come to examine a female attachment to masculine figures not just in terms of what it means for femininity, not suggesting that masculinity is established solely in terms of its opposition to femininity, but in order to examine how it is that the masculine forms its own *self-referential* system.

How does the masculine offer a form of identification for men, with other male figures, around a paradoxical and problematic male body, and how might these processes exert a pressure on definitions of masculine subjectivity? Clearly Burt Lancaster's body only provides one way into such questions, for the figuration of the male body is also caught up in narratives of masculine social subjectivity and historical presence, allowing its use as a motif for a persuasive account of relations between the community of men and their transcendence of a problematic male body. The loss that arises in that 'overcoming' of an unwelcome but essential corporeality in masculine social presence gives rise to a radical displacement; a homelessness or foreignness at the heart of the distinctions through which masculinity becomes intelligible.

While to see such signification in terms of failure may imply a *disruption* of the conventions of corporeal signification of masculinity, the proposal that it may elicit a *feminine* form of attachment also suggests the inadequacy of a model that assumes identification occurs with a like object while assuming that one may identify with a sexually differentiated figure in film. However, I want also to insist that the figuring of this form of masculinity in a male body has a determining effect on the *type* of female identification that may occur.

THE PRINCE: MASCULINITY, POLITY, NATION

As the first coda at the beginning of this piece shows, *The Leopard* (Luchino Visconti, Italy, 1963) starts with a paradox: the credo of Don Fabrizio, Prince of Salina (Burt Lancaster) seeks to tame history, to contain processes of change through the movement of possession, directed towards a restatement of convention. The film ends with the rescinding of that possession, the Prince's alignment of the 'leopards' and the 'jackals' showing a recognition of an estrangement borne of familiarity, the boundaries of self-possession no longer compelling a continual revisiting of discovery and the exercise of authority.

A film about the Risorgimento, *The Leopard* is made at the time of its centenary. It looks at the founding of the Italian State in its narrative of the containment of Garibaldi's partisan rebellion by a tactical *rapprochement* between the bourgeois ascendants and the aristocratic families.[2] The scrutiny of such origins were part of political and intellectual debate from the end of the Second World War, partly as a result of the emergence of Gramsci's influential analysis of the unification of Italy, but also provoked by the contemporary example of the defeat of the partisans at the end of the war when a 'tradition of continuity' meant the loyalists of the previous system reassumed their old positions.[3] From the early 1950s, moves were made towards an 'opening to the left', to allow centre-left government coalitions to be formed between the Christian Democratic Party and the Socialists. The first to directly involve the Italian Socialist Party was eventually established in 1963: spreading across the country and becoming established at a national level, the coalitions allowed the Socialists into power but at a cost; of alignment with a party whose recent past had been seen as anathema to anti-fascist movements; of a division of the left; and of the marginalisation of the Communist Party. As the post-war ambitions of these political movements appeared to have been finally compromised, such political alignments drew accusations of the 'Sicilianisation of Italy'.[4]

In his discussion of *Senso*, another of Visconti's Risorgimento films, Nowell Smith suggests the connection between the two moments of containment of the partisan causes is a question for a Marxist like Visconti: 'Did the revolution that might have happened in 1943-47 fail in the same way and for the same reasons as that of 1886-70? Or did it not also fail *because* the first one had failed, because the ruling class was allowed to establish a tradition of continuity, and *trasformismo* was allowed from the start to mask the conflicts that, objectively, seem to demand a revolutionary response'.[5] As a member of the Communist Party in the early 1960s, Visconti's consideration of history – and the dynamics of *trasformismo*, 'the process whereby seemingly dangerous elements were 'transformed' into stable parts of the system'[6] – would have been formed from such political questions. The concept of nation and national alignments that follow from this are clearly pursued in *The Leopard*, a film which addresses the disparities in the way national alignments are individualised, the pragmatics of historical continuity and the vulnerability of political contract to personal investments.

It is not so much the specifics of these historical pressures I wish to explore here, but the connections between national identification, political contract and masculinity. What is it about the sexual *as a problem of masculinity* which gives some legibility to these terms, allowing us to see the masculine as a *historical* problematic, a category which exceeds sexual definition and becomes one related to social subjectivity and agency, based in the relations of polity and national affiliations? It is not just that the relation between social and sexual offers masculinity a set of historical co-ordinates, but that its vulnerability is formed from the contingency – and the pragmatics – of the histories of political alliances. The instabilities of masculinity are formed by the possibility of fragmented alignments and identifications which move beyond their grounding in the 'natural': such are the dilemmas of masculinity's investment in the national. It is the establishment of civil relations that both legitimates, and puts into question, such investments. The possibility, and the evasiveness, of a *sovereign* masculinity becomes the means by which an authoritative relation to the social may be secured. How does *The Leopard*, and Burt Lancaster's Prince, allow an enactment of the instabilities of such formations of masculinity?

The opening of *The Leopard* gives us the landscape and the Prince's house. The solemn family ceremony of the House of Salina is disrupted by the news of Garibaldi's troups nearing the environs and a dead soldier found in the grounds. Even the family's authority is itself no longer securely moored, as Tancredi, the Prince's nephew, proclaims his intention to leave to join Garibaldi's redshirts and to fight 'a big duel with the King' on the side of those who threaten his own family's interests. As the Prince becomes occupied with the impact of such changes on the government of his own domain, Tancredi exhausts his political romanticism and he returns, falling in love with Angelica, the daughter of an aspirant bourgeois. Tancredi thereby overlooks the affections of Prince's daughter, who is, even by the Prince's own definition, too meek, too passive and timid for a man with as much ambition as Tancredi. Angelica, by contrast, can be seen to incite desire as much in the Prince as in Tancredi. In this masculine recognition they are separated from the women of their line, and by Tancredi's marriage the bond of a new alliance is to be made.

The film's use of the sexual as a mechanism of the social is one which addresses masculine identifications, formed in opposition to and outside of sexual exchanges which can only mirror them. This political narrative shows the development of a new order – not from the glorious redshirts and their hopes for a new Italy of the people, but instead one formed from the compromise between the aristocratic families fearful of losing their own position and traditions and the new classes embodied by Angelica's father – vain, ambitious for status, and unprincipled. The consolidation of this new political system results as much in the paralysis of will that occurs for the Prince, in his eventual recoil from the forms of government this compromise has brought, as it does in the breathless infatuation of Tancredi, whose hypocritical and arrogant condemnation of the Garibaldini to whom he had once devoted himself, at the end of the film, shows him to be a man of the future, able to adapt to changing circumstances. Thus we see the variability – the fragility – of masculinity, whose ultimate logic is to move on, to form oneself in the image of such new alliances. These are the fragmented identifications – and the cost – of an investment in the social.

It is the Prince we stay with at the end of this film: as he finally walks alone through unfamiliar streets at night, he falls to his knees, moves heavily, his introspection bows his figure. This is another view of masculinity from that of ambition, historical initiative and compromise: it is one of fragility, of hesitancy, and of the measured grace of humility. The ambivalence of his masculinity in *The Leopard* is centrally wrought through performance: a tension between the gesture and the movement shows the Prince to be uncompleted in some way, unachieved. In his combination of physical grandeur and gestural hesitancy, the particular restraint of his enactment of masculinity suggests a distance between subjectivity and presence which I want to examine as a feature not just of this narrative of masculine secession, or of Burt Lancaster's performance style, but of a further estrangement which these *reiterate*: one which is formed out of the fracture within which masculinity itself is construed.

It is in Burt's reiteration of masculinity, that we can identify the motif of the foreigner.[7] Set apart from the community of men who form 'the nation', this figure is marked by the estrangement required for the forms of national and civic identification that inform men's relation to the social, those based on the distinction of social and sexual, civic and 'natural' or familial relations.[8] As a hierarchical model of government by 'father-kings', where the 'natural order' of family life informed notions of natural authority, cedes to a modern order of civil society where equal individuals subscribe to, and are bound by, a social contract, a separation occurs. The separation of the civil realm of government from the private, familial world of particularity, and ties of blood, emotion, love and sexual passion, demands also a separation between the masculine subject of reason and the disorderly realm of women. Models of democratic government thus allow men to take up authority in the social world on the basis of their definition *against* – and separation from – the private, the corporeal or sexual, and the feminine. These distinctions at the base of modern political theory delegitimise corporeality within the social realm as they ask men to act in accordance with the public good and 'above' the demands of the body and the corporeal relations of family.

There is thus a tension created in the embodiments through which masculinity may be enacted, allowing it to become marked by a definitional instability. Masculinity's basis in the 'artificial' realm of social reproduction in the polity, as men become 'born' as social subjects, leads to a loss of the certainties allowed by the correspondence of natural, familial realms to those of government in previous, patriarchal, orders. These orders presented social destiny as following from 'natural' origin, claiming that authority and subordination depended upon (biological) birth. They were, then, truly patriarchal in political form.[9] Sovereignty in modern liberal-democratic orders is, however, created as a feature of civil right, not inherent: hence masculinity's grasp of authority is less secure, more provisional, needing to be endlessly renewed and reclaimed. The *possibility of lack of sovereignty* in liberal democracies is posed by the 'foreigner', who is denied the rights of citizens.[10]

> Is it not true that, in order to found the rights that are specific to the men of a civilisation or a nation – even the most reasonable and the most consciously democratic – one has to withdraw such rights from those that are not citizens, that is, other men?[11]

It is my particular interest in Burt's reiteration of contained and authoritative masculinity, one whose definition seems to *dismiss* the possibility of the feminine as a meaningful term, which I am pursuing here, but it is also an interest deriving from the way in which this figure elicits a form of pathos, demanding a recognition of its own estrangement and a nostalgia borne from its *separatedness*. Foreign to itself, the masculine civic individual of modern political theory and national identifications is formed through a loss of the certainties of origin and destiny brought by the dislocation of social and sexual arenas. These are the losses which move the foreigner towards the instabilities of masculine exile and mourning.

THE FOREIGNER

How does the recognition of loss inform these masculinities and make men foreigners to themselves, removed from the will for historical presence through which they may claim authority? Near the end of *The Leopard*, the weary Prince, robbed of his capacity to form the direction of historical momentum, sits with the emissary of a new democratic government, of an efficient administration, who has come to ask him – as an honourable man, a man of integrity and principle – to represent the Sicilian people in the senate, following a plebiscite unifying Sicily with the Kingdom of Sardinia. Despite his membership of the ruling class, then, his is an authority borne from the ties of respect, not birth. 'For more than twenty-five centuries', he explains, declining the offer, 'we have borne the weight of a superb and heterogeneous civilisation, all from the outside, none made by ourselves, none that we could call our own. For two thousand and five hundred years we've been a colony ... We're tired, tired and empty. Your intention is good, but it comes too late.'

To explain his heaviness to this emissary, the Prince recounts an old Sicilian expression:

> 'Even the most violent is really a wish for death.' Our sensuality, a wish for oblivion; our knifings, our shootings, a hankering after extinction; our laziness ... a desire for voluptuous immobility; that is for death again.

This is the Prince's reason for refusing the entreaty he is proffered; a plea to help remove the memory of bad government, a promise to change the climate, to enrich the landscape, and to find a way of breaking the spell of an unchanging history which is said to make the Sicilians' vanity stronger than their misery, so that they too can enter the modern world. Without his help, 'everything will be as it was before', the way open to men with no scruples, no vision: to the pragmatists of a new order that would only change towards the same; the perpetuation, not the interruption, of a history of degeneracy.

What is the recognition being effected here? What is the force of a description of a Sicilian character forged from nature and the disinclination to master its determinations? And how is the Prince situated in a story of the birth of a modern democratic state? His embodiment of authority takes him from one world to the next and creates a form of estrangement which casts him outside of the community of men, setting him apart. In emerging democracies,

> the body politic itself was represented by the sovereign 'actor' the one who speaks and acts by authority for all ... [t]he person of the sovereign represented the body politic by *performing* their unity, *speaking and acting as if they were one* by *being* one himself, undivided and indivisibly one. On the stage of public life, bearing the outward appearance of a man, acting in the name of everyone, but no-one in particular, the sovereign performed the real unity of all.[12]

This indivisibility depended on 'losing' the essential being of *maleness* and instead taking on the 'outward appearance' of 'a' man, representative of 'all' men. *Performing* the unity of all men, taking on the authority to represent the community of men, means setting oneself apart from one's own particularity, the physical body; becoming *no-one in particular*. This is different from investing the sovereign with authority on the basis of his particularity: his corporeal self, his familial status, his birth. To make a transition from 'old' authority to 'new' authority, however alluring, the Prince is confronted with a loss that derives from the new visibility of this as a *masculine* embodiment and its consequent demarcation against that which is feminine: particularised corporeal being.

By his own account inevitably compromised, tied to the old Bourbon regime by chains 'of decency if not affection', the Prince is 'a member of an unlucky generation, striding between two worlds and ill at ease in both'. One might see him simply as the father of the old regime, positioned by birth, his patriarchal sway needing to be removed for democratic ties to be established between free and equal men. But he is not just an embodiment of power. He is the beneficiary of a *colonised* land, a foreigner in both worlds: one that he commands but has not made and the other in which he looks on at the ascendancy of a new class of men and can only see himself as other to the world they will make. His own dividedness prevents his performance of this political unity as he comes to embody the contradiction at the heart of the new order: the problem of masculine sovereignty. His is the voluptuous immobility of one who *exiles himself*: his gesture of accession a solace, as the new world fails to incite the will to encounter a difference he is already privy to.

One moment in this scene gives a clue to the specifically masculine form of this exile. As the Prince corrects himself to speak not of 'Sicilians' but of *Sicily*, he prizes apart the identification that fixes men to their nationality. The enduring, unmoving *old* Sicily is formed from a violence of landscape, a cruelty of climate, an unspecified tension: national designations can here be made outside of the actions of men. Thus unfixed, their actions become formless and without issue, for if Sicily can be spoken of as distinct from Sicilians there is no coherence between place and individual men, no *polity*. Without an alignment of action to nation, masculinity becomes unmoored; it is rendered static, *unbecoming*. The consequence of this for masculine definition is the potential for a difference that opens up the space between origin and destination, location and individual locatedness. Masculinity becomes produced as a wanderingness: its travels oriented by insecure co-ordinates, it is unable to locate itself in a trajectory that escapes immobility; it is finally unable to assume a position.

Yet the promise of a *new* Sicily, a modern democratic state freed from such histories of inevitability and fixedness, masks the cost of citizenship: the loss of sexual definition. For the fraternity of citizens is made on the promise of a categorical distinction from *maleness*. As men become citizens, the unruly demands of corporeality must give way to their constitution as social subjects, whereby they must act according to the principles of reason and the public good. Woman's 'disorder' is that she cannot effect this transcendence: just as her connection to corporeality prevents her ever entering the modern body politic, so in her incapacity for justice she must be prevented from bringing the state to ruin.[13] In their entry into the civilised public world, men are reborn: not as men but as *citizens*, leaving behind the moral disorder of a too-close relation to the natural, the bodily: while distinguishing themselves from the disorder of femininity, they thereby 'lose' their manhood. The democratic gaze seeks out its others, those it defines as other, those who become exiled; *foreigners*. Signifiers of the loss at the basis of masculine civic authority and self-possession, the foreigner shows – becomes formed from – the disarticulation between the masculine social subject and the male body, embodying the threat which 'maleness' poses to the autonomous, representative, communal subject. To continue the logic of Kristeva's concept of the foreigner *as a function* of citizenship:

> Is it not true that, in order to found the rights that are specific to the men of a civilisation or a nation – even the most reasonable and the most consciously democratic – one has to withdraw such rights from those that are not citizens, that is, other men? The process means – and this is its extreme inference – that one can be more or less a man to the extent that one is more or less a citizen, that he who is not a citizen is not fully a man ... Is he fully a man if he is not a citizen?[14]

Kristeva suggests that it is through the constitution of men as citizens that the possibility of insufficient definition as a *man* is presented. But while it is true that modern liberal democracies allow the possibilty of excluding or exiling particular men, we can also see a state of exile existing within the constitution of men as citizens *per se*. For the entry into a modern political order both requires that men resist being constituted through their 'maleness' and defines those who do not make this transition to identify with a body politic, a sexless body, as lesser men – or 'not men'. It is necessary both to be male to make the transition and also to deny the foundation of this maleness: just as women may not enter the fraternity of citizens so men's entry is based on renouncing the origin and precondition of their entry, their maleness, as they take up an identity beyond sexual definition. This paradoxical construction suggests that at the base of social subjectivity's translation into civic relations lies a problematic relation to a male body: it is *both* antipathetic to citizenship (in its corporeality), *yet* its guarantor (in its lack of femininity). This means that the birth of the social is both the birth of 'men' and the death of 'maleness'. In this way, the formation of subjectivity marks masculinity, in its forging of a cultural body, one of *social*, not natural, meaning, with an estrangement and a recognition, as it both carries and denies its corporeal base. It renders men foreign from their own constitution *as* men.

How do the motifs of the foreigner and the exile become persuasive in such accounts of masculinity? For if the historical encounter enacted in *The Leopard*, between an old and a new order, presents the bonds of difference in terms of a loss that cannot be regained through possession, so too the encounters implied in the taking up of a social subjectivity entail a loss: that of a conception of the self as whole, unified and in command. It is this fracturing of coherent histories that occurs in the loss of 'maleness' brought about in the assumption of citizenship and social definition. The recognition of the self as part of a community of other men brings with it a recognition of failure: of the authenticity of the 'natural' which must now be overturned for such encounters to become subject to governance; and of a lack of *origin* as corporeal 'birth' must give way to the 'rebirth' of men into the social world. These are the losses that are necessary to bring about a story of social birth: a birth that gives men not bodies, but *presence*.

> We live by a series of encounters – with friends, lovers, books, places – but every encounter, as Jacques Derrida says, is 'separation,' a 'contradiction of logic'[15] in that it signals an encounter with something other than ourselves, a long-felt absence, that element of difference that breaks the illusory unity of the self. For the story ... is always already about the foreigner in ourselves.[16]

Kristeva's concept that the foreigner (and the foreign) is troubling because we are foreign to ourselves shows that any encounter is shot with the difference that disrupts the secure positioning of absolute presence, *self*-possession. Her argument proposes – as does that of Derrida – that this is a prerequisite of subjectivity. While the emphasis that subjectivity is 'divided in itself' is a welcome one, it has been used to investigate female rather than male subjectivity, tied to the assumption that women's subjectivity is formed from a *lack* of self-possesesion and presence-to-themselves, hence necessarily presenting a greater problem of dividedness.[17] Political theory, addressing the forms by which social subjectivity is governed, however, implies that the masculine identification with the body politic implies another kind of self-dispersal, in and across the community of men, suggesting that an oscillation between self and other, the recognition of oneself *as* other, is as central to the encounters of men as to those of women.[18] In fact it suggests that the very definition of a social subjectivity for men is the stage for such an estrangement. Citizenship as a domain of public presence, whose contours are formed from the fragmented and mobile identifications of men, becomes marked by the motif of the foreigner. What does it mean to encounter the other in an exchange that mirrors our own otherness, a foreign encounter where we risk becoming the foreigner ourselves? Clearly this is not just a question of female spectatorship, but of the terms by which masculinity provides an *object* of identification.

THE WANDERER

The displacements of masculinity's foreign encounters become articulated in the figure of the wanderer. In modern cultures this is a familiar figure, comprising amongst others the *flâneur*, the dandy and the male homosexual, whose movement through urban landscapes manifests a radical dislocation connected to new forms of social positioning.[19] Those forms of spatial and corporeal instability relating to urban narratives become *embodied* in the figure of the male homosexual and connected to those of the prostitute, whose 'monstrous' alignment with the recasting of social and sexual space – disorganising boundaries between public and private – also disorganises the co-ordinates of secure positioning for the authoritative masculine subject.[20] Such figures, and their pathological framing within sexual classifications, propose absolute correspondences between sexual and social as less than convincing. They propose the costs and pleasures of 'losing oneself' in narratives which reorganise sexual patternings to move beyond notions of self based on 'origin', 'nature' and 'authenticity'.

We can see the persuasiveness of this motif of the wanderer in a film whose central image, in my less than empirical research, is unwavering in the remembrances of men of my generation. *Lawrence of Arabia* contains very many more pressing images on reviewing, and this one hardly presses itself on me, but it passes beyond filmic representation in these men's accounts of the excitement of seeing Peter O'Toole in the desert, at the moment of his most emphatic assertion of the possibilities of identification with an 'other' culture as he changes British military uniform for the robes he is given, twirling and running in billowing white Arab dress, giggling delightedly at the wonder of corporeal disguise and exotic self-fashioning. It is not by focusing on this moment in particular that we can see in *Lawrence of Arabia* a historical moment of unravelled masculinity – although these men clearly delighted in the spectacle of Lawrence's abandonment – but rather by situating the film in 1962, in the aftermath of a decade of debate over the 'pathologies' of male homosexuality and men's insufficient masculine definition. This is also a period which saw the shattering of T.E. Lawrence's embodiment of national achievement, as questions over his part in colonial exchanges were aligned with a new form of sexual scrutiny, his legendary recoil from conventional heterosexuality becoming translated into a perverse and masochistic homosexuality.[21]

I am interested in the way *Lawrence* represents the dilemmas of an insufficiently secure national identity and a problem of masculine confidence, using T.E. Lawrence's movement between cultures as both symptom and or cause of a radical split in his psyche which leads him to become both murderous and self-damaging. This invests the moment where a western reader is compelled to collapse together the 'otherness' of his Arab disguise and his 'feminised' appearance and behaviour with a particular understanding of the relation between masculinity and the foreigner, one which is manifested in the figure of the wanderer as an unsecured subjectivity whose lack of 'home' shows not only a disaffection with national identifications but one of corporeal dislocation. The male body here becomes figured through its displacements, in the unstable image of Lawrence in an unsecured landscape, in a narrative of placelessness, as his corporeal tracings become dispersed across the immense and changing desert spaces. If the wanderer is based in a space of shifting co-ordinates, Lawrence's 'foreign' definition has, albeit tacitly, a sexual character as well as a national (colonial, racial) one. He exhibits a set of instabilities over the relation between sexual and social being, masculinity and the body: his 'problem' of being between cultures is linked to the corporeal instabilities accorded to male homosexuality; an insufficiently defined resolution between sexual body and social persona which is interpreted as a 'feminisation'.[22] As Lawrence's 'passing between' represents the differences clustering around a fragmented national masculinity and its declining cultural authority in the exchanges wrought by colonial dispossession, the *remembrance* of this moment of the foreignness of masculine encounter and exchange perhaps shows the possibility of an embrace of the foreigner, the recognition of an encounter with the foreign *as part of* the historical constitution of masculine subjectivity and definition.

The dispersed passages of the wandering body may not undermine masculine identifications so much as redefine our sense of masculinity in terms of its displacements. Stephen Greenblatt's account of the discourse of travel in a period of colonial encounter, starting from the late Middle Ages and Renaissance, suggest that it exists as a collection of anecdotes, rather than an overarching history 'that knows where it is going'. These were the writings of

> voyagers who thought that they knew where they were going and ended up in a place whose existence they had never imagined ... (writing) chronicles of exploration (that) seem uncertain of their bearings, disorganized, fragmentary ... Their strength lies ... in the shock of the unfamiliar, the provocation of an intense curiosity, the local excitement of discontinuous wonders. Hence they present the world not in statement and harmonious order but in a succession of brief encounters, random experiences, isolated anecdotes of the unanticipated.[23]

It is the will to encounter difference and the unexpected, the 'local excitement of discontinuous wonders', that allows the pleasures of displacement and dispersal in such chronicles of wandering, of exploration and discovery. Such an account of histories which have so often been characterised in terms of an all-encompassing will for possession helps us to restore to the motifs of national – colonial – masculinity a sense of the local, the discontinuous, the unanticipated and the fragmentary. Perhaps the 'unknowingness' of the anecdote as a form of history can also help us locate the histories of masculine subjectivity in more local, discontinuous and provisional ways, whose encounter with difference is not only marked by the authority of possession but by contingent gestures of wonder at the 'radically unfamiliar' and the unanticipated.[24] The *fascinations* engendered by a decentred masculinity *also* form the experience of the foreign.

In the stories of colonial encounter, as Greenblatt shows, the moment of the marvelous gives way to that of possession. The immobility of wonder, the experience of the dissolving of self as a point from which knowledge is constituted, both offers a recognition of distance and 'excites a desire to cross the threshold, break through the barrier, enter the space of the alien'.[25] Greenblatt describes two paths that overcome this immobility, each of which, he argues, is distinct and radically opposed to the other. One is a movement from a 'radical alterity ... to a self-recognition that is also a mode of self-estrangement: you *are* the other and the other is you'; the other passes 'through identification to complete estrangement: for a moment you see yourself confounded with the other, but then you make the other become an alien object, a thing, that you can destroy or incorporate at will'.[26] This model chronologises what may in fact be a play or tension in masculine encounters: in *Lawrence* we see that the recognition of oneself in the other as foreign, estranged, leads to an objectification that allows foreignness to become part of the scenario of encounter, as the will to destroy and incorporate is both 'externally' and 'internally' directed. The exchange between these paths prevents masculine exchange from simply being harnessed to a colonial project wrought from the second path, of alienating the other until it becomes an object, which Greenblatt proposes brings about 'absolute difference and absolute possession'.[27] For the *absorption into the other* remains, in the enduring forms of fascination that becomes reiterated in masculine definition and remembrance. What does it mean to find oneself in love with estrangement?[28]

THE EXILE AND THE MOURNER

The estrangement at the heart of both national identification (implied by the displacement from 'natural' origins in the exclusion of other men) and masculine definition (implied by the corporeal displacement of a citizenship which separates the body politic from the physical body) offers a dispersed form of attachment and identification. The loss implied by this form of masculinity derives from the problematic male body whose marks are those of an archaic connection now denied. This loss of 'home' becomes translated into the figure of the foreigner, the wanderer and, now, the exile, as the will to encounter can find no resolution except in the 'voluptuous immobility' of permanent and debilitating estrangement. Destruction or incorporation are simply the measure of this recognition, as the dispersal of self implied in the play of identification can only find the achievement of masculine definition elusive.

It is the pathos of such a recognition that strikes me in the final moments of *The Leopard*, one that has as much to do with my perception of Burt Lancaster as it has to do with my inclination to understand masculinity as an unravelled, unconvinced kind of construction which can only be lived discontinuously, in incomplete appropriations and local excitements, in estrangements and dislocations. The Prince's humility is inseparable from the pathos of Burt Lancaster's performance, the directing of a definitively solid corporeality towards a surrender. This is not a matter of a film part, but of a performative – and a corporeal – tension: Burt's body *enacts* the nostalgia of anecdotes already told, a loss of aim and a ceding of the central part to others, the remorse for what is past and forgotten, no longer entirely self-present.[29] Prizing apart the masculine division between male bodies and men's social constitution brings the source of such pathos into view, the loss entailed in social subjectivity and presence. Characteristically slightly bent or stooping, in surrender, entreaty, solicitous inquiry, despair or seduction, Burt's gestures *mould themselves around the encounter*, recognise the distance implied in these movements, their dependence on journey over origin, and the immobility of their ending. He forms his body in the image of the foreigner, in recognition of his estrangement. Eventually, however much it seems to move in a tender gesture towards other figures, this body is alone: it is a body of solitude. In *The Leopard*, the Prince exhibits a melancholy which progressively robs him of movement. His mourning is for that which exists still, but which is no longer his, which he no longer wants and which is not available to be given up. He can only become struck by an interminable grief for an elusive object, a foreigner in his own land.

> Melancholy lover of a vanished space, he cannot, in fact, get over his having abandoned a period of time ... the foreigner is a dreamer making love with absence.[30]

This *encounter* with loss, the recognition that masculine identifications depend on the opening up of a space which precludes a 'place' for subjectivity, prevents us seeing the imaged body simply as the end point of identificatory impulses, a 'home', with a secure sexual meaning, and instead allows it to become part of a process of reiterating subjectivity's placelessness; both eliciting an identification but also orienting it towards the nostalgia of damaged intimacy, an affiliation with estrangement and the dissolving of the fantasy of self-presence. Perhaps this is the compelling quality I am attempting to identify in the fragile opulence of Burt's body, driven by an investment not in the groundedness of physique but in the *spatiality* of subjective encounter, its *moulding* of a dispersed corporeality. Does his corporeal enactment of narratives of displacement allow him to become the focus of a tension between the wish for a reinhabitation of the spaces of our intimacies and the passionate engagement with solitude, between historical remembrance and corporeality, between presence and self-presence?[31] These are the dilemmas by which female subjectivity has so long been described, but which become visible in the spaces of masculine corporeal figuring. As self-estrangement and the melancholy wrought by displacement combine to bring an immobility to masculinity, its relation to the male body becomes struck by an alterity and it dissolves under the weight of its own need to possess that which it defines itself against. As it becomes the site of a dividedness, this masculine figure thus allows the female spectator a form of identification that recalls her own movement in difference. As maternal identification provides an alternative model of self-presence for women, re-enacted in the gestures of female corporeality, the female body becomes defined in a movement of remembrance and a relation of nostalgia, in a recognition of the loss entailed in contained subjectivity.[32] It is this set of relations that allows her to remake the figuring of masculine instabilities in such male figures, in the image of those of femininity.

THE SWIMMER

In a later film, *The Swimmer* (Frank Perry, US, 1968), Burt Lancaster plays the part of a man returning to his neighbourhood after a long absence. As disturbances of landscape evidence his presence, he emerges from his own eclipse of the camera's image, hopping over stones and plants, his naked back moving off to dive into a glittering blue pool.

The owners of this pool, his neighbours, greet him as a missed friend and in his wooing of their delight in his presence, his gestures of pleasure become ever more extravagant. 'Did you ever see such a glorious day?', he exclaims, looking up, only for his insistent and winning smile to become dazzled by the bright midday sun. As he formulates a plan to swim home across the county, from pool to pool in connecting properties, he both embraces and separates himself from their company, using them simply to talk of a home and family they know he no longer has: 'Lucinda's at home and the girls are playing tennis'. In contrast to the Prince's intelligent restraint – and its physical cost – the Swimmer – with a careless physicality in his near-nakedness in the midst of formal social occasions, his enthusiastic greeting and embrace of intimate friends now rarely seen, his grasping of their hands and his searching gaze – is caught in an unmeasured fantasy of recapturing that which is lost to him: he is a perverse mirroring of the Prince's masculine dilemma, in his obsessive commitment to a relation to absence. Finally, as he reaches his destination, he finds an abandoned and neglected home, his wife left for another man, his family gone. Hunched in the doorway of the empty house they used to live in, howling and beating against the door as the rain pours down on his almost naked, crumpled body, his is the defeat of the exile, ever to be outside a home which is, in any case, unoccupied and broken: the site of a vanished and impossible dream of a situated self which could become the end and origin of the journey.

NOTES

1 Such as those which take up Laura Mulvey's concept of 'transvestite' identification in *Duel in the Sun* to develop a general theory of identification. See Laura Mulvey, 'Afterthoughts on "Visual Pleasure and Narrative Cinema" inspired by King Vidor's *Duel in the Sun* (1946)' in *Visual and Other Pleasures*, Macmillan Press, London, 1989.

2 The film reworks the novel, *Il Gattopardo*, by Giuseppe Tomasi di Lampedusa.

3 Geoffrey Nowell Smith, *Visconti*, Martin Secker and Warburg, London, 1973, p90.

4 Paul Ginsborg in his history of the emergence of the centre-left between 1958 and 1963, outlines the changes that permitted the alignment of the Christian Democrats with the Socialist Party, and its cost for the Italian Communist Party. Paul Ginsborg, *A History of Contemporary Italy: Society and Politics 1943-1988*, Penguin Books, Harmondsworth, 1990. Thanks to Belinda McKay for

informing me of this political and intellectual context and for her recommendation of the above sources.

5 Geoffrey Nowell Smith, *op.cit.*, p90.

6 *Ibid.*, p99.

7 See Julia Kristeva, *Strangers to Ourselves*, Harvester Wheatsheaf, Hertfordshire, 1991.

8 Carole Pateman, 'The Fraternal Social Contract', in *The Disorder of Women*, Polity Press, Cambridge, 1989, p36. While Pateman argues that the separation from the private realm of biology and reproduction is necessary for men to become social subjects, I aim to chart a division between the social and sexual definition of *masculinity itself*.

9 The characteristics of these patriarchal political orders can be contrasted to the features of social models which second wave feminism has defined as patriarchal, which are too broadly grouped and too loosely identified to convey accurately the nature of modern forms of masculine authority, contributing to a fantasy of masculine sovereignty too unified and absolute to admit such instabilities as I discuss here.

10 Julia Kristeva, *op.cit.*, p2.

11 *Ibid.*, p97.

12 Kathleen B. Jones, *Compassionate Authority: Democracy and the Representation of Women*, Routledge, New York and London, 1993, p80.

13 See Carole Pateman, 'The Disorder of Women' *op.cit.*, and Moira Gatens, 'Towards a Feminist Philosophy of the Body', Barbara Caine et al, (eds) *Crossing Boundaries*, Allen and Unwin, London, 1988.

14 Julia Kristeva, *op.cit.*, p97-98.

15 Jacques Derrida, *Writing and Difference*, trans. Alan Bass, University of Chicago Press, Chicago, 1978.

16 Smaro Kamboureli, 'Of Black Angels and Melancholy Lovers: Ethnicity and writing in Canada', in Sneja Gunew and Anna Yeatman, *Feminism and the Politics of Difference*, Allen and Unwin, Sydney, 1993, p143.

17 This is an argument which can be seen in Mary-Ann Doane, *The Desire to Desire: The Woman's Film of the 1940s*, Macmillan Press, London, 1987. Jessica Benjamin, in an account that echoes some of the work of Irigaray, argues that the 'inter-subjective' is the space of female identification and its engagements: female subjectivity is so formed from the movement of difference that its dividedness may not be so antipathetic to its motifs of selfhood (see Jessica Benjamin, *The Bonds of Love*, Virago, London, 1990, and Luce Irigaray, 'And the One Doesn't Stir Without the Other', translated by Hélène Vivienne Wenzel, *Signs*, 1981).

18 At this point we may recall Kaja Silverman's important emphasis on the non-sexually specific nature of castration anxiety as she suggests feminist film theory overlooks an original primary

castration in the recognition of the self as bounded and separate from the other, prior to the sexual recognition which initiates secondary castration (Kaja Silverman, *The Accoustic Mirror*, Indiana University Press, Bloomington, 1988, p14).

19 See Elizabeth Wilson, 'The Invisible *Flâneur*', in Kathie Gibson and Sophie Watson (eds), *Postmodern Cities, Spaces, Politics*, Basil Blackwell, London, 1994.

20 Gillian Swanson, 'Drunk with the Glitter', in Kathie Gibson and Sophie Watson (eds), *op.cit.*

21 Why sexual definition might be seen as a social problem in Britain in this period, and how problems of citizenship become addressed in terms of the pathologies of sexual difference does not concern me here, except to point out that it is and they do, most markedly. This is the subject of my monograph study, *Controversial Sexualities*, Routledge, forthcoming.

22 As an example of the way psychopathological models were applied to homosexuality in this period, see Clifford Allen, *A Textbook of Psychosexual Disorders*, Oxford University Press, London, 1962.

23 Stephen Greenblatt, *Marvelous Possessions: The Wonder of the New World*, Clarendon Press, Oxford, 1991, p2.

24 *Ibid.*, p6.

25 *Ibid.*, p135.

26 *Ibid.*

27 *Ibid.*

28 Kristeva connects her early work on melancholy with the foreigner in her discussion of the foreigner as a 'melancholy lover', Julia Kristeva, *op.cit.*, p9.

29 Stephen Greenblatt links nostalgia to the anecdote already told, *op.cit.*, p139.

30 Julia Kristeva, *op.cit.*, p9.

31 Gaston Bachelard, *The Poetics of Space*, Beacon Press, Boston, 1964, p5-9.

32 I am thinking of the work of Luce Irigaray and earlier work by Julia Kristeva, in particular, here. See Luce Irigaray, *op.cit.*, and Julia Kristeva, 'The Maternal Body', translated by Claire Pajaczkowska, *M/F*, Nos. 5&6, 1981. Both stress, to different degrees, the extent to which this physical closeness to the maternal brings about the potential for psychosis as well as a form of embrace of the other which prevents the neuroses of masculine subjective definition.

'Mad About the Boy': Masculinity and Career in *Sunset Boulevard*

Sarah Street

Noël Coward's lyrics 'Mad about the boy ... the sleepless nights I've had about the boy'[1] are the words of the 1963 hit record by Dinah Washington, which is now also the soundtrack for a recent Levi jeans cinema and television commercial with a gigolo theme: a young man dives in and out of a succession of swimming pools in the fleeting gaze of rich, admiring older women. But he pays them no attention and in the end stands triumphant on a diving board with a young athletic female swimmer. In a celebration of youth and beauty, they both dive off the board simultaneously, in a climax of Olympian symmetry. The significance of the lyric for my purposes is that in Billy Wilder's *Sunset Boulevard* (US, 1950) Norma Desmond/Gloria Swanson inscribes 'Mad About the Boy' on a cigarette case gift to her very own gigolo, down-at-heel screenwriter-in-hiding Joe Gillis/William Holden who begins and ends the film as an inert body in Norma's swimming pool. The same preoccupation with the role of the gigolo informs both usages of the lyric, and in this essay I will be concerned with its significance in the film. *Sunset Boulevard* is usually interpreted as a film about Hollywood victims: sound's replacement of silent cinema, figured in the charismatic but pathetic older star who has trapped her screenwriter victim in a vast, crumbling mansion.[2] However, to see Joe purely as *her* victim is, as I shall demonstrate, a reading which accords very much with his voice-over narration and glosses over the heart of the film's reflection on self-loathing and other effects of male prostitution.

Considering the film in terms of its genre, its representation of masculinity and its mise-en-scène, particularly the costume and accessories, I will also show how the cigarette case and inscription symbolise Joe's masculine humiliation at being a

223

gigolo and I will read *Sunset Boulevard* as a horror movie/film noir with a fascinating exploration of masculinity at its core.

Sunset Boulevard describes an overwhelming male anxiety about age, mortality and career. In post-war USA, lack of career success was taken as a sign of failure; not to have made one's way in a man's world was not to be fully a man: career and success were means of affirming masculinity. But rather than take responsibility for his career failure the film noir hero would, typically, 'put the blame on Mame'.[3] Like other noir heroes, Joe's own weakness allows his destruction by the *femme fatale*[4]: his end is pathetic, 'poor dope, he always wanted a pool'. Her end is madness, 'the dream she had clung to so desperately had enfolded her'. Joe's voice-over expresses his self-disgust and the film as a whole comments on the contingent nature of career: Joe's outdated screenplays don't sell and Norma's career was dependent on silent pictures.

SUNSET BOULEVARD AS JOE'S HORROR FILM, *THE NAKED AND THE DEAD*[5]

Just as the construction of the *femme fatale* in film noir tells us much about male anxiety, the 'monster as woman' in the horror film performs the same function.[6] *Sunset Boulevard* is a good case study of a mix of genres, both exposing the dilemmas of the central male protagonist. This masculine bias is made explicit by Joe's voice-over narration. However, as with other films which use this technique, we can't always trust what we are told.[7] In many ways *Sunset Boulevard* appears to be *Joe*'s picture (he has the controlling voice-over; he is the central protagonist), but his *ambiguous* authorship allows us to maintain a critical distance from his 'story'. The voice-over serves as a revealing pointer to Joe's psyche, his sense of self and his perception of being both a screenwriter and reluctant gigolo, caught in an awkward 'masculine/feminine' space.[8] That space is, literally, Norma's house: she is the owner and she is also Joe's employer, thus placing him in the subservient role more usually assigned to a woman. His often hysterical voice-over is further evidence of Joe's 'feminised' position, more typically associated with female protagonists. There are many references to Joe feeling trapped and contained by Norma's various 'spaces': his first small bedroom; the chimp in its tiny coffin which prefigures Joe's own collapse into the swimming pool; Norma's car which has replaced his own and Norma's bedroom. His sense of claustrophobia, for example, is emphasised when he comments on the number of photographs of Norma all over the house: 'How could she breathe in that house crowded with Norma Desmonds'. At New Year, when Norma has arranged for an orchestra to play at an intimate party for herself and Joe, his voice-over complains: 'I felt caught, like that cigarette contraption on her finger'. It is interesting how Joe articulates his fear of being in her grasp, a predicament further emphasised by the number of shots of her hands and references to their claw-like appearance.

Since Joe has made his version of events clear from the outset (he claims to be the 'true' author of the narrative which is about to unfold who must get his word in 'before you hear it all distorted and blown out of proportion'), we have to ask what lies behind his interpretation. An example of a clear dichotomy between what we hear and what we see comes early on in the film when Joe stumbles on Norma's house. We are *told* that it resembles Miss Havisham's decaying residence in *Great Expectations* before we *see* Norma behind the blinds wearing dark glasses. In its anxiety to control the narrative, the voice-over has impressed upon us the sex of the owner as well as her age and 'condition', seeking to deny us independent judgement and diffusing tension between word and image.

As a screenwriter and movie-buff, Joe's perceptions are best understood in terms of genre. When Paramount rejects his screenplay about baseball, he leaves the office making a bitter joke about his next film being titled *The Naked and the Dead*. In 1950, baseball screenplays were not deemed to have box-office potential, indicating a shift in studio attitudes towards more socially-conscious subject-matter. He is clearly out of touch with current trends. From Joe's point-of-view *Sunset Boulevard* might well bear the title *The Naked and the Dead*. The film opens with his corpse in the swimming pool (originally his voice-over was to be explicitly addressed to an 'audience' of corpses in the morgue).[9] His ambition has been stripped of value and his masculinity humiliated by dalliance with a wealthy, older woman who re-clothes him and won't let him out of her sight; by the end of the film he is victim to *his own* self-loathing and pity for Norma. He is, in fact, both naked and dead.

The film Joe wants us to see emerges as horror, with him trapped in Norma's 'Sunset Castle', a fall-guy who has unwittingly stumbled into his own worst nightmare.[10] In genre terms this posits him as innocent victim (horror), whose weaknesses as a man are also foregrounded (film noir). The horror references are plentiful: Joe speaks 'from the grave'; he is revolted by rats scuttling in the empty swimming pool; Norma's house is dark and mysterious; she is burying a dead chimp when Joe arrives; Max (a proto-typical horror butler) behaves as if Joe's visit was expected; Max plays eerie organ music; Norma entertains 'the waxworks'[11] and Joe refers to her as a 'sleepwalker'.[12] Under Wilder's direction, John F. Seitz's camera zooms in and out to create the suspense associated with horror, as Joe tells us: 'queerer things were yet to come'. As a young man Joe finds this situation repulsive: his horrific scenario is aptly described by Simone de Beauvoir: 'as men see it, a woman's purpose in life is to be an erotic object, when she grows old and ugly she loses the place allotted to her in society: she becomes a *monstrum* that excites revulsion and even dread'.[13] The word 'monstrum', with its particular connotations of evil and portent, sums up Joe's vision of Norma as a blood-sucking vampire.[14]

What emerges, therefore, is a picture of horror, seen from Joe's point-of-view: he feels humiliated and undignified by his status as a gigolo, and instead of escaping from a hostile Hollywood, he is forced to face his ignominious status in the castle of a '*monstrum*'. Not only is the '*monstrum*' female, she is also sexually demanding. It is this latter aspect which Joe finds most abhorrent, that there is a clear sexual dimension to his work on Norma's script. His feelings of self-disgust become all the more acute when he offers his body without loving Norma.

JUST A GIGOLO

Career and professionalism, key concerns of the 1950s white western male, are both at issue in *Sunset Boulevard*. Joe Gillis is a failing screenwriter who can't sell his latest script, 'Bases Loaded'. He has moved from a local newspaper office in Ohio to make his fame and fortune in Hollywood, but foreshadowing his 'career' as a gigolo, he is forced to demean himself by begging the studios to produce his scripts. He feels that he has no choice, because a return to Ohio, 'back to the smirking delight of the whole office', would be a public admission of failure, a surrender to suffocating small-town life and values.

Joe epitomises the standard image of Hollywood screenwriters as undervalued, underpaid and often forgotten.[15] He makes a cynical comment to this effect: 'audiences don't know somebody sits down and writes a picture, they think the actors make it up as they go along'. At Paramount he has to pretend that other studios are interested in his work, but to no avail. Although he decides to 'take advantage' of a producer who 'had always liked me', the script analyst, Betty Schaeffer, pronounces his baseball script 'flat and trite', without social awareness or feminine interest. The film gives the impression that for Joe screenwriting is an 'unmanly' occupation, far removed from the traditional hardware associated with the film business. Perhaps Joe is compensating for his association with the less 'masculine' aspects of film-making by writing 'hardboiled' baseball scripts. Furthermore, in the era of 'the woman's picture', there is no room for his Alan Ladd 'hardball' script – unless it can be turned into a Betty Hutton softball musical. It is interesting that it is Betty Schaeffer who rejects his script: she goes on to play an important part in the narrative. She befriends him, encourages him to write scripts again and finally acts as a catalyst for Joe's rejection of his role as Norma's gigolo.

When his agent refuses to lend him money Joe is forced to contemplate losing his car; the repossession of a car represents restriction, humiliation and worse, in Los Angeles. The terms used to describe the effect are emasculating: 'like having my legs cut off'. Joe takes refuge in Norma's mansion when his car has a blow-out on Sunset Boulevard and he is just able to reach her empty garage.

Once ensconced in the house, he finds that she too has been wounded by Hollywood, and by sound pictures in particular. He is struck by a common bond linking their fates: she reminds him of his own failure and 'feminised' position, and therefore we get a distorted picture of her through his eyes. The comparison between the two is clearly inappropriate because she was a star who is well-loved and remembered, almost worshipped, when she returns to Paramount, whereas Joe lurks outside, never having made his mark. Humiliation at career failure haunts him all over Norma's house. Evidence of her former stardom and talent is emphasised by pictures, film screenings and her impressive improvisational act. By contrast, Joe has no successful past to look back on. Once inside the mansion his career as a screenwriter merges with the more unsavoury role of being a gigolo, so much so that towards the end he tells Betty that he has given up professional screenwriting altogether. It is as if he has swapped occupations and entered the more secretive world of male sex work, symbolised by Norma's gift of the cigarette case engraved with the telling inscription: 'mad about the boy'.[16] Whereas Noël Coward's lyrics refer to women idolising an unattainable male film star, in *Sunset Boulevard* they are used with irony since it is *Norma* who is in a position to demand sexual favours from Joe.

The repossession of Joe's car signifies his loss of independence, and the items he gains – jewels, clothes, trinkets – his dependence.[17] It is significant that whereas the clothes have been made-to-measure, the jewels have been 'borrowed', handed down from 'Madame's former husbands', thus giving Joe the status of simply one in a succession of gigolos, a fact which cripples his sense of individuality. The emblems of his gigolo status are dress and certain key accessories. When Norma presents the cigarette case to Joe his voice-over tells us that he feels caught, ashamed to admit his position as a kept man, complaining: 'What right do you have to take me for granted?' 'What right?' she retorts ironically, 'Do you want *me* to tell you?'

There are many references to Joe's expensive clothes. When he goes to the New Year party his former workmates comment on his splendid attire. Norma takes him to buy a new set of clothes and the male sales assistant correctly assumes that because of her conspicuous wealth and her confident influence over his appearance she is an older woman accompanied by her gigolo. Joe's humiliation is complete when the assistant remarks that 'if the lady's paying' he might as well have the most expensive of everything. Ironically, despite *Sunset Boulevard*'s bleak presentation of Joe's gigolo role the Paramount press book included stills of 'debonair William Holden which will gain the co-operation of dress-hire agencies and mens' wear shops' in marketing the film.[18] The male viewer was thus targetted in an ambiguous address regarding Joe, his position as a gigolo to a certain extent compensated by his handsome looks and glamorous appearance and, of course, his voice-over control of the narrative.

Joe's inability to earn a living is accentuated by Norma's conspicuous wealth. There are many references to Joe's 'houseboy' status: when the 'waxworks' come to play cards he sits looking bored 'on call' behind her, emptying the occasional ashtray; he never has any cash; he can't pay his rent and his car has to be towed away, signalling the disappearance of his last trace of independence. In terms of the horror genre we might conclude that Joe has sold his body and soul to the aged *monstrum* who has cut him off from an independent manhood.

AGE AND AGEISM, MORTALITY AND IMMORTALITY

Sunset Boulevard was unusual for its time in that it depicted a relationship between an older woman and a young man. In its anxiety to encourage exhibitors to forge tie-ins with local dress-shops and department stores, the Paramount press book for the film stressed Swanson's youthful appearance as well as her glamorous outfits. At the same time, however, the posters posited Swanson as an ageing, mad creature staring into nothingness with Joe and Betty locked in a desperate embrace above her. Reviewers picked up on the themes of youth and age: *Picture Post* used a series of stills to show 'Swanson as she used to be' in 1923 juxtaposed with her in *Sunset Boulevard*, as 'the forgotten star who cannot believe she is obsolete both as an actress and as a woman ... Swanson's performance is deliberately and magnificently grotesque'.[19] The sardonic *New Yorker* review noted that the authors 'have a pretty unhealthy contempt for ageing stars'.[20]

As I have already indicated, remarks about age are plentiful in *Sunset Boulevard*. The social unacceptability of Joe's relationship with Norma and his embarrassment at being 'kept' by her both undermine his masculinity. After the disastrous New Year party, for example, Joe leaves, and his voice-over confides in us: 'I *had* to be with people my own age'. When Betty, ('nothing like being twenty-two'), asks him about the inscription on the cigarette case, Joe passes Norma off as 'a middle-aged lady, very generous, very foolish'. Joe's perception of Norma has a clear physical dimension. Despite his frequent comments about her age and seclusion, Norma is clearly still attractive. From an early point he realises that romantic involvement is on the agenda, despite his protestations to the contrary. Joe's 'twenty-twenty vision' doesn't prevent him from noticing her extraordinary eyes and charismatic presence. In fact many of his point-of-view shots are ambiguous in their vision of Norma as faded star/lover. When Joe takes on the task of re-writing her screenplay he looks her over several times as he hatches 'a little plot' of his own. Yet again, the audience must adopt a critical stance as far as the voice-over is concerned. Joe is not a helpless victim imprisoned in a mad-house, but a man who is disappointed by his lack of career success and humiliated by his resort to what he sees as, effectively, male prostitution: he is as much his own victim as Norma's, or Hollywood's, or Ohio's.

MASCULINITY AND MAX

Max is an important counterpart to Joe in the film's delineation of masculinity. Joe becomes Norma's gigolo because he has failed to earn a living as a screenwriter; 'trapped' in her castle there are no other models of masculinity except Max, who has given up his directorial career and his status as her husband in order to become her servant. He is, however, a portentous figure who appears to know what will happen next, exercising a great deal of control over the lives of Norma and Joe. When Joe is installed in his first room Max tells him that he already made up the bed because he was expecting him. Max is instrumental in keeping Joe at Norma's house. He collects his belongings from his apartment and allows Joe's car to be towed away. When his friends try to reach Joe on the telephone Max tells them that he is not there. It is Max who seems to understand that Norma has been a recluse too long to be able to bear the news that the public are no longer interested in her. When Joe confronts her with the truth she turns to Max. His motives for protecting Norma from the reality of her lost stardom are less selfish than Joe's: what is at stake for Joe is shelter from the law and poverty, whereas Max loves Norma and feels responsible for putting her into motion pictures. Joe is shocked to learn that Max 'discovered Madame' when she was sixteen and was both her first director and her first husband. He has, therefore, been indispensable to her in several different roles, and it is significant that Max's final role is as director of her dramatic 'scene' for the newsreel cameramen. It is all the more shocking to Joe that Max started off in a dominant position with Norma (he discovered her; directed her; married her) but still ended up being her servant, whereas he himself began by being in *her* employ and 'just a gigolo' with no independent status. Max is no longer of sexual interest to Norma which makes Joe's moral self-loathing all the more acute because whereas Max loves her, Joe does not.

Joe's perceptions of Max, therefore, are determined by his masculine fear of complete subservience to a woman, even to the extent of facilitating her desire for a younger man. Although Joe's dilemma reflects the centrality of career and success to representations of masculinity in popular cinema of the 1950s, it is important to remember that the model of masculinity represented by Max accords very much with 1950s notions of putting a woman on a pedestal, worshipping her, but not allowing her to take control of her own life. Even though Max is selfless in his indulgence of Norma's desires he will not help her to face the outside world or encourage her to be independent. Her delusion of still being a popular film star with a glamorous young lover at her side is totally dependent on Max's co-operation.

Max is often the bearer of crucial information and engineers Joe's participation in key events. He informs Joe of Norma's history and draws attention to her suicide attempts. When Max tells Joe that 'Madame' has attempted suicide several times in 'melancholy moments', Joe assumes that, despite Max's phoney fan letters, the cause is her lost stardom. Joe then realises that both he and Max have been dishonest in not challenging her delusions. Joe performs the gigolo role reluctantly but nevertheless despite several opportunities never leaves Norma. There are no locks on the doors, though she does resort to emotional blackmail. The first time Joe escapes, for example, he rushes back on learning from Max that Norma has attempted suicide.[21] Even though Joe pities Norma and is clearly trying to stifle the nurturing/feminine aspect of his personality, it is important not to underestimate the use he has made of her; his self-disgust at allowing himself to become a gigolo and his fear of ending up like Max. Faking 'being in love' with Norma in the New Year reconciliation scene is Joe's way of preventing another suicide attempt (significantly, his back is to the camera when he goes to her bed), but his full acceptance of the gigolo role only fuels her fantasies of a return to the screen with her own special Valentino in the background. From that point on the emphasis of the film shifts to Joe's self-punishment and his complete humiliation. But all the time Max is in the background, witnessing Joe's emasculation for the greater good of Norma's desire.

Joe's encounter with Betty is also illustrative of his rejection of the model of masculinity represented by Max. After Joe's clandestine screenwriting meetings with Betty she falls in love with Joe and Norma's jealousy eventually brings the three together. After a scene laden with Joe's self-disgust during which he explains his gigolo status to Betty, he finally walks out on Norma, leaving her to commit suicide. He feels that he does not deserve Betty as much as his friend Artie, even though Betty loves Joe, not Artie. For Joe, Betty is the opposite of Norma: she is young, uncomplicated and optimistic about work and life in general. The self-loathing that is the consequence of his position as gigolo, however, renders him incapable of responding to her love. Unlike Max, he is not able to privilege the *woman*'s desire. He can only allow it to reflect on himself and his predicament. It is the revelation of his situation to Betty, a woman who loves him and who has encouraged him to revive his screenwriting career, which finally gives Joe the courage to leave Norma, making way for the excessive noir/horror ending of tragedy and madness. It is as if he feels 'marked' by his prostitution, considering himself henceforward morally unfit to love Betty. His prostitution has made him feel part of the space represented by Norma's house, it is his 'prison', a space he feels condemned to occupy under the unrelenting gaze of Max.

To return to Noël Coward's lyric, there are, clearly, much more than 'traces of the cad about the boy' in *Sunset Boulevard*. It seems that Joe is caught between different worlds and conflicting masculinities which he finds impossible to reconcile. The 'masculine/feminine' space he occupies in the narrative proves to be intolerable: he cannot accept Norma's world where he is 'feminised', reduced to being an obedient gigolo or, like Max, surrendering everything to be her servant; nor can he suffer the humiliation of being an 'ordinary man', returning to his copy-desk and his stifling life in Ohio as a failed screenwriter who had tried his luck in Hollywood and failed. Nor can he respond to Betty's 'pure' and selfless love, since, as a gigolo, he had 'prostituted' himself. All he *can* do is seek to 'set the record straight' for us, the audience, by means of his voice-over control of the narrative. But though he has the voice-over at his disposal the film denies Joe total control over the narrative, sound *and* image. As my film noir/horror analysis has shown, the dilemma for his masculinity posed by career failure and his lapse into male prostitution are most clearly expressed by his construct of Norma as a '*monstrum*', a horror movie creature from the *real* film he has written: *The Naked and the Dead*.

NOTES

I would like to thank the following for their comments on drafts of this paper: Pat Kirkham, Sue Simkin, Melissa Sydeman and Janet Thumim.

1 Noël Coward, *The Lyrics*, Methuen, London, 1983, pp129-132.
2 For example, a recent summary of the film by Michael Billington in his review of Andrew Lloyd Webber's musical version of *Sunset Boulevard*: 'Joe Gillis, a Hollywood hack on the run from creditors, winds up in the baroque mansion of forgotten silent star Norma Desmond. In a world of lost illusions, she employs him to work on her unfilmable Salome script. He is drawn into her web of fantasy, becoming her lover, household pet and finally the fatal victim of her overwhelming vanity', *The Guardian*, 14 July 1993.
3 'Put the blame on Mame' is the song Rita Hayworth sings in *Gilda* (US, 1946). The lyrics refer to how men frequently blame women for their misfortunes.
4 Bruce Crowther, for example, calls Norma 'one of the most grotesque of all *femmes fatales*' in *Film Noir: Reflections in a Dark Mirror*, Columbus, London, 1988, p128.

5 *The Naked and the Dead* is the title of Norman Mailer's 1949 novel and is also the title of a film directed by Raoul Walsh (1958).

6 For male anxiety in film noir see Frank Krutnik, *In a Lonely Street: Film Noir, Genre, Masculinity*, Routledge, London, 1991 and Barbara Creed's *The Monstrous-Feminine: Film, Feminism and Psychoanalysis*, Routledge, London, 1993, which deals with the woman in horror films.

7 See Robert Stam, Robert Burgogyne and Sandy Flitterman-Lewis, *New Vocabularies in Film Semiotics: Structuralism, Post-Structuralism and Beyond*, Routledge, London, 1992, pp97-100.

8 See Amy Lawrence, *Echo and Narcissus: Women's Voices in Classical Hollywood Cinema*, University of California Press, Oxford, 1991, p164.

9 See Maurice Zolotow, *Billy Wilder in Hollywood*, Limelight, New York, 1992, p165.

10 Charles Brackett (co-screenwriter on *Sunset Boulevard*) revealed in an interview that they first thought of Norma as 'a kind of horror woman' (undated; British Film Institute microfiche jacket on *Sunset Boulevard*).

11 Norma's group of friends from the silent era who were played by themselves: Buster Keaton, Anna P. Nilsson and H.B. Warner.

12 Danny Peary, *Cult Movies*, Vermilion, London, 1982, is one of the few books to suggest horror as the genre of *Sunset Boulevard*.

13 Simone de Beauvoir, *Old Age*, André Deutsch, London, 1972, pp122-123. The word *monstrum* means 'an evil omen, a monster', deriving from the Latin *monitum*, to warn.

14 Danny Peary, *op.cit.*, compares *Sunset Boulevard* with *Dracula's Daughter* (1936), a horror film about a female vampire. For further reading on the 'monstrous feminine' see Barbara Creed, *op.cit.*

15 See Ian Hamilton, *Writers in Hollywood, 1915-1951*, Heinemann, London, 1990.

16 Richard Dyer discusses how the hero in film noir is often engaged in sexual 'work' in his essay 'Homosexuality and Film Noir', in *The Matter of Images*, Routledge, London, 1993, pp67-68.

17 Wilder and Brackett had already dealt with the gigolo theme in *Hold Back the Dawn* (1941), starring Charles Boyer. In more recent films like Schrader's *American Gigolo* (1980), a gigolo is associated with ambiguous sexuality; excessive attention to clothes and he is portrayed as an aimless person who is cured by meeting the 'right girl' in the end.

18 Press-book, *Sunset Boulevard*, British Film Institute Library.

19 Catherine de la Roche, *Picture Post*, 19 August 1950.

20 Philip Hamburger in *New Yorker*, 19 August 1950.

21 Although Amy Laurence, *op.cit.*, argues that Joe stays because of Norma's charisma and because he sympathises with her.

'Maybe He's Tough But He Sure Ain't No Carpenter': Masculinity and In/competence in *Unforgiven*

Janet Thumim

The shortcomings of Sheriff Little Bill Dagget/Gene Hackman's carpentry, noted and condoned by his deputies, are measured against his competence in being a man: it is his acknowledged 'toughness' which earns him the fear and respect of his fellows. As the narrative unfolds, however, this very toughness is continually put under the spotlight of audience attention – it is observed, recorded, analysed, questioned. This exploration, this measurement of masculinity is couched in terms both of being tough – equated with fearlessness, brutality, single-mindedness – and of competence since the paradigm for masculinity in the western is the gunfighter who must, by definition, be competent – else he's dead. What is so interesting about this western – Clint Eastwood's 'return' to the classic western – is the way in which competence is privileged, being examined not only in the context of gun-fighting and toughness, but also in relation to other and diverse activities – carpentry, farming, story-telling. The idea of competence, as foregrounded in this film, invites a meditation on history – the stuff of the western – calling into question both the morality and the veracity of propositions about America's past as delivered in western myths. That this is not a new project is clear in the near ubiquitous reference, in reviews of the film, to the western before 1964 (which

Eastwood, with Sergio Leone, 'colluded in undermining'[1]) and particularly to the John Ford/John Wayne films, and often specifically to *The Searchers* (John Ford, US, 1956). The conflicting generic demands of melodrama and realism produced fractures in the episodic narrative of *The Searchers*, most striking in Ethan/John Wayne's *volte-face* when he catches up with Debbie/Nathalie Wood near the end of the film and, against all expectations, rescues her despite what he regards as the defilement of her life as Scar's squaw. In *Unforgiven*, however, the two modes are woven together so intricately that each becomes a part of the other: the truthfulness of the melodramatic axis is measured against its consequences in a realist discourse, and the adequacy of a realist account is constantly checked in terms of its moral implications. The marker of the interchange, the place where the two axes intersect, is in the idea of competence, hence this film suggests competence is central to masculinity. *Unforgiven* is not only a classic western, it is also *about* the western and thus, necessarily, it is also *about* masculinity in both its personal and its public, or social, manifestations. The complex moral and epistemological questions it poses reach far beyond the confines of the genre or of the historical moment, 1880, in which it is set – it is not simply (if it were simple) a matter of making a western as powerful and compelling as *The Searchers* or *Shane* (George Stevens, US, 1953), or *Rio Bravo* (Howard Hawks, US, 1959), but of insisting on our attention to the meanings underlying the myths of the west – for America, for men, for all of us.

An on-screen title informs us that the film is set in Big Whiskey, Wyoming, in 1880. A cowboy, visiting the town brothel euphemistically named Greely's Billiard Hall, is mocked by a whore and is so enraged that he responds by slashing her face. The Sheriff, Little Bill Daggett, dispenses summary justice by ordering the cowboys to compensate the Saloon and Billiard Hall owner, Skinny/Anthony James, for his loss of the whore's earnings. Outraged by what they see as an *un*just refusal to consider compensating the woman herself, Delilah/Anna Thomson, the whores put up a bounty for anyone who will avenge her by killing the cowboy. This sets the narrative in train, and a succession of bounty hunters is expected in town. Amongst them is Will Munny/Eastwood and his erstwhile partner Ned Logan/Morgan Freeman, brought out of their farming retirement by the young Schofield Kid/Jaimz Woolvert who wants to prove himself against what he imagines to be the 'truth' of the legendary western heroes of whom he has heard (as we have) so many stories. English Bob/Richard Harris is also attracted by the bounty and, accompanied by his 'biographer', the writer Mr Beauchamp/Saul Rubinek, arrives in town first, only to be beaten and humiliated by the Sheriff who is determined not to allow a re-run of the mythic western free-for-all in his town. Eventually Will, Ned and the Kid track down and kill the cowboy and his partner, and Ned is caught and beaten to death in reprisal. This event triggers Will's anger – not the professional bounty hunter now, but the moral outrage of an avenging partner – and in a final and spectacular set-piece he shoots the Sheriff and deputies before returning to his two children, his run-down pig farm and his wife's grave. An end title informs us that he subsequently disappeared and was said to have 'prospered in dry goods' in San Francisco.

CARPENTRY AND COMPETENCE

> I don't deserve this, to die like this
> I was building a house.

Even as the butt of Will Munny/Eastwood's rifle hovers above Little Bill/Hackman's chin in the final scene, Little Bill laments his unfinished house. The gun fighting, violent sheriff, survivor of the legendary tough towns whose names he invokes like a litany punctuating set piece displays of his sadistic violence – 'Kansas, Missouri, Cheyenne ...' – was looking forward to a peaceful old age. He thought he would sit on his porch, the violence and competencies of his life now behind him, smoking a pipe as he watched the sun set over the lake. The film's imbrication of melodrama and realism is invoked in the Sheriff's last words: his mode of death is undeserved – the moral axis – because he was engaged in a practical and forward looking enterprise, he was building a house – he was participating in the functional here-and-now of realism.

In this film the men keep talking. But what do they talk about? They talk of desire, fear, power and death; of the past, of remembering and forgetting and knowing. These concerns weave in and out of talk about competence and incompetence, about gun fighting and, above all, about stories of the old west in which these two terms, competence and gun fighting, are synthesised. When the Schofield Kid rides up to Will Munny's pig farm in search of 'the worst, meaning the best' gun fighter to be his partner and is witness to a grey-haired and muddy display of half-heartedness and incompetence in pig handling, he is disappointed. He finds, he thinks, nothing but a 'broken down old pig farmer'. When Will Munny, recognising his limits as a pig farmer in an eloquent sigh as he leans on the pigs' corral, decides after all to join the Kid in his bounty hunt, he can't even mount his horse. His struggle to gain control of the animal is a recurrent motif – part tragic, part comic – of the narrative. Is he also engaged in a struggle to control his own 'animal' self, formerly responsible for the acts of violence, brutality and drunkenness of which his recently deceased, God-fearing, law-abiding wife Claudia had 'cured' him? Was it through her agency that he was able to control himself? The interesting question of what it was about him that elicited her support – something her mother, as a title tells us, could never understand – isn't answered. The film is not about its women. The tragedy in the motif of Will's struggle with his horse is the consequence of the man of action's loss of prowess, its comedy is based in the unlikely spectacle of his *in*ability even to reach first base – to get on his horse. As in the classic clown's device, laughs are in response to the clever performance of incompetence: here is a simultaneous recognition and undercutting of skill. The audience's laughter both applauds the clever performance and delights in the carthatic ridicule of 'prowess'. Will Munny's problems with his horse are excessive and, as if to underline the point, the narrative also delivers this spectacle to excess. When Will and his partner Ned catch up with the Kid they discover that, despite his extravagant claims the Kid's eyesight is so poor he can only hope to hit close range targets – he is practically blind: a blind gun fighter, too, is a comic absurdity. But these are not only comic moments for the audience but also serious and disabling deficiencies in the skills on which each character depends for his livelihood. All the central male characters are shown to be deficent in a skill that they themselves value and need. Their inadequacies are not just shown in passing, revealed at a tangent to some more pressing concern of the narrative, they are emphatic – leitmotifs, almost: Will's falling off his horse, the Kid's near blindness, the Sheriff's diabolical carpentry.

The event that sparks off the narrative concerns a man's inadequacy: when Delilah, who 'didn't know no better' – who was too inexperienced to have learned never to laugh *at* a man – giggled at the sight of her cowboy client's 'teensy little pecker', his enraged, almost anguished response was to slash her to bits. In its attention to the question of in/competence, the film proposes a distinction between the moral axis, good:bad, and the functional one, competent:incompetent. Social order requires a balance of the moral and the functional, which the Law attempts to negotiate. Woven through the fabric of the film is Will's refrain, sometimes assertive, sometimes questioning, sometimes plaintive, that 'I ain't like that no more'. He has changed: he has *been* changed by dear departed Claudia since, for Claudia, to be a skilful gunfighter is to be a bad man. So Will claims that he is no longer a Bad Man, a gunman. It isn't his competence that is at issue but his motivation, which he understands as pertaining to the realm of the moral. Hence one of the serious questions posed in the film is the relation between these two axes. Competence (gun-fighting, love-making, carpentry) is *necessary* to a convincing demonstration of masculinity, but moral rectitude (right action, responsible concern for the self and others, the knowing use of hindsight and foresight) marks maturity. Does this produce a paradox? How can competent masculinity be marked as mature? Is it, perhaps, a question not so much of knowing how to act, but of knowing when? 'I ain't like that no more' doesn't mean Will *can't* operate competently as a gun fighter, but that he *can* distinguish judiciously as to when such skill is appropriate. Will's lesson is eventually learned by the Kid who, initially full of bravado, is so chastened by the actual experience of violent bloodshed that he is ready to accept his inadequacy, to relinquish both his share of the bounty and his gun: 'I'd rather be blind and ragged than dead'.

But Little Bill's is a more complex and fractured character, living with crude, pragmatic and often flawed judgements – rough and ready, one might say, like his carpentry. It is in this character that the film's dialectic of melodrama and realism is most finely balanced. His inadequate justice, his barely controlled sadism, not to mention his complete oblivion to the shortcomings of his woodworking skills, exist in an utterly convincing tension with his avuncular bonhomie and the engaging pleasure he takes in building his house. Like John Wayne's Ethan Edwards in *The Searchers*, Little Bill is at once appealing in his verisimilitude and anachronistic in his values. Ethan knows how to track and, eventually, to find Debbie, he knows what to expect from the various renegades from the old west encountered during the long search – but he doesn't know how to fit into the settled, social Texas of post-civil war, post-frontier America. Little Bill knows how to deploy terror in his exercise of control, but he can't acknowledge the justice of the whores' complaint. How does the narrative resolve the conflict it proposes? The future, it would seem, is to belong to the survivors, the repressed Will, 'prospering in dry goods in San Francisco' and the near-blind, ragged Kid. Little Bill's 'mature' masculinity is inadequate now, it's a fiction. As Sheriff, in his negotiation of the moral and functional imperatives, he has failed. He has been incompetent in his delivery of the Law, and he's been out-gunned by a bounty hunter.

GUN FIGHTING

> But the Duck was faster and hot lead blazed from his smoking six guns.

While questions of skill, competence and adequacy might loom large in men's private assessment of themselves and their peers, the issue of gun fighting is also about competition, dominance and power – overtly about the relations *between* men. No matter the size of the pecker – the gun can be depended on to spurt hot lead on demand. One of the attractions of Little Bill's complex character is his apparent recognition of this, and the consideration of motive and consequence evident in his discussions with – or rather his monologues addressed to – the writer/observer Mr Beauchamp. Little Bill, Sheriff of Big Whiskey, Wyoming, in 1880, and Gene Hackman, accomplished veteran of Hollywood, seem to be laughing in unison over the extract from Mr Beauchamp's dime novel, *The Duke of Death*. We're invited to smile, too, at Little Bill's mispronunciation; but from his position of power he dismisses Mr Beauchamp's correction – command of language (and story-telling, and history, and myth-making) is secondary, for Little Bill, to command of the situation at hand. But as the narrative unfolds Little Bill's rough and ready approach, his crude pragmatics, is found wanting. His summary and fatally mistaken dispensing of justice, avoiding the 'fuss' of a trial and compensating Skinny for his 'investment' rather than Delilah for her cut-up face, turns out to have been as incompetent as his carpentry. Though his opponent, Will, reminds him that 'deserve's got nothing to do with it' before delivering the final shot, still the elegant narrative composition balancing, as it does, classic western oppositions, attributes and motives in a harmony fit to delight any structuralist,[2] invites an explanation for his death.

What kind of man do Eastwood as director and Hackman as actor construct, in their production of Little Bill? His easy-going pleasantness is succeeded by a chillingly passionate violence perceived by observers both on screen and in the films' audiences as bordering on the pathologically sadistic. Philip French, reviewing the film in the *Observer*,[3] wrote:

> The middle-aged Daggett disarms Bob and with a sadistic glee destroys him physically and mentally as an example to others.

and, in a similar vein, Sue Heal's *Today*[4] piece described the character as

> the terrifying Hackman who will brook no vigilantes in his town and treats all-comers with an unbridled physical force that turns law-keeping into abuse.

In three set-piece scenes, each more savage and distressing, Little Bill's beatings of the would-be bounty hunters English Bob, Will Munny and Ned Logan are the object of meticulous, lavish – some would say excessive – filmic attention. There are other depictions of violence from the initial slashing in the brothel to the shoot-outs at the Bar T and the final showdown at Greely's Saloon, but the camera, in these other scenes, doesn't dwell on victim or aggressor in such lascivious detail but rather delivers an atmospheric interpretation of western motifs. Little Bill is distinguished amongst the film's male characters by his engagement with physical brutality – and it is indeed a physical engagement as he whips, kicks and punches his victims. The only time we see him using a gun it is as a club.

As most reviewers have noted, however, the film also goes out of its way to deglamorise the violence typical of the genre.[5] Not only is Little Bill's physical brutality clearly coded as excessive, but also the gunfights which the film delivers are notable for the attention paid to the fear, suffering, anxiety and, again, the incompetence which, it would seem, were their real and inevitable accompaniments. The excessively long drawn out shooting of the first cowboy, Davey, during which Ned cannot shoot and the Kid cannot see, is an example. The dying cowboy calls piteously for water and Will, apparently exasperated by the western's demands for clean and callous dispatchings, breaks all the rules when he calls to the cowboy's comrades to bring him water, promising not to shoot while they do. Not for this film the gunfights sanitised in long-shot which contributed to the cultural status of early western heroes. The competitive strategy of the gunfighter is to inspire fear in his opponent, and fear is evidence of weakness, if not of submission. The film is relentless in its delineation of fear, noting it in heroes, villains and bystanders alike, and, in so doing, problematising those categories. It is no longer clear, by the end of the film, who *were* the heroes, villains or bystanders, nor even, perhaps, what a hero is. From reminiscences about 'the west' of history and legend, the narrative proceeds to 'replay' a paradigmatic western event, emphasising all the discomfort, anxiety and pain conventionally omitted in the interests either of glamour or of a lascivious dwelling on spectacular brutality and bloodshed – such as in Peckinpah's *The Wild Bunch* (US, 1969).

The careful cataloguing of the signs of fear is worth recalling – partly because the implicit acknowledgement of the protagonists' frailty is productive in the interests of a realist re-assessment of the western legends, and partly because they account for the survivors' rejection of the 'meaner than hell cold-blooded goddamn killer' role. Will, once the most cold-blooded killer in the west, will prosper in dry goods, and the Kid, avid consumer of western stories and would-be dandy and gun-fighter, vows never to touch his Schofield model Smith and Wesson again. The sweating and shaking deputy, standing in the Sheriff's office, a framed picture of a stag visible on the wall behind him, argues that anyone can be scared. The almost palpable presence of fear is brilliantly suggested in the following scene when, as Mr Beauchamp reaches into his shoulder bag for the book which will substantiate his claim to being a writer, the tense silence is broken first by the sound of the nervous deputies' clicking rifles, and then by the trickle of liquid forming a pool on the ground by his feet as his bladder gives way. But it isn't only novice deputies and visiting writers who experience fear in the face of western (or should I say masculine?) violence and lawlessness. English Bob, bloody, beaten and imprisoned, knows enough to be frightened by Little Bill's cat and mouse game as he instructs Mr Beauchamp in the subtler intricacies of gun fighting. Will, in his delirious fever, sees grotesque and terrifying visions from beyond the grave and tells Ned 'I'm scared of dying', his admission closely followed by an acknowledgement that this fear is somehow shameful (emasculating?) 'don't tell anyone the things I said, don't tell my kids'. And then there is the Kid, whose quest for the reality behind the western myth fuels the narrative, and whose own admission of fear is in many ways a more cathartic moment than the final shoot out, or than Will's operatic departure from Big Whiskey. It is the Kid's acknowledgement of his fear which allows his (and the audience's) recognition of the tawdry and brutal reality underlying the western fiction. The narrative's project, to re-educate the Kid, raised as he has been on stories of the west (stories of the masculine) is in a sense completed here in the scene between the man and the youth under the lone pine. What follows – Will's resumption of his discarded persona as the most cold-blooded killer in the West – can be seen as the last repeat of the western melodrama's tragic chorus. Suddenly carpentry, pig farming or even dealing in dry goods, even though they may not enjoy such spectacular sound, lighting and effects, seem preferable alternatives.

The film's articulation of fear is amplified by its recognition of the multiple and intricate connections, in the masculine psyche, between sexuality and violence. It is this, the powerful opening scene suggests, that makes for such a heady concoction when a private inadequacy is played out in a public contest – particularly when the terms are guns and whiskey. The links, for masculinity, between sexuality and power (the latter *always* coded as violence in the western) are acknowledged in several references to the penis. It is the 'teensy little pecker' that is the initial cause of all the trouble; Two Gun Corcoran is so called, Little Bill tells Mr Beauchamp, not because he carried two guns but because 'he had a dick that was so big, it was longer than the barrel on that Walker Colt', and Ned refers to the Kid's penis as his 'pistol', when they make their precipitous escape from Greely's billiard hall. But whereas reference to the analogic relation between the penis and the gun is no doubt intended to amuse, to be a lighter moment in the textual construction – albeit (as Delilah discovered) a comedy fraught with danger – there is, I think, a more profound and more troubling relation between male sexuality and the exercise of violent power lurking beneath the surface of the film, half acknowledged, half concealed. Here I return to the film's excessive concentration on the details of Little Bill's grotesque and barely controlled physical attacks.

After the first of these, when he has finished kicking English Bob around the main street of Big Whiskey he is suddenly 'spent', his power and energy wasted. Limp and alone, his opponent vanquished, he returns the gaze of the shocked onlookers as if seeing them for the first time and, irritated by their intrusive presence at his 'post-coital' depletion, sends them away:

> What are you all looking at?
> Go on, get out of here, scoot.
> Go on, mind your own business.

When he whips Ned, stripped to the waist and gripping the cell bars, the camera lingers perhaps just a little too long on the extreme close up of Ned's face, Little Bill's face just behind, whispering threats. Is it Ned's shallow breathing, his glistening skin, or is it Little Bill's intensity, his whispering, that lends this scene such a sexual charge? Little Bill's violence is not expressed through the stand off, the shoot out, the exercise of skill and cunning in hunting, tracking, aiming and so on, but in the sweaty intimacy of (almost) hand to hand combat – except there's no combat here, just beating, which is what makes the scenes so hard to watch. Once again I'm reminded of Ethan Edwards in *The Searchers*, and the grim retribution he exacted from his opponent, Scar. What is less clear is how far the film is condoning or even legitimating the dubious pleasures of spectacularly sexualised violence, how far the propitiatory jokes about guns and penises are offered as a mask, a cover for a more disturbing model of male sexuality, one which requires a powerless partner (should I say victim, opponent?)

STORY-TELLING

> Hell, I even thought I was dead but I found out it was just that I was in Nebraska.

Whereas the classic western characteristically glamorises violence and romanticises the arduous frontier life, this film works to deconstruct, even to undermine those myths. The emphasis on competence as the measure of moral adequacy in the melodramatic mode and of functional adequacy in the realist mode requires the film's protagonists to evaluate each other's past and present actions – to deliver the measurement. Thus the very processes of storytelling, of men's talk, are at the centre of the film, embodied in the characters of the writer/observer Mr Beauchamp, author of *The Duke of Death* and in the would-be gun fighter – we might say the consumer of western fictions – the self-styled Schofield Kid. Both these characters propose 'histories' which are corrected by the central pair of protagonists Little Bill Dagget and William Munny. Through this device of doubled pairs of storyteller and listener the film draws attention to the gap between the event and its recounting, and hence to the formation of the story – and of history. Various sources purveying western myths are emphasised in our glimpses of the newspaper, the *Cheyenne Gazette*, the book, *The Duke of Death*, in the traces of the Kid's Uncle Pete and his reminiscences, in Little Bill's eyewitness corrections to English Bob's falsified accounts and, finally, in Mr Beauchamp's faltering attempt to begin a history of the massacre he (and we) have just witnessed.

Mr B: You killed five men. You're single-handed.
Will: Yeah.
Mr B: That's, ah, that's a Spencer rifle, right?
Will: That's right.
Mr B: Who, er, who d'you kill first?
       When confronted by superior numbers an experienced gunfighter will always fire on the best shot first.
Will: Is that so?
Mr B: Yeah. Little Bill told me that.
       Then you probably killed him first, didn't you.
Will: I was lucky in the order.
       But I've always been lucky when it comes to killing folks.
Mr B: Is that so?
       Who was next?
       It was Clyde, right?
       It must have been Clyde. Well it could have been Deputy Andy.
Will: All I can tell you is who's going to be last.

In this way the audience itself is implicated in the recording, preservation and recycling of stories and their transformation into myths – both the myths of the western *and* the myths of the masculine. It is impossible to ignore the film's demads that its audiences consider the politics of storytelling as well as its consequences for culture and history – for social formation. At the same time it *is* a story and it is *about* stories.

Storytelling assumes this crucial importance once hindsight allows the recognition, frequently reiterated by both Will Munny and Little Bill in their re-tellings, that the protagonists of the legendary events were too drunk to shoot straight half the time, let alone to remember who shot who, and why. Thus the film works to reveal, as we have seen, not only the complex and unsettling links between male sexuality and violence, and their centrality to the western genre, but also the uncertain and provisional understandings of reality embodied in both contemporary and historical accounts of western history. As Philip French put it in the *Observer* review[6] 'it is a meditation on history and the American experience, and an allegorical commentary on the state of the union'. So men's fictions are laid bare. Could this be the offence implied in the film's resonant title?

There is a clear distinction, in *Unforgiven*, between 'men' and 'boys', between those (men) who remember the real west because they were there, they have earned their status as 'men' by virtue of their survival which has required their competence as gunfighters, and those (boys) who know *of* the west, but do not *know* it. The older characters – Little Bill, William Munny, English Bob, legends in their own time – must educate, discipline and protect the younger ones – the group of deputies, the 'hardworking' cowboys, the Kid and, through the figure of the writer, the readers of the future – the audience for the stories. It is here that the implied synonymity between 'the west' and 'the men' is instrumental in defining masculinity. Herein too lies the film's fascination for the female audience, because in deconstructing the myths of the west the film is also obliged to deconstruct the myths of the masculine. Just as the 'teensy little pecker' summarises, retrospectively, the in/ adequacy: sexuality: violence matrix at the centre of patriarchy's construction of the masculine, so the resonances of the initial event, the cowboy cutting Delilah's face, constitute a paradigm for western storytelling. The pivotal scene in the melodrama/ realism dialectic ordering the narrative is the meeting between Will and Delilah, when he first sees her for himself. He is recovering from a fever contracted after his ride to Big Whiskey in torrential rain and his brutal beating at the hands of Little Bill in Greely's Saloon. For three days he's been hovering, delirious, near death. His old, stubbled, bruised face half buried in unwholesome blankets is seen in medium shot, in the shadows of a dilapidated shed. Delilah, her scars healed but still visible, is tending him. She seems a little hesitant, awkward, frightened perhaps, an ordinary woman in her dull coloured dress and enveloping cloak, from the homestead or wagon train of any western. But to him she is, as he says, a 'beautiful woman with scars' – his summary, in itself redolent of melodrama's central paradigm, invites the audience to take a second look at the scene. Now the characters' latent meanings to each other, and to us, come to the fore. She is beautiful because she has suffered; he is frightening because he is unknown. The symbolic possibilities of melodrama transform the characters, the landscape, they shift the focus of our attention. But as our attention is shifted, realist and melodramatic codes are simultaneously in play, and realism's damaged man/scarred woman are balanced by melodrama's threatening male/suffering female, the equation offered as exemplary of patriarchy's masculine and its feminine Other.

The films opens with a low lit medium close-up of a cowboy 'riding', in the whores' own parlance, a semi-clothed woman. The rhythmic creaking of the bedsprings is interrupted by the sounds of cries and commotion from the adjacent room which the couple (and the camera) run to investigate. All is chaos: the medium and close-up shots of the dimly lit and crowded interior make it impossible to distinguish people and actions; a claustrophobic urgency pervades the scene. Silence and order are achieved by a threatening gun to the head of the enraged cowboy whose 'pecker' had so amused the sadly ignorant Delilah. Thus, in the very construction of this scene the film suggests the impossibility of answering the question 'what happened' in any but the most partial manner. The contingency of truth is subsequently demonstrated through the various (and varying) accounts both of the incident and of Delilah's face, which punctuate the film. Alice/Frances Fisher, in her fury at Little Bill's misogynist prioritising of Skinny's property rights over Delilah's own rights, refuses Davey's conciliatory offering: 'She's got no face and you bring her a goddamn mangy pony?' The Kid, in his efforts to enlist Will as his partner, claims that Delilah's eyes, ears and 'teats' were slashed, as well as her face and, as in a game of Chinese whispers, this version is repeated, with elaboration, to Ned. Delilah's narrative function here recalls that of Debbie in *The Searchers*, whose seizure by Scar and his band motivated the long search chronicled in that film. Both Will and Ned, seasoned gunfighters though they are, are shocked by the story they hear:

Ned: All right, so what did these fellas do?
       Cheat at cards?
       Steal some strays?
       Spit on a rich fellow?
       What?
Will: No, they cut up a woman.
Ned: What?
Will: Yeah.
       Cut up her face, cut her eyes out, cut her fingers off,
       Cut her tits.
       Everything but her cunny I suppose.
Ned: Well I'll be darned.
       Well – I guess they got it coming.

The retribution required by moral order leads, just as it did in

The Searchers, to the quest, the contest – but though it is *activated* by the woman it really concerns the *exchange* between men, self-appointed as executors of the Law. When, somewhat later, we get to see Delilah's scarred face for ourselves we are invited to compare our view with others' descriptions. Alice says she's got 'no face'; Skinny says she's so ugly no-one would pay for sex with her; Will when he finally meets her takes her, in his delirium, for an angel. Later, as the film shifts effortlessly from realism to melodrama, he calls her a beautiful woman with scars – the version with which the audience is invited to concur. Both Delilah herself in the flesh, as it were, and references to her in the accounts of other characters appear repeatedly throughout the film, insisting by their presence on the relativity of truth in that continuous relay and replay of record and interpretation which constitutes the social world. This paradigmatic tale, Delilah's 'story', allows fragments of other stories – 'I was in the Bluebottle Saloon in Wichita the night English Bob shot Corky Corcoran....'; or 'You remember the night I shot that drover in the mouth and his teeth came out through his head ...'; or 'You were *there*, at ...?' – to reverberate around the cavernous space the film creates with its sweeping landscapes, its cyclic time marked by the passing of seasons, its echoing fictions counterpointed with rolls of thunder.

Whether Little Bill is in Death, Nebraska, or Big Whiskey is, in the Wagnerian climax, immaterial. Despite some reviewers recognition of a 'feminist streak'[7] patriarchal order is, on the evidence of this film, secure enough to risk if not a little giggle at its pecker, at least some navel-gazing. The fact that to today's audiences – or at any rate to this audience member – the whores' outrage, if not its consequences, is utterly convincing and justifiable is a credit to Eastwood's recognition of a feminist agenda. It's certainly a development from the narrative pretext of *The Searchers* which was to prevent an unthinkable miscegenation. But the misapprehension of those men sympathetic to a feminist agenda who thought that Eastwood could produce a 'feminist western' is amply demonstrated in the film's ultimate *in*ability to sustain a female character central to both the moral and the functional axes of the film. With the possible exceptions of William Wellman's *Westward the Women*, (US, 1951) and the flawed but alluring *Ballad of Little Jo* (Maggie Greenwald, US, 1993), the western and feminism seem to be contradictory terms. Women, though certainly not absent from the film, are freely acknowledged in their classic role, marking the boundaries of the masculine. Delilah's mishap motivates the contest, and she and her 'sisters', the whores at Greely's saloon and billiard hall, mark the progress of their revenge, standing silently together in the windblown garden or on the raised wooden sidewalk, watching, waiting, subject to the outcome. Claudia's gravestone frames the narrative and the whores' revenge gets it moving. In between it's men's talk.

My thanks to Gill Branston, Pat Kirkham and Lee Thomas for helpful comments on earlier versions of this essay.

NOTES

1 *Sunday Times*, 13 September 1992, p22-23.
2 For example, Will Wright, *Sixguns and Society*, University of California Press, 1975.
3 *The Observer*, 20 September 1992, p53.
4 *Today*, 18 September 1992, p33.
5 See, for example, review articles on the film in *Cineaste*, December 1992; *Literature/Film Quarterly*, Volume 21, Number 1, 1993; *Films in Review*, December 1993; *Sight and Sound*, October 1992.
6 *The Observer*, 20 September 1992, p53.
7 For example, Amy Taubin in *Village Voice*, 18 August 1992, p52; Jonathan Romney in *New Statesman and Society*, 18 September 1992, p31-32; Alexander Walker in *Evening Standard*, 17 April 1992.

From Proletarian Hero to Godfather: Jean Gabin and 'Paradigmatic' French Masculinity

Ginette Vincendeau

The French cinema has traditionally privileged male stars, though few of them have achieved international recognition; for instance, great popular comics like Fernandel, Louis de Funès and Bourvil, never exported well. The stars who did export tended to fit received ideas of the 'French lover', either boulevard dandies like Maurice Chevalier or romantic heroes – Gérard Philipe, Charles Boyer, Louis Jourdan – or the playboys of the New Wave era such as Alain Delon, Jean-Paul Belmondo, and Jean-Pierre Léaud. In terms of box-office and resonance in French culture, however, the two most important French male stars are Jean Gabin and Gérard Depardieu. Not coincidentally, both embody what seems to me a paradigmatic type of masculinity in French cinema, that of the rebellious and occasionally tragic 'proletarian hero', who in his middle age becomes a strong patriarchal figure. It is my contention that Gabin both created and epitomised this paradigm, to which many other male stars, including some mentioned above like Delon and Belmondo, conformed at one point or another, while others offered derivations on the pattern, for instance Yves Montand and Lino Ventura. Depardieu most clearly fits the paradigm, despite the significantly different cinema he works in; he rose to stardom precisely at the end of the era of mass cinema to which Gabin belonged. This article examines the Gabin image across his career, concentrating on his construction and representation of 'paradigmatic' French masculinity, with

249

reference to its impact on other prominent French stars, especially Depardieu.

Gabin rose to prominence in the mid-1930s in a number of classic films: Jean Renoir's *La Grande illusion* (France, 1937) and *La Bête humaine* (France, 1938), Julien Duvivier's *La Belle équipe* (France, 1936) and *Pépé le Moko* (France, 1937), Jean Grémillon's *Gueule d'amour* (France, 1937), and Marcel Carné's *Quai des Brumes* (France, 1938) and *Le Jour se lève* (France, 1939). Rarely has an actor been the star of so many canonical films in such a short period. Gabin was lucky to work with the most talented directors of his time, but, in turn, he was central to their construction of a 'proletarian' masculinity which met with huge popular and critical approval. The Gabin persona of this period, commonly referred to as a 'myth', is brilliantly summed up by André Bazin's phrase 'Oedipus in a cloth cap'[1]. He condensed a precise, if stylised, populist (rather than strictly proletarian[2]) universe through looks, gestures, clothes, and accent. This was the world of the Parisian working class and the artisan, the 'little people' found in many French films of the period, notably those directed by René Clair and Pierre Chenal. At the same time, the 'ordinary' proletarians Gabin played were involved in 'tragic' stories of romantic love and desires, generally doomed, for rebellion and escape. As a way of symbolising, or motivating, his tragic destiny, his characters regularly integrated a criminal element: he murdered someone, was a gangster, or committed suicide.

Gabin's 1930s 'myth' exported well, insuring his place in international film history. He can be seen, for instance, in the Museum of the Moving Image in London, gazing soulfully out of a window, alongside Michèle Morgan, in a blown-up still from *Quai des brumes*. But, if in Anglo-American film studies the 1930s proletarian rebel remains the dominant element of the Gabin persona, in France a more mature image gradually replaced it. From 1931 to his death in 1976, Gabin featured in almost 100 films: the canonical ones were all made during the 1930s, but he subsequently starred in another 64 films. At the beginning of the war Gabin went to Hollywood, where he made two films (*Moontide*, Archie Mayo, US, 1942, and *The Imposter*, Julien Duvivier, US, 1943), before joining the Free French army. Rebuilding his career in the late 1940s was difficult, despite a 1946 film, (*Martin Roumagnac* Georges Lacombe) and a much-publicised affair with co-star Marlene Dietrich. When he regained his popularity, it was in a different incarnation, as a 'godfather' figure in thrillers, beginning with

Jacques Becker's brilliant *Touchez pas au grisbi* (France, 1954). There followed many more thrillers, populist dramas and comedies. Whatever the genre, though, the visibly older and stockier Gabin played autocratic patriarchs, seemingly the opposite of his pre-war persona, or even, as many see it, a reactionary betrayal of it – a reading underlined by the fact that most of his post-war films were mainstream rather than auteur movies.

His popular audience, however, stayed loyal to him. Gabin became nothing short of a national hero, whose death was compared with that of Général de Gaulle, and who now has his own museum.[3] His trajectory, from rebellious proletarian to godfather/patriarch, and the tremendous popular loyalty he elicited, have been seen in two ways: as a homology of the political context (Gabin embodying the increasingly conservative ethos of his mass audience moving into the consumer society) or as evidence of the 'bad taste' of spectators craving mainstream films in the heyday of auteur cinema; in this respect, Gabin's undisguised contempt for the New Wave did not help. Such ideological analyses are as fascinating as they are problematic. My own argument is that there are far more continuities between Gabin's pre-and post-war image than these readings imply and, indeed, that a major feature of the paradigm is the reconciliation of the apparent contradiction between the rebellious proletarian and the 'godfather'. This is true of the three main components of Gabin's masculinity, which I will consider in turn: 'ordinariness', his oscillation between subject and object, and his incorporation of the feminine. Under each of these headings I will look at how the paradigm put in place by Gabin overdetermines the dominant type of masculinity in French cinema, as illustrated by Depardieu and a number of other male stars.

AN ORDINARY MAN

Contrary to many cinematic representations of the male coded as excessive or distanced – from Rudolf Valentino and the romantic heroes of costume dramas such as Gérard Philipe, to the muscle men of the *peplum* – Gabin embodied 'ordinary' masculinity. The vast majority of his films belong to realistic genres and his image is anchored in the quotidian, in terms of milieu, language and iconography, of characterisation, and of his 'minimalist' performance style. In the 1930s, by contrast with other prominent French stars who used an emphatic, theatrical style, Gabin adopted a sober form of acting 'for the camera', characterised by economy of movement and a non-declamatory elocution, which led to frequent comments of 'non-acting' and consequently to the inscription of 'authenticity' as central to his persona. These features and techniques naturalised his characters to the point of erasing their construction. The close relationship perceived between the real Gabin and his screen image, especially in terms of his *origins* (working-class and farming), together with the generic features of his films especially around the Popular Front, produced this aura of authenticity and proletarian/populist 'ordinariness'. Thus, although he rapidly became a high-profile member of the *tout-Paris*, with the concomitant luxury lifestyle widely reported in fan magazines, Gabin was – and still is – adored by his audience as the perfect representation of an *ordinary* man. The railwaymen's union awarded him a prize in 1938 for his 'truthful' portrayal of a train driver in *La Bête humaine*. When French railworkers went on strike in 1987, they still referred to *La Bête humaine* as the model of good working practice.[4] The aura of authenticity and ordinariness attached to Gabin's star persona produced some fascinating contradictions. As a wealthy landowner bent on accumulating land in Normandy in the 1960s and 1970s, Gabin elicited, unbelievably, more popular sympathy than the farmers he evicted.

Gabin's 'ordinary masculinity' was reinforced, on screen, by a populist topography of the masculine which included barracks and prisoners' camps, workshops and factories, and train engines, as well as leisure spaces connoting the masculine and the popular: boxing rings, racing and cycling tracks, football grounds, and, in practically every film, the café which was, in France (in Gabin's lifetime) a traditional surrogate home, coded and 'lived' as masculine. The predominance of male characters, their gestures, the dialogue, all establish these locations as both class and gender specific. Women may be passing through and, even, occasionally, 'invited', but they are usually on sexual display or out to create trouble – the Viviane Romance character in *La Belle équipe* for example.

When Gabin's mass popularity returned in 1954, it was, as in the 1930s, thanks to a genre which placed him at the centre of a male group: the thriller (or *policier*): I have already mentioned *Touchez pas au grisbi*, but there were also *Razzia sur la chnouf* (Henri Decoin, France, 1955), *Le Rouge est mis* (Gilles Grangier, France, 1957), *Maigret Tend un piège* (Jean Delannoy, France, 1958), *Mélodie en sous-sol* (Henri Verneuil, France, 1963), *Le*

Clan des Siciliens (Henri Verneuil, France, 1969), amongst others. Just as the cafés of the 1930s showed that Gabin and his mates were their legitimate inhabitants, so the night-clubs of the 1950s and 1960s also belonged to them. Women now appeared, as 'artistes' and/or call girls, for instance the Jeanne Moreau and Dora Doll characters in *Touchez pas au grisbi* (there are exceptions in the self-effacing 'motherly' figures who occasionally run such places, but their narrative roles are minimal). To the typical topography of the 1930s, other post-war films added courtrooms and police stations, and, gradually, spaces associated with different classes, such as night-clubs, cabarets, plush bourgeois flats and executive offices, lawyers' or doctors' consulting rooms, and so on, leading to the accusations of *embourgeoisement*. It is remarkable, however, and in my view paradigmatic, that Gabin transcended such a class decor and maintained his 'proletarian' image. There were two main reasons for this. First, his performance style retained many elements of his original persona: his looks, the way he walked and still spoke with a working-class Parisian accent, retained enough class codes evoking 'the popular', even when he was dressed in bourgeois suits. Secondly, the proletarian-criminal element of his 1930s 'mythical' image was recast to suit the illegitimate social climbing aspect of the thrillers which, in a different way, mixed 'genuine' working-class characters with criminals. All Gabin's thrillers from the 1950s onwards, as well as his other films of the period (populist dramas, bourgeois psychological dramas) explicitly drew – in terms of performance, dialogue and narrative – on his 'popular' origins, connecting him to his 1930s image as well as to his contemporary popular audience.

The 'popular' community to which the Gabin persona referred became increasingly nostalgic, as the post-war films moved towards a greater emphasis on the individual, and traditional communities were dismantled in the modernisation of France that was then taking place. The post-1968 Depardieu,[5] frequently coded as a proletarian (as in *Les valseuses*, Bertrand Blier, France, 1974, and *Loulou*, Maurice Pialat, France, 1980), was so in even more marginal terms. His group was not much more than a bunch of disaffected marginals whose own families and groups of friends were in the process of collapse. Still, the strength of the paradigm can be felt in the crucial role played by notions of authenticity and ordinariness in his persona, where 'popular' origins are called upon as a guarantee of social authenticity and 'Frenchness'. Like Gabin, Depardieu's early success was based on what was perceived as a perfect overlap between his real life circumstances as a petty criminal from a small provincial town, and his parts as rebellious 'yob'. Twenty years on, the release of *Germinal* (Claude Berri, France, 1993) has been surrounded by prominent references by Depardieu to the relevance of his own social origins in relation to his casting as the miner Maheu. The same point can be made about Montand, whose peasant patriarch in *Jean de Florette* and *Manon des Sources* (Claude Berri, France, 1986) has been strongly linked to his own antecedents as a poor Italian immigrant. Now that most of Depardieu's parts and his public identity have moved up the social scale, his image still draws on his origins to construct a persona coded as 'ordinary', in the sense of unaffected and fundamentally non-bourgeois. This is true for instance, in Bertrand Blier's *Trop belle pour toi* (France, 1989), where he plays an executive moving in wealthy circles. His pairing with the elegant Carole Bouquet in this film, as with Catherine Deneuve in *Le Dernier métro* (François Truffaut, France, 1980) or *Fort Saganne* (Alain Corneau, France, 1984) emphasizes his 'earthiness', compared with these female stars with a very bourgeois image; Gabin's earlier pairing with stars Michèle Morgan and Mireille Balin functioned in a similar way.

SUBJECT AND OBJECT, HERO BUT 'VICTIM'

As well as being economically responsible for the existence of most of his films, Gabin, from *La Bandera* (Julien Duvivier, 1935) onwards, was the driving force of their narrative. But whereas classical narrative structure suggests that he will, as a male protagonist, occupy the place of a goal-oriented hero, most of his 1930s and 1940s films showed him as a victim, a character struggling vainly to maintain control over live and events. He was often 'paralysed', unable to move, portrayed as trapped, in enclosed spaces, behind bars, railings, window frames or banisters. Dreams of escape were always doomed. From the 1950s onwards, he became seemingly a figure of great authority, but on closer analysis his patriarchal power was constantly threatened, his trajectory often blocked. Despite apparently victorious endings, and characters that range from mafioso godfather (*Le Clan des Siciliens*), to farming patriarch (*La Horse*, Pierre Granier-Deferre, France, 1970, *L'Affaire Dominici*, Claude Bernard-Aubert, France, 1973) to head of state (*Le Président*, Henri Verneuil, France, 1961), the narratives of these films predominantly present Gabin's male power as threatened and in crisis. His main narrative characteristic is thus to oscillate between the status of dominant hero and that of suffering 'victim'.

Similarly, whereas male heroes are supposed to actively relay the male spectator's look towards a female object, Gabin, especially in the 1930s, was the overt object of that look. His films hardly belonged to 'women's genres', and he was careful to emphasise the roughness of his features (for instance he refused to have his hair highlighted or back-lit, thinking blonde hair 'effeminate'). Yet lighting and framing greatly glamorised his face, especially his eyes, and the camera consistently gave him more close-ups than the heroines of his films, even when these were played by stars of equal status.[6] Despite its naturalism and minimalism, his performance also contained a strong element of ritualised spectacle: in the 1930s there were songs, but also spectacular entrances and exits, and most famously, the 'explosions of anger' during which his laconic, restrained heroes would suddenly rant and shout in a fit of rage. Whether or not Gabin insisted on having such outbursts built in into his contracts as legend has it, they functioned as a mise-en-abyme of his whole performance, emphasising his to-be-looked-at-ness. I should add that in the pre-war films, this 'objectification' had a strong erotic function which chimed with current popular cultural concerns. Dime novels, soft porn magazines, and popular songs of the pre-war period typically emphasised the erotic appeal of the proletarian hero. Among the canonical 1930s films, *Pépé le Moko* and *Gueule d'amour* provide the most extreme examples of this spectacular function, fundamental to a definition of proletarian virility which, as Pierre Bourdieu[7] and other analysts of male behaviour have observed, requires a public arena in which to exhibit itself.

In the post-war period, as Gabin aged and moved into different genres, there were inevitable shifts in his visual treatment. The narcissism of the glamorous proletarian/ hoodlum was deflected away from his person, yet symbolically retained in two ways. In the thrillers, especially those of the 1950s and early 1960s, it was displaced on to the iconography of the genre. Silk suits, gleaming cars and the paraphernalia of nightclub life – champagne bottles, crystal glasses, young and beautiful women – were all adjuncts of the male hero and a reflection on his status; as in the first cabaret scene in *Touchez pas au grisbi*. As time went on, this was distanced further, and relayed through the figure of a young handsome hero positioned as a symbolic 'son'; here Gabin took on a double 'godfather' role, on and off screen, playing mentor to a new generation of male stars – especially Belmondo and Delon – who recalled the glamour of his own youth, and embodied the narcissistic iconography of the whole thriller genre. This is particularly clear in the three films with Delon, especially the first, *Mélodie en sous-sol*. In this film, Gabin teaches Delon the tricks of his trade as they prepare a heist in the casino at Cannes. The handsome young Delon, cruising for women on the sea front in dark glasses and open-top cars, is an updated, consumerist, version of the dashing young Gabin, who seduced Mireille Balin in the very same location in *Gueule d'amour*. The narrative allows Gabin, through Delon, to re-live his young erotic life; at the same time, he retains narrative superiority, as Delon, his 'pupil' ultimately botches the job. *Le Clan des Siciliens* features Gabin as the Godfather of a Sicilian mafioso family, in which the surrogate son Delon physically performs the criminal and erotic exploits which evoke the young Gabin of *Pépé le Moko*. Gabin played mentor in such a way to other young male stars, notably Belmondo in *Un Singe en hiver* (Henri Verneuil, France, 1962) and Lino Ventura in several thrillers of the 1950s and 1960s. These shared the male narcissistic structure of the Gabin-Delon films, allowing the ageing star to retain power symbolically, while re-living his youth through the younger, sexually active male character, who is nevertheless a pale 'shadow' of himself. *L'Air de Paris* (France, 1954), a little-known populist drama directed by Marcel Carné, in which Gabin trains, and becomes obsessed with, a young boxer, foregrounds most explicitly the homo-eroticism of this narcissistic structure, especially as all these films marginalise women.[8]

How does Depardieu insert himself in this paradigm? The two stars appeared together in three films: *Le Tueur* (Denys de la Patellière, France, 1972), *L'Affaire Dominici* (Claude Bernard-Aubert, France, 1973), and *Deux Hommes dans la ville* (José Giovanni, France, 1973). Their distance in age and status at that point – Gabin at the pinnacle, Depardieu an unknown – means that their on-screen interaction is limited. Depardieu plays a young criminal in *Le Tueur* and *Deux Hommes dans la Ville*, with no real contact with Gabin. On the other hand, *L'Affaire Dominici* (based on the real murder of a British family in Provence), features Depardieu as Gabin's grandson who, along with his father and uncle, turns the patriarch over to the police. It would be fanciful to see much direct influence in these Gabin-Depardieu contacts. It is a fact, however, that in all three films Depardieu plays characters who are both proletarian and criminal, and that these are the roles he soon developed into his major star persona, in a clear echo of pre-war Gabin. *Les Valseuses, Loulou, La Lune dans le caniveau* (Jean-Jacques Beineix, France, 1983) all focus, in different modes, on Depardieu as eroticised proletarian and or semi-criminal. In *Mon oncle d'Amérique* (Alain Resnais, France, 1980), the connection is made explicit; Depardieu, a struggling travelling salesman, explicitly evokes the young Gabin in fantasy 'flashes' made of short extracts from Gabin's films. Equally, in *Fort Saganne*, a French colonial drama set in the Sahara during World War I, Depardieu with blonde hair and a dashing uniform directly suggests the Gabin of *Gueule d'amour*. Depardieu undoubtedly has had a more versatile career than Gabin, partly reflecting the varied generic spectrum of popular French cinema, incorporating for instance 'new' genres such as the heritage film and even Hollywood comedies. However, in many of his key films, Depardieu's masculinity is clearly within the paradigmatic model constructed by Gabin. A dominant male protagonist, even a macho figure (given the increased naturalism of the French cinema since the 1970s), he is also presented as a 'victim', a blocked and objectified character, for instance in *Loulou* and *Police* (Maurice Pialat, France, 1985), as well as several Blier films such as *Trop belle pour toi*. Other French male stars could be cited here as belonging to this paradigm. One of the most famous is Yves Montand, in such films as Alain Resnais' *La Guerre est finie* (France, 1966) or Claude Sautet's *Vincent, François, Paul et les autres* (France, 1974, also featuring the young Depardieu). Equally, though Alain Delon through the 1970s featured predominantly as a tough, American-style gangster, later roles have returned him to the familiar terrain of French 'victim males', for instance in Blier's *Notre histoire* (France, 1984). Following on from what can be summed up as an 'active/passive' duality in paradigmatic French masculinity, I now turn to the third, and in some respects, most striking aspect of the paradigm, that of the incorporation of the feminine.

MASCULIN-FÉMININ

Though Gabin may have been the concentrated object of the look in his films, he was undoubtedly, at the same time, its bearer vis-à-vis female characters, his power and appeal being located in this dual position.[9] In his 1930s films, women functioned quite explicitly as his mirror images, with the effect that he took on 'feminine' characteristics, rather than the other way round. The similarity between his character and that of his lover Françoise (Jacqueline Laurent) in *Le Jour se lève* has frequently been noted, and the pattern informs most of his canonical films of that period, for example *La Bandera, La Bête humaine, Pépé le Moko* and *Gueule d'amour*. Symbolically, Gabin and his 'feminine doubles' were placed in the same impotent, child-like position vis-à-vis authority (or the 'law of the father'), emphasising his proletarian lack of power on the social scale.[10] Importantly in view of the central criminal component of the Gabin persona, the doubling function of the women means that their murder or oppression (by him) is primarily seen, at the narrative level, as symbolic of his own destruction. This is reinforced by the fact that the murders (for instance of Séverine in *La Bête humaine* and of Gaby in *Gueule d'amour*) take place while he is 'not himself': crazed by the alcoholism of his ancestors in the first case, destroyed by destitution and jealousy in the second case, but generally during his 'explosions of anger', thus presented as 'unavoidable' and therefore more authentic.[11] His victimisation of the heroines is thereby adduced to *his* 'tragedy', the coding of these female characters as *femmes fatales* serving to justify his male violence. Gabin's star persona in relation to his portrayal of masculinity thus served to mask his oppression of female characters, foregrounding instead his own suffering, characterised, as is frequent in French culture, as social as well as psychic, thus doubly 'justified'. In this respect, the paradigm put in place by Gabin directly applies to the young Depardieu in films such as *Les Valseuses, La Lune dans le caniveau*, and especially in *Loulou*.

From the 1950s onwards, different patterns emerged in terms of Gabin's relationships to women. First of all, pairings with women his own age tended to produce extremely misogynist narratives. Mature women appear in humiliating or monstrous positions, embodied by actresses of lesser star status: bitter, dull 'kill-joys', pointedly childless or else horrific mothers. Secondly, a small but significant number of films paired him with a major female star who automatically took a larger part in the narrative, notably: Isa Miranda in *Au delà des grilles* (René Clément, France, 1948), Marlene Dietrich in *Martin Roumagnac*, Danielle Darrieux in *La Vérité sur Bébé Donge* (Henri Decoin, France, 1952), Simone Signoret in *Le Chat* (Pierre Granier-Deferre, France, 1971, Sophia Loren in *Verdict* (André Cayatte, France, 1974). All of these end in tragedy for the woman and/or Gabin, as if the confrontation with woman as 'equal' was unbearable. The remarkable and harrowing, *Le Chat*, in which Gabin and Signoret fight a grim and silent mortal battle in the prison of their home – their relationship broken down to the point that they communicate only in writing – is the extreme expression of this pattern. Either way, 'feminine' values of tenderness, nurturing and vulnerability, are ascribed to the Gabin character and his male friend(s). A particularly telling example is *Un Singe en hiver*, in which the relationship between the two central male characters (Gabin and Belmondo) is presented with such warmth, while those between men and women are so full of hatred and bitterness, that the spectator is left with only one conclusion: the ideal woman is a man, the ideal woman is Gabin! What emerges is that the Gabin persona incorporates the feminine, concurrently signifying the redundant nature of women. A different version of this phenomenon is evident in another type of male-female relationship in Gabin's post-war films, where he is paired with a young woman.

In their famous *Panorama du film noir américain*, written in the mid-1950s, Raymond Borde and Etienne Chaumeton rather unkindly said: 'Before the war, Gabin was wonderful in populist versions of *amour fou*. Today he fucks. And – this is no accident – he always fucks women who are much younger than him.'[12] By ascribing to him the responsibility for this formula, Borde and Chaumeton conveniently forgot its long history in French culture, from fairy tales and the classical novel, to the cinema. From the 1950s to the 1970s, Gabin occupied and eventually epitomised the ultimate place for mature male actors in popular French cinema, that of the powerful but troubled patriarch, a place previously filled by the likes of Harry Baur, and Raimu, and subsequently by Ventura, Montand, Belmondo and Delon, and now Depardieu. The father figure, in Gabin as in his predecessors, is both a seducing symbolic father (*French Cancan*, Jean Renoir, France, 1954, *Des Gens sans importance*, Henri Verneuil, France, 1955; *En cas de malheur*, Claude Autant-Lara, France, 1958; and others) and a nurturing father, actual or symbolic (*Rue des Prairies*, Denys de la Patellière, France, 1959; *Des Gens sans Importance*). The seducing father nurtures his 'daughters'; for instance in *En Cas de malheur*, Gabin treats Bardot, his lover, like a little girl (feeding her, blowing her nose, etc). Conversely, the nurturing, actual, father displays overt or oblique desire for his daughter, as for instance in *Rue des Prairies*. The result of this seductive-nurturing duality, together with the absence, marginalisation or demonisation of actual mothers, was that the Gabin persona encompassed in a naturalistic way the father and the mother, the masculine and the feminine, offering a fantasy of 'universal' identification, continuity and nostalgia for the lost paradise of youth.

The incorporation of the feminine (while eliminating or marginalising women) is perhaps the feature of the paradigm epitomised by Gabin which most obviously applies to Depardieu. Depardieu, who frequently declares that he 'is a woman', like Gabin evokes and valorises feminine values, so long as *he* embodies them. Thus he too can offer the fantasy of the complete, male/female, father/mother, so successful in Gabin's persona. This is true in comedies, where he often functions as both 'nurturing father' and dominant partner of male duos (*Les Fugitifs*, directed by Francis Veber in 1986 is a good example), and in dramas such as *Police*. Now, in the mid-1990s, the middle-aged Depardieu would seem to be taking up the father position developed in Gabin's later roles, as can be seen in Tony Gatlif's *Rue du départ* (1986), and *Mon Père ce héros* (Gérard Lauzier, France, 1991), remade as *My Father, the Hero* (Steve Miner, US, 1994).

The paradigmatic masculinity constructed by Gabin and which has had so much impact on other French male stars since, draws its strengths both from deep rooted elements in French culture – classical literature as well as popular forms, and the cinema itself – and of course the charisma and talent of the stars themselves. Its power may also be seen to derive from its 'mythical' (in the Lévi-Straussian sense) capacity to reconcile apparently antagonistic elements: the rebellious young proletarian on the one hand, and the patriarchal authority figure on the other. This is achieved around the notion of crisis: the young Gabin and Depardieu dramatise the conflict, and ultimate 'failure' of the proletarian rebels, while endowing them with charisma and glamour. Conversely, the stars as patriarchs dramatise the older man's loss of power, while retaining the narrative centrality of the patriarchal hero. Thus charismatic male stars within the Gabin model have been able to pursue long careers, since the passage from youthful rebel to authority figure is smoothly made and 'naturalised' for the audience. Depardieu's career so far would seem to confirm the pattern.

Another powerful way in which the paradigm 'works', is because of its integration of 'passivity' and 'femininity' in the definition of masculinity thus constructed, which produces the effect of a 'universal' figure. This puts female, not to say feminist, spectators in an ambivalent position. Figures such as

Gabin and Depardieu present a version of masculinity undoubtedly more acceptable than many traditional male heroes, especially in Hollywood cinema, but it is a model of masculinity which implies the elimination of women. Here, however, a feminist analysis must take cultural and historical contexts into account. As Gabin's precedent and the continuities between Gabin and Depardieu show, 'masculine-feminine' versions of masculinity have a long history in French culture; they cannot simply be understood as a postmodern or post-feminist development, as has been argued.[13] Though it is certainly regrettable that women rarely find adequate representation within this system, it also explains why film stars such as Gabin and Depardieu have historically appealed to female as well as male spectators. The success of this male paradigm may be evidence of one way in which patriarchal French culture reconciles the valorisation of femininity-as-difference with male hegemony, but it is also a way in which female spectators are offered the possibility of a strong investment in narratives which champion 'feminine' qualities, albeit in male guise.

NOTES

1 André Bazin, 'The Destiny of Jean Gabin', in Mary Lea Bandy (ed), *Rediscovering French Film*, Museum of Modern Art, New York, 1983, pp123-124. For a detailed analysis of Gabin's 'myth', see Claude Gauteur and Ginette Vincendeau, *Jean Gabin/Anatomie d'un Mythe*, Nathan Université, Paris, 1993. The best Gabin biography is André Brunelin, *Gabin*, Robert Laffont, Paris, 1987.

2 Though I will on the whole refer to it as 'proletarian', in so far as it is the dominant description of Gabin within established film history.

3 The museum is situated in the town hall of the village of Mériel, north of Paris, next door to Auvers-sur-Oise, where Vincent Van Gogh is buried.

4 See Michèle Lagny, 'The fleeing gaze: Jean Renoir's *La Bête humaine* (1938), in Susan Hayward and Ginette Vincendeau (eds), *French Film, Texts and Contexts*, Routledge, London, 1990.

5 For a detailed analysis of the Depardieu persona, see Ginette Vincendeau, 'Gérard Depardieu: the axiom of contemporary French cinema', *Screen* 34/4, Winter 1993, pp343-361.

6 Detailed statistics are available in Gauteur and Vincendeau, *op.cit.*, pp124-125.

7 See Pierre Bourdieu, *La Distinction: Critique Sociale du Jugement*, Les Editions de Minuit, Paris, 1979; translated as *Distinction: Social Critique of the Judgement of Taste*, RKP, London, 1986.

8 For a further analysis of *L'Air de Paris'* 'homosensuality', and its place within the Carné oeuvre, see Edward Baron Turk, *Child of Paradise*, Harvard University Press, Cambridge, Massachusetts, 1989, pp384-386.

9 Similar in this to Rudolf Valentino, as analysed by Miriam Hansen, *Babel and Babylon: Spectatorship in American Silent Film*, Harvard University Press, Cambridge, Massachusetts,1991, chapter 3.

10 See Ginette Vincendeau, 'Community, Nostalgia and the Spectacle of Masculinity – Jean Gabin', *Screen*, 26/6, November-December 1985, pp18-38.

11 On the question of lack of control as 'authenticity', see Richard Dyer, '*A Star is Born* and the construction of authenticity', in Christine Gledhill (ed), *Stardom: Industry of Desire*, Routledge, London, 1991, pp132-140.

12 Borde et Chaumeton, *Panorama du Film Noir Américain*, Les Editions de Minuit, Paris, 1955, p168.

13 See Tania Modleski, 'Three Men and Baby M', in Modleski, *Feminism Without Women*, Routledge, London, 1991, pp76-89.

Changing Places?
Men and Women in
Oliver Stone's Vietnam

Margaret O'Brien

Oliver Stone's stated purpose in the making of *Heaven and Earth* (1993) is to change places: man with woman and the USA with Vietnam. He attempts to reverse the concentration on the sufferings of men at war and on the scars inflicted on the American soldier by the Vietnam conflict in *Platoon* (1986) and *Born on the 4th July* (1989) by the telling of a Vietnamese woman's own story. But he scarcely scratches beneath the surface.

This article will argue that all three films display a central concern with American masculinity under threat and that each in turn reveals a progressively deepening sense of unease about its very survival. I shall focus on a pattern of dualities – of male/female, USA/Vietnam and soul/body – which is evident in all the films, despite their generic and narrative differences. I will further argue that these are often gendered oppositions, bound up with underlying assumptions about masculinity and femininity and that they are re-worked rather than revised in *Heaven and Earth*.

Of the three Vietnam films *Platoon* alone can be placed firmly in the war film genre. The battlefield milieu, the spectacle of combat and the emphasis on heroics and endurance tempered by the reflection that 'war is hell' and the ordinary soldier is worth more than the absent politician or the cynical general, are all there.[1]

The narrative structure is also familiar: within the snapshot approach to the telling of a collective war story a platoon of young draftees is joined by a raw college boy who has enlisted for idealistic reasons. Yet *Platoon* is not a straightforward rendition of the patriotic war film.[2] Made in the aftermath of a massive and humiliating defeat for the USA and in the context of doubts about the integrity of both the military leadership and the American soldier, it attempts to retrieve the honour of the ordinary 'grunt' and to rescue the notion of individual heroism within a 'realistic' and honest portrayal of the war.

Bitterness against the American military élite who drafted a largely working-class army to fight an unjust and unwinnable war underpins the narrative voice of *Platoon*. It is spoken by the hero, Taylor/Charlie Sheen, in voice-over based on Stone's personal experiences and echoed by the men throughout.

'Well, here I am anonymous all right, with guys nobody really cares about. They come from the end of the line most of 'em, small towns you never even heard of ... Brandon, Mississippi; Pork Beach, Utah; Waltham, Pennsylvania. Two years high school is about it. Maybe, if they're lucky, a job waiting for them back in a factory. But most of 'em got nothing. They're poor, they're the unwanted yet they're fighting for our society and our freedom. It's weird isn't it? They're at the bottom of the barrel and they know it. Maybe that's why they call themselves grunts, 'cos they can take it. Can take anything. They're the best I've ever seen, the heart and soul.'

Yet Stone's project of 'telling it like it was' necessarily involves the inclusion of the everyday brutalities perpetrated by American soldiers on the Vietnamese. He contextualises this by constructing a Vietnamese 'hell' whose jungle landscape and dangerous inhabitants, human or otherwise, combine to present with convincing authenticity an alien environment within which the occasional atrocities of the 'grunts' are made understandable.

Taylor's initiation into combat in the jungle ambush sequence illustrates this graphically. The tension is built up through Taylor's eyes, a succession of sinister nocturnal images – a stone Buddha, a lizard and a strange steamy mist out of which looms the ghostly silhouettes of the Vietcong. The ambush is bungled and one of the platoon is killed by a 'friendly' grenade. The men are left with the sergeant's chilling reminder of their own possible fate, 'Remember what it looks like.'

The members of the platoon are just 'ordinary guys', plunged into the strange nightmare world of the Vietnam War. Their path into good or evil is influenced by the model of masculinity they adopt: the platoon is divided into two 'families', the Heads and the Rednecks, each with its own father figure and rival role model.

One is the sergeant, Elias/Willem Dafoe whose attractive-ness to Taylor alternates between the paternal (when the new young volunteer collapses from heat exhaustion en route through the jungle, Elias in a protective gesture takes his pack) and the homoerotic (when he is initiated into the world of off-duty hedonism Elias offers Taylor his 'smoke' through the barrel of a rifle suggestively cocked into his mouth.) Elias is the good warrior of frontiersman tradition: he is heroic, he refuses sadism against the Vietnamese, and although he expresses doubts about the validity of the war he carries on for the sake of his men. The other father is Sergeant Barnes, the leader of the Rednecks. Heavily scarred and unambiguously going for victory at any cost, he is sadistic to Vietnamese civilians and to his men.

In these two figures the ordinary soldier, the 'heart and soul' as described by Taylor, is offered a symbolic choice of good and evil, of alternative models of masculinity. For Stone's tale is very much concerned with the spiritual side of what it means to be a warrior. Incongruously, after the massive, spectacular battle and cathartic slaughter of the final sequence of the film we are offered a spiritual conclusion by Taylor in voice-over. 'We did not fight the enemy, we fought ourselves and the enemy was in us.'

Much of the narrative focus on the conflict between good and bad warrior centres on the life and death struggle between Elias and Barnes for the possession of Taylor's soul. At one point Taylor is on the verge of joining Barnes. The men occupy a Vietnamese village and come close to a My Lai-type massacre of its inhabitants. This sequence graphically portrays the near unbearable pressure which releases the latent brutality of the men and which is only contained by the arrival of Elias. The subsequent 'war' within the platoon leads to the final self-sacrifice of Elias in the cause of 'good' masculinity. Treacherously wounded by Barnes, he is shot to pieces by the Vietcong, his endurance tested and triumphant, his arms outstretched in a final pose of crucifixion.

Taylor's heroism grows from this moment. In the final battle he both excels in bravery against colossal odds and executes Barnes. His spiritual quest now has a meaning.

In *Platoon* the Vietnam War, problematic though it is, has enabled Taylor to move from boyhood to manhood, his moral choices made. In *Born on the 4th of July* a more profound unease about the war leads to the near destruction of its hero Ron Kovic/Tom Cruise whose tragic journey from expectation to reality involves a crossing and recrossing of the line between active and passive hero.

The sufferings of Kovic 'the boy who yearned to be an American hero' but who came back from Vietnam in a wheelchair, take on a more disturbing meaning than those of Taylor. This is partly a matter of the rhyming of sexual with national identity in *Born on the 4th July*: the pain of Kovic's impotence and paralysis caused by his 'mistakes' are a reflection of America's pain over 'mistakes' in Vietnam, and the ravages wrought on his body mirror the disturbances inflicted on the American body politic.

And, it is partly because this is a 'coming home' film, with a hero both literally and metaphorically castrated, that no easy solutions to the crisis of American masculinity which this represents can be offered.

Stone's treatment of masculinity in action are particularly interesting. A marked contrast emerges between the idealised war games of American boyhood and the war scenes in Vietnam. The extended pre-credit sequence shows a group of small helmetted boys armed with sticks enacting an ambush in the sunbathed woods of Massapeque, Long Island. They are noisy, but disciplined, brave and in control of themselves and their environment. The sequence is conventionally shot with lavish music and the voice-over supports the evocative nostalgia of the images.

The subsequent Vietnam War scenes reveal the yawning gap between this ideal of masculinity and what emerges as the reality of war. Paradoxically, the real war is shot as fantasy: ghostly figures and disembodied sounds inhabit a nightmare orange hazed landscape reflecting both the individual experience of the hero and Stone's vision of Vietnam. In this strange other world, Kovic unwittingly takes part in a massacre of women and children and in the confusion that follows he shoots and kills a new recruit in his own command.

The scene of his own near fatal wounding again depicts the confusion and dreamlike quality of combat. 'Is it hell or is it purgatory?' mutters one 'grunt' as the soldiers fan out before the Vietcong attack. Chaos follows: shots, exploding helicopter, Kovic's frenzied bravery as he fires in response to his first wounding and then the final shot in slow motion.

Once he is rendered inactive the sufferings of Kovic are played out as melodrama: crippled and castrated he is returned to his family which becomes the site of intense emotional conflict.

The representation of Kovic's mother as a key player, the culprit almost, in the construction of his masculinist and militarist fantasies has already been established. She is shown to be a sexually repressed American 'mom' whose aspirations are

266

vicariously centred on her son: she dreams of him becoming a great leader like Kennedy, she is the driving force behind his struggle to excel in sport and she rebukes her mild husband when he expresses doubts about their son volunteering for the war. Her overvaluation of Ron's masculinity is contrasted with her inability to cope with its loss. On his return home from Vietnam she is embarrassed by his 'failure' and, again in contrast to the father, is unable to feel sympathy with his psychic and sexual pain. 'Don't say penis in this house', she screams when during a family row he drunkenly rails against his loss of 'maleness'.

Kovic, then, cannot be re-integrated into his own family. Nor, because of his sexual lack, can he form normal heterosexual relations and establish a new family. And his sojourn with the 'family' of Vietnam vets in Mexico where the men spend their time gambling, whoring and reliving their nightmares in a drug induced fusion of despair and hedonism does not exorcise his demons. His salvation is eventually found in the public sphere. In a series of set pieces which recreate the spectacle and excitement of American politics, Kovic becomes the radical voice of the veteran experience. At the Republican Convention he steals the scene from Nixon as he puts the anti-war case to millions on television.

The final sequence of the film sees his true 'coming home'. As the acclaimed author of the most powerful memoir of the war,[3] he is about to take the platform at the 1976 Democratic Convention. Meaning is restored to politics and his own life.

It is only now that the values of the Founding Fathers invoked by the Democratic leaders can be confidently re-asserted. And as Kovic is wheeled on stage to address the nation a series of flashbacks recall his childhood – sport, war games, flag waving, the family watching Kennedy on TV with his mother's strangely prophetic words. 'I had a dream, Ronnie. You were speaking to a large crowd, you were saying great things.' In the light of his own, and America's, history the memories are not purely ironic; they have a healing power; they give a new inflection to, but at the same time hold together, the values of American masculinity.

Le Ly, the heroine of *Heaven and Earth*, inevitably follows a different national, gender specific route through the turmoil of the Vietnam War. Her experience of resistance, torture, rape, sleeping with the enemy and eventual emigration are extreme manifestations of women's relationship to war so tellingly described in the two volumes of Hayslip's autobiography, *When*

Heaven and Earth Changed Places and *Child of War, Woman of Peace*.[4] Not surprisingly, given the source text, Stone represents these issues in melodramatic form: *Heaven and Earth* is a lavish and sweeping 'epic drama' with the family at its centre. But in the process of telling Le Ly's story, 'no more and no less', as Stone claims, a curious shift takes place. The authorial voice of Hayslip is filtered in such a way that her more 'masculine' traits and exploits – heroic action in war, entrepreneurial success and social action – which so intriguingly co-exist with her romantic and spiritual philosophy are played down.

For, unlike the heroes of *Platoon* and *Born on the 4th July* Le Ly/Hiep Thi Ly is a heroine who does not articulate her pain. The device of the voice-over, effectively used in *Platoon* to reveal Taylor's feelings about the war and its meaning, is here an awkward amalgam of autobiographical detail, political history and religious testimony. It is left to the male voices – her husband's, her brother's and her father's – to reflect from their different perspectives on the legacy of pain left by the war.

Despite Le Ly's dominance of screen time in *Heaven and Earth* it is the figure of her American husband, Sergeant Steve Butler/Tommy Lee Jones who is arguably at the centre of the narrative. This is partly a matter of directorial choice: Stone selected Hiep Thi Le, a young unknown, from amongst 16,000 Viet Kieu (Vietnamese abroad) because, as he said 'There was a light about her' and he decided against any professional coaching of his discovery in order to 'leave her as natural as possible'.

Hiep's exquisite beauty and 'naturalness' are deployed by Stone to create an icon of 'timeless' Oriental femininity. Visually set apart from her betel-chewing peasant mother and coarser sister, the filmic Le Ly comes over as curiously distant from the grand events and emotional drama which surround her. For me this is less a problem of performance, as some critics have suggested, than a failure on Stone's part to create a flesh and blood heroine with her own narrative voice.

Steve Butler, on the other hand, carries with him a whole history of cinematic connotations, because of Tommy Lee Jones' filmic persona and also because of what his character represents in terms of American masculinity at war in Vietnam. For Le Ly he personifies the ambivalence felt by Vietnamese women towards the American invader. This ambivalence is signposted early on in the story. The first sighting of the Americans, as witnessed by Le Ly when they land in Ky La, her village, is a dramatic and wondrous moment. (That the

Americans are introduced as a powerful force from out of the sky, giants stepping out of monster birds, places them in structural opposition to the cave dwelling Vietcong who only operate in dark places. They emerge at night to mete out punishment to collaborators: in Le Ly's case she is raped at the edge of a deep hole in the earth, as punishment for her supposed treachery).

The motif of 'rescue from the sky' is repeated in a key sequence which shifts the focus of the narrative from Le Ly to Steve. She has by now moved from peasant girl through city life on the margins of the American economy (entailing unmarried motherhood, poverty and prostitution) to marriage with Steve for the protection of her children and the possibility of escape to the USA. It is the final stage of the war and of the North Vietnamese attack against the South and the base which houses the families of the marines is in imminent danger. In a set piece sequence which captures the confusion and the thrill of war, the marine helicopters swoop down to the rescue. Steve relinquishes his place for his family and Le Ly is borne away, clutching Steve's note which identifies her as the mother of his children in her hand. This is the high point of Steve's heroism. His subsequent return home to America, however, sees a disintegration of his marriage and his manhood.

At first, he is still Le Ly's protector and her ally against the casual racism meted out to Vietnamese immigrants. His passionate outburst at a family Thanksgiving dinner reveals the guilt of the Vietnam veteran and the rage of the returning soldier against those who weren't there.

'Thankful? Let me tell you about thankful! In Da Nang when we drove by the hospitals, past poor people our bombs had blown to pieces, they'd wave, girls and boys without legs would wave to us in our jeeps, like goddam tourists on the way to the beach, because they were happy to be alive, they were happy to see us who'd put them there where they were. There's twenty of them dead for every one of us!'

But as Steve gradually slips into gun-obsessed alcoholic despair it emerges that he is deeply implicated in even worse war atrocities. In a scene when he threatens Le Ly's life and attempts to take his own, he confesses in graphic detail to his own war crimes of murder and torture while engaged in 'black ops' for the Marines.

'The more I killed the more they gave me to kill. Do you know what it's like doing that? It's like being eaten inside out by a bellyful of sharks. You gotta keep moving, you gotta keep hitting, 'cause if you stop the fuckin' shark'll eat you alive.'

Steve represents in extremis the cumulative despair of the Vietnam veteran. The end of their marriage (bound up with his past rather than Le Ly's), his own guilty memories and the disappointments of 'coming home' drive him to suicide. And his tragedy, especially when viewed as the culmination of Stone's concern with the psychic injuries inflicted on American manhood by the War, becomes the dramatic centre of the film.

The problem of Steve's suffering and its meaning is unresolved in *Heaven and Earth*. When Le Ly consults a Vietnamese mystic after Steve's suicide, to mediate for her with the world of the dead, she is reassured that Steve forgives her and that his soul wishes to be taken to a Buddhist temple. Yet the optimism scarcely registers, either metaphorically or in terms of the narrative: the final image of Steve, naked, slumped over the wheel of his van and covered in blood and glass is one of a man alone, broken by his suffering and destroyed by his demons.

Heaven and Earth presents a version of American masculinity so battered and scarred by the Vietnam War that it blows its brains out. In *Born on the 4th of July* what makes Kovic a more complex hero than Steve, and what gives his suffering a different and richer meaning, is the anchoring of his masculinity in the larger struggle over American national identity and the desire for a better America. The interesting question, then, which arises from Stone's attempt to shift the emphasis from the USA to Vietnam in *Heaven and Earth* and to represent a 'different' national identity is how he relates the Vietnamese national experience to his female heroine and her male compatriots.

The Vietnam Stone creates in *Heaven and Earth* is a land of spectacular beauty in contrast to the 'alien hell' inhabited by Taylor and Kovic. And he is at pains to show the community and the culture of which Le Ly is a part. A series of shots introduces us to a revised and lovingly constructed Vietnam: rice-planting in the fields, yellow-robed monks and traditional theatre. This is the world of home, work and religion and the context for a story which at last humanises the victims of the war. And the repeated attacks on, and brutal invasions of, that community, like the crimes committed against the heroine, are shown with affecting intensity.

Patterns of identification of heroine with nation can be traced through *Heaven and Earth*. In the opening and closing sequences in particular Le Ly is strongly associated with the landscape and the timeless cycle of birth and death. The film opens with the child Le Ly planting rice and feeling her belly 'where babies come from' and the final images return to the same landscape where the woman Le Ly, dressed in white, walks through the graveyard of her ancestors.

But there are problems in creating a heroine (and a country) with such abstract qualities. And the fact that her journey through life is increasingly shaped by the Buddhist beliefs articulated by her father removes the necessity to seek an explanation for the agony of Vietnam. When Le Ly speaks of suffering it is to universalise the experience. 'Different skin, same suffering' was her response to Steve's anguished confessions of his war crimes. And the final words of her voice-over impose a[n exclusively] religious meaning on all that has gone before:

> ... the gift of suffering is to bring us closer to God. Lasting victories are won in the heart not in this land or that.

It is left to Le Ly's father and brother to reflect, in different ways, on the sorrow of war through the specificity of the Vietnamese experience. Her father, whose eloquence on the subject of Vietnam's struggle to retain a sense of nationhood in the face of centuries of invasion made such an impression on the young Le Ly, is eventually destroyed by grief for his missing sons and the destruction of his community. But in his final meeting with Le Ly he re-asserts the fundamental importance of love of family and ancestors over all else, and thus maps out his daughter's subsequent path in life.

Bon, Le Ly's soldier brother, is shown to be a less palatable version of Vietnamese manhood. In a significant moment, the family celebration of Le Ly's return after fifteen years, his bitter outburst (reminiscent of Steve's) exposes the legacy of the American invasion. His harsh words, both troubled and troubling, relive the story of the aftermath of the war – more fighting with the Chinese and Cambodians and intense privation and loss for the family. But Bon is tainted by his association with the Vietcong and his post-war employment in the Communist bureaucracy: he is grim-faced, unforgiving and suspicious of reconciliation with the West as personified by his 'American' sister. His persona is set against that of his brother Sau, who never returned from the war and who remained the subject of Le Ly's dreams of a lost childhood and a more joyful Vietnam. Clearly Bon cannot represent the future of Vietnam. Nevertheless, his harsh testimony is more than a disruption of the family reunion: it is the disturbing intrusion of a national history which cannot remain untold.[5]

Overall the Vietnam which is presented to us by Stone in *Heaven and Earth* has a curiously elusive identity. This is not just a matter of Stone's evasion of the political history of Vietnam. It is also, crucially, to do with his representations of the feminine and the masculine. In *Heaven and Earth* the heroine suffers, survives and finds spiritual renewal, but ultimately she remains mysterious and unknowable. The American male figures in all three films on the other hand, although exposed in all their contradictions, have an interiority and a capacity for action and change.[6] For them Vietnam becomes the symbolic site of the quest for personal and spiritual identity and the terrain on which a bitter struggle over American identity is fought: Stone's Vietnam remains bound up with his notions of masculinity.

NOTES

Thanks to Pat Kirkham and Andy Medhurst for their helpful comments on this essay. Special thanks to Michael Comber.

1 For a fuller discussion of Hollywood's Vietnam films from *The Green Berets* (1968) to *Rambo* (1985) see Michael Comber and Margaret O'Brien, 'Evading the War: the Politics of the Hollywood Vietnam Film, *History*, June 1988.
2 See John Newsinger, 'Do You Walk the Walk?': Aspects of Masculinity in Some Vietnam War Films in Pat Kirkham and Janet Thumim (eds), *You Tarzan: Masculinity, Movies and Men*, Lawrence and Wishart, London, 1993.
3 Ron Kovic, *Born on the 4th July*, Corgi, London, 1990.
4 Le Ly Hayslip, *When Heaven and Earth Changed Places* and *Child of War, Woman of Peace*, Pan, London, 1993.
5 For a powerful and poetic account of the savagery of war and the pain of memory as experienced by a North Vietnamese soldier, see Bao Ninh's novel *The Sorrow of War*, Secker and Warburg, London, 1993.
6 ' "Masculinity", although rarely attainable, is at least known as an ideal. "Femininity", within the terms of the argument, is not only unknown but unknowable.' Geoffrey Nowell Smith, *Minnelli and Melodrama*, in Christine Gledhill (ed), *Home is Where the Heart Is*, BFI, London, 1987.

'Nothing Is As It Seems': Re-viewing *The Crying Game*

Lola Young

How has sexuality come to be considered the privileged place where our deepest 'truth' is read and expressed?[1]

This essay is focused on three areas of interest suggested by Neil Jordan's fantasy, *The Crying Game* (UK, 1992): firstly, the relationship between the representation of racial difference and sexuality; secondly, the possible meanings of the text's use of cross-dressing and thirdly, the ways in which the press reviews of the film, treated these themes. One reason for concentrating on these areas is to consider the question of how a generally conservative and anti-intellectual British press responded to a film which ostensibly posits a radical sexual politics and attempts to address questions of national, racial and political identity and commitment.

The notion that it was the sexual conundrum at the centre of *The Crying Game* which held the key to the film's meaning was fundamental to most discussions of it. Perverse sexuality – epitomised by homosexuality and transvestism – figured through an interracial relationship involving two men would not appear, on the face of it, to be obvious material for mainstream cinema, yet *The Crying Game* was a critical and – after a slow start – box-office success. Through the use of a narrative device which was not only clever in terms of its dramatic execution but also in terms of the allusion to, and concealment of that plot development in the reviews, the film generated much speculation about the sexual secret at its core.

Even before filming on *The Crying Game* began, controversy about the casting was reported. It was claimed by the film's producers that Forest Whitaker would attract the necessary North American finance because he was a star of international repute. Members of the actors' union, Equity, argued that a black British actor should be given this rare opportunity to take a major role in a British film but the financial argument won, and the African-American was cast as a black soldier from north London. Apparently, a deal was struck between Equity and the film-makers that if Whitaker was accepted by the union, a role of similar status would go to a black British actor. The *Daily Telegraph* reported that, on hearing that 'the role eventually offered was that of a transvestite, Equity reversed its position.'[2] It would appear that a feminised man did not count as sufficient recompense.

The Crying Game begins as a story about the kidnapping of Jody/Forest Whitaker, a black soldier in the British army serving in Northern Ireland. Enticed by a politically motivated young white woman, Jude/Miranda Richardson, Jody is taken hostage by Irish political activitists. Jude has no sympathy for Jody and treats him brutally, but it is Fergus/Stephen Rea who has the main responsibility for guarding Jody. They strike up a relationship as a result of which Fergus promises to visit Jody's partner who lives in London. The photograph which Jody shows to Fergus is, apparently, of an attractive young black woman. Whilst trying to escape, Jody is killed, not by his captors but, significantly, by the British troops who are searching for him. Fergus manages to escape the raid, eventually crossing over to England. Once in London, he searches for and finds Dil/Jaye Davidson, Jody's lover. Dil and Fergus come to depend on each other and embark on a sexual relationship. Before long it is revealed that, anatomically, Dil is a young man, and the relationship temporarily breaks down. Jude turns up in London and makes it clear that in order to compensate for his previous lack of political commitment, Fergus has to participate in what is effectively a suicide mission: he must shoot a judge. In order to protect Dil whom Jude threatens, Fergus agrees but is prevented from carrying out the deed by Dil. The assassination goes ahead anyway and Jude seeks revenge for yet another betrayal on Fergus' part. Jude is shot by Dil and Fergus takes responsibility for the crime. In prison, Fergus is faithfully visited by Dil.

TRANSSEXUAL/TRANSVESTITE ... TRANSGRESSIVE?

One of the principal constituents of the film as far as most reviewers were concerned was the promise of a shocking revelation: that this shock turned out to be both sexualised and racialised made it all the more intriguing. Interestingly, though, reference to the racialisation of sexual transgression was rarely explicit in the critiques. In fact, both within the film and the reviews, 'race' is the great unspoken, the repressed discourse which returns, represented by two black male sexual transgressors.

Bisexuals, homosexuals and transvestites have to be read as transgressive forms of sexual expression because, despite attempts to discuss and understand the complexities and inconsistencies of sexual identity, society remains conservative in regard to the roles and behaviour considered appropriate for women and men. The boundaries of such behaviour – whether in the social or the sexual realm – are still rigorously monitored and policed.

Attitudes to sexual norms are anchored by the external evidence of gender offered by clothing, hairstyle, physical bearing and so on. Wearing clothes considered as inappropriate to one's sex is often read as a disruption of sexual boundaries, a rebellion against the constricting conformity of societal norms. Interestingly, both within and outside of cinematic representation, it is male to female transvestism to which most frequent reference is made. Cross-dressed men signify a defiance of sexual norms and assume an emblematic status that cross-dressed women do not enjoy.

In a sense, both transvestites and transsexuals contest the fixity of sex ascription, albeit in different terms. Whereas it is acknowledged that many male transvestites are heterosexual or bisexual, and that they often spend time – because of both societal pressures, and personal choice – dressed in men's clothing, male transsexuals express the necessity to be regarded as female. Transsexualism is used to refer to those who feel that the way in which they experience their gender is at variance with their biological/anatomical sex: those who attempt to 'pass' as members of the opposite sex.[3] Whether the character of Dil is transvestite or transsexual is not really elaborated in the text but in the context of a discussion of the metaphorical status of gender cross-identification, it may be important, since transsexualism indicates the absence of choice in the matter of gender identification and the impossibility of a return to biologically defined sexual origins. Transsexualism speaks of necessity rather than choice. However, the very lack of clarity regarding Dil's sexual trajectory adds another layer of ambiguity to the film and the sense that it is an understanding of his/her sexuality and others' attitudes towards it that will facilitate our understanding of the text.

The trope of 'passing', which informs an interesting essay by Judith Shapiro on transsexualism, is most often associated with racial passing which refers to a 'light-skinned' black person who can 'pass' as white. Such ambiguous racial positioning may serve to re-confirm the legitimacy of racial categorisations whilst simultaneously problematising it. With regard to 'race' the act of passing, whilst potentially undermining absolutist notions of racial categorisation, is ultimately necessary because of these fixed, prescriptive racial taxonomies.

Passing – whether racial or sexual – has radical potential in terms of its unsettling of defining norms framed by social, scientific, and legal discourses, and in terms of undermining the privileging of visual proof and knowledge. What you see may not actually be what you get, something made clear on a number of occasions during *The Crying Game*. However, not every act of passing may realise that radical potential since there are frequently deeply conservative elements involved. For women with black ancestry who claim whiteness – and most fictional accounts of 'passing' do refer to women – denial of the past and fear of the future characterise their experience. In regard to cross-dressing, it is often the case that representations of men passing as women assume the most conspicuously 'feminine' accoutrements – false eyelashes, heavy amounts of coloured eyeshadow, over-elaborate coiffures and so on: these excessively 'feminine' external signifiers take on a performative, parodic role which do not necessarily suggest convention-breaking notions of womanhood.

The notion that it is somehow necessarily politically progressive to adopt the external appearance of the Other is problematic. However, Shapiro posits that:

> ... we might see male to female transsexualism in Euro-American society as reflecting the fact that those who intentionally move down in the system are more threatening to its values than those seeking to move up. The latter may constitute a threat to the group concerned with maintaining its privileges, but the former constitute a threat to the principles on which the hierarchy itself is based.[4]

This analysis oversimplifies what is at stake, especially when racial difference is implicated in the sex/gender matrix, since ideologies of racial and cultural inferiority and superiority inform social and gender hierarchies. Further, it may also be the case that 'moving up' is profoundly disruptive because it undermines the essentialist claims of the exclusivity of the dominant, privileged group: the privilege based on the external signs of 'race' or sex is demonstrated as being something which is appropriated rather than a natural and inevitable situation. 'Moving down' is not inherently more radical or subversive, as it may be read as a surrendering of power in order to abdicate responsibility. In addition, with regard to the transsexual, there is also the point that beyond the anatomical external characteristics of gender, it is implied that there are distinctive female and male essences which struggle to emerge from within the confines of the inappropriately genitalised body.

In her critical account of the stage play *M Butterfly* – a narrative concerned with the fallibility of visible 'proof' of gender identity, and racial fantasies/cultural stereotypes regarding sexuality – Marjorie Garber notes

> ... the fact of transvestism as both a personal and a political as well as an aesthetic and theatrical, mode of self-construction. Once again, as so often, the transvestite is looked through or away from, appropriated to tell another kind of story, a story less disturbing and dangerous, because less problematic and undecidable.[5]

Garber points to a 'category crisis' (i.e. a failure of definitional distinction) once a borderline which has been assumed impervious but that becomes permeable, permits crossings from one (apparently distinct) category to another. Once again, the trope of 'passing' is invoked to indicate the fluidity of sexual positions which defy reductionist ascriptions of masculinity or femininity. The presence of the undefinable sexual subject – the transvestite – in a text, in a culture, Garber claims, may signal a crisis of definition elsewhere.[6] The 'crisis' suggested but not elaborated in *The Crying Game* is linked to 'race' but not explicated in racial terms.

With regard to cinematic play with transvestism, many of the roles which call upon men to play women have not done so in a manner which explicitly calls into question their heterosexual, masculine integrity. When Tony Curtis dresses as a woman in *Some Like It Hot* (Billy Wilder, US, 1959) it is clear that his pursuit of Marilyn Monroe is not sisterly. The situation with Jack Lemmon's cross-dressing in the same film, is rather more complicated, since we are left to ponder what will become of his relationship with an elderly rich, male suitor. Even in this instance though, Lemmon's performance is conducted with a good deal of knowingness about his deception which is, after all, economically expedient: the joke is on the old man, who in the quest for the perfect female partner, falls for a man in drag.

Other often cited examples of male cross-dressing in mainstream popular cinema where the male concerned makes clear his heterosexuality are Cary Grant in *I Was a Male War Bride* (Howard Hawks, US, 1949) and Dustin Hoffman in *Tootsie* (Sidney Pollack, US, 1982). More recently, in *Mrs Doubtfire* (Chris Columbus, US, 1993), despite proving that he is better at mothering than his wife, Robin Williams, in the central role, retains his heterosexual masculinity throughout.

According to Chris Straayer, in these instances '[A]t the level of performance, feminine garb ironically both accentuates the male's secondary sex characteristic, thus signalling his 'nature', and keeps his biological genital out of view.'[7] In the case of Dil however, this does not hold true. In this instance, it is his femininity which is consistently emphasised, suggesting that 'he' is really 'she'. Furthermore, Dil's male genitals are fully exposed and the sexual incongruity foregrounded. Straayer argues that the absence of the penis invisibilises male sexuality, whereas women's sexuality is inscribed on the female body through constant exposure of the secondary sexual characteristics such as breasts:

> the historic absence from view of the penis in cinema has allowed the male body an independence from sexual anatomical verification. It is his charging about that has identified a male film character as male, yet it is his penis that has invested him with the cultural right to charge about – the signifier *in absentia*.

Straayer contends that the male cross-dresser has 'the *potential* for an intense double signification of sexuality, containing both macho male sexuality via the unseen penis, and female sexuality displaced onto visible display via masquerade.'[9] The masquerade which is evidenced in *The Crying Game*, is of a different order: here the intensity of the signification of sexuality is achieved through the penis being stripped of its macho resonance as a consequence of its appropriation by the (constructed) femininity of Dil.[10]

Dil's physical image as both feminine and phallic helps to negate the disturbing notion of sexual difference and castration anxiety. It is significant that the big secret that reviewers were asked to withhold from the public was the sighting of a *black* man's penis. One of the few close-up images of a penis outside of pornographic films just happens to be that of a homo/transsexual black man masquerading as a woman: three kinds of Otherness captured in one. The anxious desire to look at the dimensions of the black male's penis is satisfied by its disclosure, and, as the black penis belongs to an ersatz woman, it is rendered harmless by its feminisation.

CRITICAL INTERVENTIONS

> To understand the real social/sexual meanings of drag ... I would argue that you must look not so much at the *men* who dress as women, or the *women* who dress as men, but at the 'feminine' or 'masculine' characteristics they adopt, and the values placed on these, no matter who 'wears' them.[11]

It is necessary to look at the men involved, however, when considering how racial identity is implicated in the cross-dressing in *The Crying Game*. In both *M Butterfly* and *The Crying Game*, the cross-dressing men are doubly Other because they are Chinese and black respectively. At work here are not only gender stereotypes but racial ones too. In order to develop this point further, it is instructive to examine how Dil/Davidson is discussed in the reviews.

Jaye Davidson's film acting debut caused a stir, eliciting much praise: 'stunning' was a well-used term but quite what Davidson contributed apart from sexual enigma is hard to elicit from the citations. *Gay Times*' commented that 'the film really belongs to newcomer Jaye Davidson as Dil; the impact of this, her debut film appearance, will be at least equal to that made by Cathy Tyson in *Mona Lisa* (Neil Jordan, GB, 1986).'[12] The comparison is appropriate since Jaye Davidson is dressed and made up to be similar in appearance to Cathy Tyson's performance as Simone, and the shoot-out towards the end of *The Crying Game* bears similarities to that of *Mona Lisa*. *Gay Times*', positive review was somewhat reticent about the sexual games played in the film, refusing to mention the 'secret'. Such a strategy may be read as being consistent with the film's rejection of sexual essentialism, although it could be argued that such a ploy is undermined by referring unproblematically to Dil/Davidson as 'she'. By not engaging with the question of gender and sexual identity, and making only one reference to racial identity, however, this account of the film serves to highlight the fact that, without the racialised sexual shock, the text has little allure.

Fascination with Dil/Davidson is demonstrated in *Forum Art* where Hilton Als writes, 'One image that is in between: Jaye

Davidson. Between colored and not colored, male and not female, kindness and not kindness.'[13] Designated by Als as racially liminal, Dil/Davidson becomes a literalisation of the phallic mother as Als asks 'Would I eventually ask Jaye Davidson the baby question I ask of everyone: Are you my mother?'[14] It is Dil/Davidson's perceived 'in betweenness' that allows him to become a screen onto which these fantasies of maternal and sexual desire may be projected.

In the same magazine, Molly Nesbitt in a discussion of both Sally Potter's film *Orlando* (GB, 1993) and *The Crying Game*, states that 'The Body without Organs is a beyond. A friendly, forthcoming beyond that can help explain how an Irish man who loves women can continue to love a man who appears with a woman's surface.'[15] Fergus is seemingly attracted by Dil's intriguing manner and the 'surface' of her/his body as well as being motivated by the guilt he feels at having been involved in Jody's death. Notably, however, this character elaboration is only accorded to Fergus by Nesbitt: apparently no explanation is required of Jody's motivation, even though the narrative demonstrates that he too 'loves women'. In any case, according to normative perceptions rather than being a body 'without organs' Dil has an excess of sexual organs.

The actor who played the transvestite Chinese spy in *M Butterfly* was billed in such a way that his gender could not be identified. Similarly, the sexual ambiguity of the name 'Jaye' Davidson served to obscure gender signs. It was reported that the film – the original working title of which was *The Soldier's Wife* – was made on a closed set and that no-one was allowed to divulge the 'secret' of Davidson's anatomical sex. This play on gender/sexual ambiguity was further emphasised in reviews of the film, where apparently critics were requested not to divulge Dil/Davidson's sex. To further confound the speculation, it was suggested that Davidson should be nominated for an Oscar under the 'best supporting actress' category. Undoubtedly these strategies ensured a good deal of publicity for, and curiosity about, the film.

In Jonathan Romney's *Sight and Sound* review – which begins by mistakenly attributing both the accounts of an allegory about a scorpion to Fergus rather than acknowledging that the first telling is by Jody during his captivity – Jody's remark to Fergus about his posting in the British army is quoted: 'I get sent to the one place where they call you a nigger to your face' which constitutes a rare explicit reference to black/white antagonisms in the text.[16] Leaving aside the question of the lack of correspondence of this remark to black people's actual experiences, the fact that this comment is singled out as being a summary of 'the film's theme of perceived identities and their naming' is of interest since it does not appear to me to be given a great deal of significance in the course of the narrative.[17] Rather it seems more like a necessary but reluctant acknowledgement of the contradictory position of black soldiers in the British armed forces, fighting for a country which often rejects them and renders their presence problematic. However, locating the racial politics both of the film and its critics is not easy since racial themes are so under-elaborated that they constitute a structuring absence.[18]

The film's publicity clearly emphasises its potentially controversial themes but, despite this, it was not generally perceived in the press as politically controversial. This is quite an achievement for a film which features Irish Republicanism. In fact, I suspect that the absence in the text of a distinctly articulated political position contributed to the film's appreciative reception by most reviewers. There is certainly evidence of this in Sheridan Morley's review when he claims that the film is 'about personal politics, about states of mind rather than states on a map.' And again, as he states, 'This is not a film about the IRA or Northern Ireland except in its early sequences: rather it is a film about what we mean when we take on people and assignments'.[19] The political is adeptly reconstituted as the non-threatening personal, in contrast to the listings guide, *What's On*, which somehow manages to claim that the film 'deals with politics and race and sexual obsession ...'.[20] By keeping interracial sexual relationships, homosexuality, transvestism and the moral corruption of the judiciary to the realm of the private, individual act and choice, *The Crying Game* is on much safer ground.

This desire for a 'safe' text is not confined to the British press: in the New York publication *Village Voice*, Georgia Brown claims that *The Crying Game* 'handles the matter of race in a refreshingly natural way. Jody is black and so is Dil. But only in the opening scene, when drunken Jody drapes himself around the blond Jude (at a carnival in Northern Ireland where everyone else is white) was I conscious of him as a black man.'[21] Brown's sigh of relief is almost audible here, relief that she was not forced to think of Jody's predicament as a lone black man in a hostile environment. The insinuation here is that treating 'race' in a 'natural' way means not drawing attention to structures of dominance and subordination, or to individual and communal acts of racism. Dil *is* in an interracial sexual relationship with Jody's former captor Fergus, but the focal point for the audience's view of the relationship is not that of racial difference but that of transgressive sexuality. Significantly, for Brown, Jody's blackness is troublesome and obtrusive when he engages in a heterosexual act with a 'blond' white woman. When his head is obscured by a sack or when he is implicated in a sexual relationship with a black male transvestite, he is not so dangerous.

Brown positions Fergus as 'the product of a racist culture' and also quotes Jody's line about being called a 'nigger' to his face. She continues 'yet he's [Fergus] a gentleman to the core and doesn't seem to make distinctions according to race' – all of which serves to allay Brown's racial anxieties. It is a tribute to Jordan's script and direction and to Stephen Rea's acting that several critics point to Fergus' humanity and *kindliness*, overlooking his participation in terrorist activities and the fact that he was instrumental in Jody's death.

Despite citing a lack of pretension in the treatment of racial difference here, Brown manages to reconstruct *Crying Game* as a 'racial allegory', explaining that 'Jody and Dil are twins, extensions of each other, magical and real.' There is a brief moment when Brown questions whether the two black characters are merely marginal, not autonomous subjects but mysterious objects constructed for the white male gaze. Fergus is redeemed by his behaviour towards Jody and Dil: the process of his humanisation is demonstrated by his benevolence to black people who are indeed otherwise marginal. The black man's role – in the character of Dil and Jody – is to draw out Fergus' sexual and political ambivalences. In this sense Dil represents an intensification of the common function assigned to black women, black men, and white women: that of a backdrop for white male experiences.

It was refreshing to read Cynthia Heimel's statement: 'I personally think that the appearance of a bigger-than-life penis right in our faces is what got everyone excited'. She links this fascination with the phallic to women's lack of substantial roles in the cinema in general.[22] Philip French describes Miranda Richardson's characterisation of Jude as 'sexuality transformed into lethal politics' implying that for her, political commitment is a sublimation of sexual energy which accounts for her intense fanaticism. Jude's shrill characterisation as the ideologically dogmatic political gangster's moll, wielding a retributive gun stands in stark contrast to Dil, the soft voiced transvestite version of femininity.

One of the few female reviewers of *The Crying Game* in the British press, Anne Billson, also comments on the representation of women in the film. Referring to the men's relationships, she argues 'it's no wonder they go in for this male bonding, when the token women on display are such dubious specimens.'[23] The 'best woman' turns out to be Dil: after all, Dil is faithful to Fergus to the end, and after, whilst Jude uses her sexuality to deceive Jody and abandons Fergus when he fails to demonstrate his political commitment.

The awe and fascination engendered by the film is hyperbolically exemplified by Terrence Rafferty's review in the *New Yorker*.[24] The critical appreciation is titled 'Knight in Armor' which gives an indication of the mythical status that Rafferty confers on the film. *The Crying Game* is compared to various literary categories – myths, legends, short stories, fables and fairy tales – and to dramas. The film's alleged universal appeal is further emphasised by Rafferty's emphatic use of the all-encompassing 'we' which is deployed to conceal his imperial 'I'/eye. The sense of Rafferty's imperial I/eye meshing with that of Jordan's is suggested in the following: 'Jordan keeps trying to see to the bottom of things, to plunge into the mysteries of his own nature, and in recent films his vision has seemed to cut through the murk and shadows of modern life like a searchlight beam.'[25] Rafferty's task as a critic is analgous to that of Jordan since Rafferty guides 'us' through the 'dark interior', consisting of black, homosexual and female sexualities. Perhaps Rafferty's presumptuous use of 'we' indicates an over-identification with what he describes as Jordan's task – to assist 'us' in 'our' understanding of the mysterious processes of sexual identification and identity. As is so often the case, these 'explanations' are necessary in order to explore the central enigma of white, male sexuality. It is that theme which is constantly and obsessively explored in texts, and although *The Crying Game* attempts to shift the parameters of this discussion, it still foregrounds white male experience at the expense of others.

The significance of the sexual revelation is rarely in doubt, although some reviewers attempted to underplay it. Although he fixes on the sexual shock, a 'huge, jaw-dropping surprise – a revelation that changes utterly our understanding of everything that has gone before', Rafferty claims that the revelation is not merely a narrative device. Similarly, Sheridan Morley's critique for the *Sunday Express* is full of praise for Jordan's drama but the giveaway is the italicised, indented paragraph which states:

The plot turns on two shocks of stunning impact, neither of which it would be fair to reveal, and either of which I defy you to forecast.[26]

He observes later, in similar style:

Nothing is now what it may have seemed at the outset.

The Crying Game self-consciously presents us with a disruption of sexual binarism whilst evading and failing to address racial binarisms. It may be the case that the attempt to problematise sexual categories is intended to make audiences question national and racial dichotomies, but it is on the visual, sexual spectacle of the male cross-dresser that the film is fixated. Jody's brief, physical relationship with Jude is both a diversionary tactic to lead us to an assumption of his heterosexuality, and a reiteration of assumptions about that black male sexuality which is apparently unable to resist the temptations that white women offer. Black women are apparently so troublesome that they have to be written out completely, replaced by a black man 'passing' as a woman.

The narrative is centrally concerned with a white male identity, that of a man whose political affiliations have afforded him companionship and a heterosexual relationship but little by way of coherent political philosophy or emotional commitment. Black men here are serviceable Others, created in order to form a setting against which Fergus may explore his personal and political dilemmas. Jordan compulsively re-explores some of the same ground tentatively covered in *Mona Lisa* regarding black sexuality, a point emphasised by the similarity of the look of Cathy Tyson and Jaye Davidson. Unfortunately, *The Crying Game* is too preoccupied with its own fantasies to be able to effectively comment on, and engage with that fascination and its provenance.

Given the current state of the press, I suppose it is not surprising that none of film critics writing on *The Crying Game* that I read, appear to have developed a perspective on 'race', gender and sexuality as both discrete and intersecting areas of discussion in contemporary cinema: serious, perceptive, and accessible film criticism is currently very scarce indeed.

NOTES

1 Lawrence D Kritzman (ed), *Michel Foucault: Politics, Philosophy,*

Culture: Interviews and Other Writings, 1977-1984, Routledge, London, 1988, p110.

2 The *Daily Telegraph*, 21 October 1991, p3.

3 For an extended discussion of the significance of transsexualism, see Judith Shapiro 'Transsexualism: Reflections on the Persistence of Gender and the Mutability of Sex'; Julia Epstein and Kristina Straub (eds), *Body Guards: The Cultural Politics of Gender Ambiguity*, Routledge, London, 1991, p248.

4 *Ibid*, p270.

5 Marjorie Garber, 'The Occidental Tourist: *M Butterfly* and the Scandal of Transvestism' in Andrew Parker et al. (eds), *Nationalisms and Sexualities*, Routledge, 1991, p123.

6 *Ibid.*, p125.

7 Chris Straayer, 'The She-man: Postmodern Bi-sexed Performance in Film and Video', *Screen*, Volume 31, Number 3, Autumn 1990, p262.

8 *Ibid.*, p262.

9 *Ibid.*, p263.

10 The notion of 'feminine masquerade' is a concept developed by Joan Riviere in her often cited essay, 'Womanliness as Masquerade' published by Hendrik M Ruitenbeek (ed), *Psychoanalysis and Female Subjectivity*, College and University Press, New Haven, 1966.

11 Judith Williamson, *Consuming Passions: The Dynamics of Popular Culture*, Marion Boyars, London, 1987, p47.

12 *Gay Times*, October, 1992, pp78-79.

13 Hilton Als, 'A Fan's Notes', *ArtForum*, Summer 1993, p95. This is not a review of the film but a rather self-indulgent eulogy centred on Dil/Davidson.

14 *Ibid.*, p95.

15 Molly Nesbitt, 'Apart Without a Face: *Orlando* and the *Crying Game*', *ArtForum*, Summer 1993, p95.

16 *Sight and Sound*, November 1992, p40.

17 *Ibid.*

18 This term is useful in considering how some issues and representations are both present and absent. For an explanation of the term, see Richard Dyer's '*Victim*: Hegemonic Project' in *The Matter of Images: Essays on Representation*, Routledge, London, 1993, p105.

19 Sheridan Morley, *Sunday Express*, 1 November 1992, p45.

20 *What's On*, 28 October 1992, p8.

21 *Village Voice*, 1 December, 1992, p24.

22 See *The Independent on Sunday*, 28 March, 1993, p43.

23 See *The Sunday Telegraph*, 1 November, 1992, p41.

24 *The New Yorker*, 16 November, 1992, pp127-130.

25 Terrence Rafferty. *Ibid.*, p130.

26 Morley, *op.cit.*

Notes on Contributors

Gill Branston lectures in the Centre for Journalism Studies, University of Wales, College of Cardiff and is currently working on *The Media Student's Book* for imminent publication.

Lesley Caldwell teaches Social Theory and Psychoanalysis at the University of Greenwich. She is preparing a book on the Italianness of Italian cinema.

Christine Geraghty lectures in Media and Communications at Goldsmiths College, University of London. She has written a number of essays on British cinema and her publications include *Women and Soap Opera* (1991).

Christine Gledhill is Principal Lecturer in Media and Cultural Studies, Staffordshire University. She has edited *Home is Where the Heart is* (1987) and has co-edited *Nationalising Femininity: Culture, Sexuality and Cinema in World War Two* (forthcoming).

Pat Kirkham is Professor of Design History, De Montfort University, Leicester. She co-edited *You Tarzan: Masculinity, Movies and Men* (1993) and, with Judy Attfield, also produced *A View from the Interior* (1989).

Rikki Morgan lectures in the School of Creative, Cultural and Social Studies, Thames Valley University and is co-authoring a book on contemporary Spanish cinema with Barry Jordan.

Griselda Pollock is Professor of Art History at the Centre for Cultural Studies, University of Leeds.

Susannah Radstone directs the MA in Cultural Studies at University of East London. Her current project is a book, *From Confession to Remembrance: Fiction and Film 1970-1990* to be published next year.

Charlene Regester lectures at the University of North Carolina, Chapel Hill, USA. She is co-editor of the Oscar Micheaux Society Newsletter.

Kathleen Rowe is Assistant Professor of English at the University of Oregon, USA and author of *The Unruly Woman: Gender and the Genres of Laughter* (1995).

Helen Stoddart lectures in the Department of English, University of Keele.

Gillian Swanson lectures in the Faculty of Humanities, Griffith University, Australia and is co-editor of *Nationalising Femininity: Culture, Sexuality and Cinema in Britain in World War Two* (forthcoming).

Sarah Street lectures in Film and TV in the Department of Drama, University of Bristol and her most recent publication is 'Hitchcockian Haberdashery' in *Hitchcock Annual* (1995).

Janet Thumim lectures in Film and TV Studies in the Department of Drama, University of Bristol. She published *Celluloid Sisters: Women and Popular Cinema* (1992) and co-edited *You Tarzan: Masculinity, Movies and Men* (1993).

Ginette Vincendeau is Professor of Film Studies at the University of Warwick. She is the editor of the *Encyclopaedia of European Cinema* (1995) and author of the forthcoming book, *Pépé le Moko*.

Margaret O'Brien is Head of Education at the BFI, South Bank, London. She has edited, with Allen Eyles, an oral history of cinema-going, *Enter the Dreamhouse* (1993).

Lola Young lectures in Media and Cultural Studies at Middlesex University. She has written widely on 'race', gender and representation and her book *Fear of the Dark: 'Race', Gender and Sexuality in Cinema* is forthcoming.

Film Index

General Index